OECD Skills Studies

Skills Matter

FURTHER RESULTS
FROM THE SURVEY OF ADULT SKILLS

OECD
BETTER POLICIES FOR BETTER LIVES

This work is published under the responsibility of the Secretary-General of the OECD. The opinions expressed and arguments employed herein do not necessarily reflect the official views of the OECD member countries.

This document and any map included herein are without prejudice to the status of or sovereignty over any territory, to the delimitation of international frontiers and boundaries and to the name of any territory, city or area.

Please cite this publication as:
OECD (2016), *Skills Matter: Further Results from the Survey of Adult Skills*, OECD Skills Studies, OECD Publishing, Paris.
http://dx.doi.org/10.1787/9789264258051-en

ISBN 978-92-64-25804-4 (print)
ISBN 978-92-64-25805-1 (PDF)

Series: OECD Skills Studies
ISSN 2307-8723 (print)
ISSN 2307-8731 (online)

The statistical data for Israel are supplied by and under the responsibility of the relevant Israeli authorities. The use of such data by the OECD is without prejudice to the status of the Golan Heights, East Jerusalem and Israeli settlements in the West Bank under the terms of international law.

Photo credits:
© aleksandr-mansurov-ru/iStockphoto
© Don Pablo/Shutterstock
© Jamie Grill/Getty Images
© Jaroslav Machacek/Shutterstock
© Konstantin Chagin/Shutterstock
© Lightspring/Shutterstock
© momentimages/Tetra Images/Inmagine LTD
© Ocean/Corbis

Corrigenda to OECD publications may be found on line at: *www.oecd.org/about/publishing/corrigenda.htm*.

Foreword

In a world in which millions of people are unemployed while many employers complain that they cannot find qualified workers something is obviously out of balance. One of those issues is the match between the supply of and demand for skills. Governments need a clearer picture, not only of how labour markets are changing, but of how well-equipped their citizens are to participate in, and benefit from, increasingly knowledge-based economies. The Survey of Adult Skills, a product of the OECD Programme for the International Assessment of Adult Competencies (PIAAC), is providing that picture. It captures information about adults' proficiency in literacy, numeracy and problem-solving skills, and whether and how those skills are used on the job and throughout life.

Skills Matter: Further Results from the Survey of Adult Skills expands on the data and analysis examined in the *OECD Skills Outlook 2013: First Results from the Survey of Adult Skills* by including data from nine additional countries that conducted the survey in 2014-15. The results show that poor skills severely limit people's access to better-paying and more rewarding jobs. The distribution of skills also has significant implications for how the benefits of economic growth are shared within societies. Put simply, where large shares of adults have poor skills, it becomes difficult to introduce productivity-enhancing technologies and new ways of working, which in turn stalls improvements in living standards. Importantly, the results show that skills affect more than earnings and employment. In all countries, adults with lower skills are far more likely than those with better literacy skills to report poor health, to perceive themselves as objects rather than actors in political processes, and to have less trust in others.

The report also finds that acquiring relevant skills is certainly key, but may not be enough to integrate successfully in the labour market. Skills must be used productively, not only to keep them from atrophying, but also to reap some of the intangible benefits of skills proficiency that contribute to adults' general well-being. For example, this report shows that the intensity with which workers use their information-processing skills in their jobs is related to the likelihood of being satisfied at work.

Going forward, the OECD is working with governments to develop national skills strategies that ensure that their citizens are equipped with the right skills for 21st-century economies and use those skills productively. We know that skills matter for both workers and employers; now it's time to get the balance right.

Angel Gurría
OECD Secretary-General

Acknowledgements

The Survey of Adult Skills (PIAAC) is a collaborative endeavour involving the participating countries, the OECD Secretariat, the European Commission and an international Consortium led by Educational Testing Service (ETS). This report was prepared by Miloš Kankaraš, Guillermo Montt, Marco Paccagnella, Glenda Quintini and William Thorn, with the assistance of Vanessa Denis, Paulina Granados Zambrano and François Keslair.

Marilyn Achiron, Marika Boiron, Jennifer Cannon, Cassandra Davis and Marta Encinas-Martin, provided valuable support in the editorial and production process. Administrative assistance was provided by Sabrina Leonarduzzi.

The international Consortium was responsible for developing the assessment instruments and preparing the underlying data under the direction of Irwin Kirsch.

The development and implementation of the project was steered by the PIAAC Board of Participating Countries. During the implementation of the 2nd round of the Survey of Adult Skills (2011 to 2016), the Board was chaired by Aviana Bulgarelli (Italy) from 2016, Patrick Bussière (Canada) from 2014 to 2015 and Dan McGrath (United States) from 2010 to 2016. A full list of the members of the Board together with the names of the National Project Managers, experts, members of the international Consortium and staff of the OECD Secretariat who have contributed to the project can be found in Annexes C and D of *The Survey of Adult Skills: Reader's Companion, Second Edition* (OECD, 2016).

Table of Contents

READER'S GUIDE 13

EXECUTIVE SUMMARY 17

CHAPTER 1 **OVERVIEW: WHY SKILLS MATTER** 19
Proficiency in information-processing skills among adults 23
Proficiency and socio-demographic characteristics 24
Information-processing skills and well-being 26
Information-processing skills and the labour market 26
- Proficiency in information-processing skills and labour market outcomes 26
The use of information-processing skills at work 28
- Mismatches of qualifications and skills 29

CHAPTER 2 **ADULTS' PROFICIENCY IN KEY INFORMATION-PROCESSING SKILLS** 33
Reporting the results 37
Proficiency in literacy 38
- Levels of literacy proficiency across countries and economies 39
- Literacy-related non-response 42
Reading components 42
Distribution of proficiency scores across countries and economies 44
- Mean proficiency scores in literacy 44
- Variation of proficiency scores within countries/economies 46
Proficiency in numeracy 48
- Levels of numeracy proficiency across countries/economies 48
- Literacy-related non-response 50
Distribution of proficiency scores across countries/economies 50
- Mean proficiency scores in numeracy 50
- Variation of proficiency scores within countries and economies 52
Proficiency in problem solving in technology-rich environments 53
- Levels of proficiency in problem solving in technology-rich environments across countries and economies 54
- The proportion of adults without basic ICT skills 54
The relationship among the three proficiencies 56
Comparison of the results from the Survey of Adult Skills with those of previous surveys 59
Summarising performance across countries and economies 61
Summary 63

CHAPTER 3 **THE SOCIO-DEMOGRAPHIC DISTRIBUTION OF KEY INFORMATION-PROCESSING SKILLS** 67
Overview of socio-demographic differences in proficiency 68
Differences in skills proficiency related to educational attainment 70
- Proficiency in literacy and numeracy among low- and high-educated adults 70
- Proficiency in problem solving in technology-rich environments among low- and high-educated adults 72
- Skills and education among younger adults 73
Differences in skills proficiency related to age 75
- Proficiency in literacy and numeracy among older and younger adults 77
- Proficiency in problem solving in technology-rich environments among older and younger adults 79

Differences in skills proficiency related to gender..81
- Proficiency in literacy and numeracy among men and women..81
- Proficiency in problem solving in technology-rich environments among men and women....................83

Differences in skills proficiency related to country of origin and language...............................84
- Proficiency in literacy among native- and foreign-born adults..84
- Proficiency in problem solving in technology-rich environments among native- and foreign-born adults...........86

Differences in skills proficiency related to socio-economic background.....................................87
- Proficiency in literacy among adults with high- and low-educated parents...88

Adults with low proficiency...89

Summary..91

CHAPTER 4 **HOW SKILLS ARE USED IN THE WORKPLACE**...95

Measuring skills use in the workplace and in everyday life..97

Levels of skills use in the workplace and in everyday life...98

Why skills use at work matters..100
- Skills use, wages and job satisfaction..100
- Skills use and productivity 101

The link between proficiency and use of information-processing skills.....................................102

The variation of skills use at work..104

The distribution of skills use, by workers' gender, age and educational attainment 105
- Gender..105
- Age 106
- Educational attainment...107

The demand side: How firm and job characteristics influence skills use..................................109
- Industry, firm size and sector 110
- Type of contract 111
- Work organisation 113

Summary 116

CHAPTER 5 **THE OUTCOMES OF INVESTMENT IN SKILLS**...119

Skills proficiency, labour market status and wages..120
- Proficiency and employment..121
- Literacy proficiency, education and employment..122
- Proficiency and wages..123
- Literacy proficiency, education and wages...126

Mismatch between workers' skills and job requirements, and its impact on wages..................129
- Mismatch in the Survey of Adult Skills..130
- Overlap between skills, field-of-study and qualifications mismatch 134
- How mismatch interacts with proficiency and other individual and job characteristics....................136
- The effect of mismatch on wages...141

Skills and non-economic outcomes...144
- Trust..144
- Volunteering..146
- Political efficacy..146
- Health..147

Summary..148

ANNEX A **SKILLS MATTER: FURTHER RESULTS FROM THE SURVEY OF ADULT SKILLS, TABLES OF RESULTS**...........153

ANNEX B **SKILLS MATTER: FURTHER RESULTS FROM THE SURVEY OF ADULT SKILLS, ADDITIONAL TABLES**.........157

BOXES

Box 1.1   Key facts concerning the Survey of Adult Skills (PIAAC) 20

Box 2.1   A context for cross-national comparisons of adult proficiency 35

Box 2.2   Reading on a screen or on paper: Does it affect proficiency in literacy?...................................38

Box 2.3   Comparing results among countries/economies and population subgroups...............................44

Box 2.4   Adults who "opted out" of taking the computer-based assessment 56

Box 2.5   Skills proficiency among adults in the countries/economies that participated in Round 2 of the Survey of Adult Skills (PIAAC).........62

Box 4.1   Measuring the use of information-processing skills in the Survey of Adult Skills 97

Box 5.1   Measuring qualifications, skills and field-of-study mismatch in the Survey of Adult Skills......132

Box 5.2   The STEP Skills Measurement Study: A skills survey in low- and middle-income countries..........143

FIGURES

Figure 1.1   Snapshot of performance in literacy, numeracy and problem solving 22

Figure 1.2   Average and variability of numeracy scores 23

Figure 1.3   Literacy proficiency, by educational attainment...25

Figure 1.4   Impact of education, literacy proficiency and reading use at work on wages..........................26

Figure 1.5   Contribution of education, literacy and numeracy to the variation in wages 27

Figure 1.6   Correlation between labour productivity and the use of reading skills at work........................29

Figure 2.1   Per capita GDP, USD 36

Figure 2.2   Population with tertiary education 36

Figure 2.3   Population without upper secondary education 37

Figure 2.4   Foreign-born population as a percentage of total population..37

Figure 2.5   Percentage of respondents taking different pathways in the Survey of Adult Skills (PIAAC) 39

Figure 2.6   Literacy proficiency among adults...41

Figure 2.7   Relationship between literacy proficiency and performance in reading components................42

Figure 2.8   Performance in reading components..43

Figure 2.9   Comparison of average literacy proficiency 45

Figure 2.10   Distribution of literacy proficiency scores..46

Figure 2.11   Average and distribution of literacy scores 47

Figure 2.12   Numeracy proficiency among adults 49

Figure 2.13   Comparison of average numeracy proficiency 50

Figure 2.14   Distribution of numeracy proficiency scores...51

Figure 2.15   Average and distribution of numeracy scores 52

Figure 2.16   Proficiency in problem solving in technology-rich environments among adults......................55

Figure 2.17   Socio-demographic characteristics of adults with varying levels of ICT experience 56

Figure 2.18   Relationship between literacy and problem solving in technology-rich environments................57

Figure 2.19   Relationship between numeracy and problem solving in technology-rich environments................58

Figure 2.20   Changes in literacy scores in IALS, ALL and PIAAC surveys 60

Figure 2.21   Changes in numeracy scores in PIAAC and ALL surveys..60

Figure 2.22   Summary of proficiency in key information-processing skills 61

Figure 3.1   Socio-demographic differences in literacy proficiency..69

Figure 3.2   Differences in literacy proficiency, by educational attainment 71

Figure 3.3   Problem-solving proficiency, by educational attainment 72

Figure 3.4   Differences in literacy proficiency by educational attainment, young adults aged 16-24 73

Figure 3.5   Differences in literacy proficiency by educational attainment, young adults aged 20-24 74

Figure 3.6   Relationship between skills proficiency and age..76

Figure 3.7   Age differences in literacy proficiency 77

Figure 3.8   Problem-solving proficiency among younger and older adults 79

Figure 3.9   Relationship between literacy and problem solving in technology-rich environments, by age 80

Figure 3.10   Gender differences in literacy and numeracy proficiency 81

Figure 3.11   Gender gap in literacy and numeracy, by age 82

Figure 3.12   Problem-solving proficiency among women and men 83

Figure 3.13   Differences in literacy scores between native- and foreign-born adults 85

Figure 3.14   Differences in literacy scores, by immigrant and language background 86

Figure 3.15   Problem-solving proficiency among foreign-language immigrants and non-immigrants 87

Figure 3.16   Differences in literacy proficiency, by parents' educational attainment 88

Figure 3.17   The proportion of adults who are low performers 89

Figure 3.18   Low performers: Synthesis of socio-demographic differences 90

Figure 4.1   Information-processing skills used at work 99

Figure 4.2   Information-processing skills used in everyday life 100

Figure 4.3   Labour productivity and the use of reading skills at work 101

Figure 4.4   Skills use at work and skills proficiency of the working population 102

Figure 4.5   Skills use at work, by proficiency level 103

Figure 4.6   Explaining information-processing skills used at work 104

Figure 4.7   Information-processing skills used at work, by gender 105

Figure 4.8   Information-processing skills used at work, by age group 107

Figure 4.9   Information-processing skills used at work, by educational attainment 108

Figure 4.10   Information-processing skills used at work, by sector 110

Figure 4.11   Information-processing skills used at work, by firm size 111

Figure 4.12   Information-processing skills used at work, by contract type 112

Figure 4.13   Skills use, by High-Performance Work Practices 114

Figure 4.14   High-Performance Work Practices, by type of practice 115

Figure 5.1   Mean proficiency in literacy, by labour force status 121

Figure 5.2   Effect of education and literacy proficiency on the likelihood of being employed 123

Figure 5.3   Distribution of wages, by literacy proficiency level 124

Figure 5.4   Effect of education, literacy proficiency and use of reading at work on wages 127

Figure 5.5   Contribution of education, literacy and numeracy to the variation of hourly wages 128

Figure 5.6   Contribution of education, literacy and numeracy to the variation of hourly wages, by age group and gender 129

Figure 5.7   Qualification, literacy and field-of-study mismatch 133

Figure 5.8a   Overqualified workers who are mismatched by literacy or field of study 135

Figure 5.8b   Field-of-study mismatched workers who are mismatched by qualification or literacy 135

Figure 5.9   Overqualification, by individual and job characteristics 136

Figure 5.10   Overskilling in literacy, by individual and job characteristics 138

Figure 5.11   Field-of-study mismatch, by individual and job characteristics 140

Figure 5.12   Effect of qualification, literacy and field-of-study mismatch on wages 142

Figure 5.13   Literacy proficiency and positive social outcomes 145

Figure 5.14   Private health expenditure and association between literacy and self-reported health 147

TABLES

Table 2.1   Description of proficiency levels in literacy 40

Table 2.2   Description of proficiency levels in numeracy 48

Table 2.3   Description of proficiency levels in problem solving in technology-rich environments 53

Table 4.1   Indicators of skills use at work and in everyday life 97

Table 4.2   Industries with highest and lowest skills use at work 109

Table 5.1   Glossary of key terms related to mismatch 131

Follow OECD Publications on:

🐦	*http://twitter.com/OECD_Pubs*
f	*http://www.facebook.com/OECDPublications*
in	*http://www.linkedin.com/groups/OECD-Publications-4645871*
You Tube	*http://www.youtube.com/oecdilibrary*
OECD Alerts	*http://www.oecd.org/oecddirect/*

This book has...   *StatLinks* 📊

A service that delivers Excel® files from the printed page!

Look for the *StatLinks* 📊 at the bottom of the tables or graphs in this book. To download the matching Excel® spreadsheet, just type the link into your Internet browser, starting with the *http://dx.doi.org* prefix, or click on the link from the e-book edition.

Reader's Guide

Data underlying the figures

Detailed data tables corresponding to the figures presented in the main body of the report can be found in Annex A. These figures and tables are numbered according to the corresponding chapters, and include an abbreviation in brackets to denote one of the three direct measures of skills for which there are data in the Survey of Adult Skills (PIAAC) – literacy (L), numeracy (N) and problem solving in technology-rich environments (P). As an example, Figure 3.1 (L) denotes the first figure in Chapter 3 based on the literacy scale and it has Table A3.1 (L) as a corresponding data table in Annex A.

Annex B includes other detailed data tables that either correspond to figures included in boxes or to citations in the main body of the report, but for which no figure was provided.

Unless otherwise stated, the population underlying each of the figures and tables covers adults aged 16-65.

Web package

Figures included in the report and the corresponding data tables contained in Annex A and B present data for only one of the three direct measures of skills, either literacy (L), numeracy (N) or problem solving in technology-rich environments (P). A more complete set of data tables can be found at www.oecd.org/site/piaac/. This web package includes all the figures and tables included in the report as well as data tables for the other skills domains referred to but not examined in the report. The package consists of Excel® workbooks that can be viewed and downloaded by chapter.

StatLinks

A *StatLink* URL address is provided under each figure and table. Readers using the pdf version of the report can simply click on the relevant *StatLinks* url to either open or download an Excel® workbook containing the corresponding figures and tables. Readers of the print version can access the Excel® workbook by typing the *StatLink* address in their Internet browser.

Calculating international averages (means)

Most figures and tables presented in this report and in the web package include an OECD average in addition to values for individual countries or sub-national entities. The average in each figure or table corresponds to the arithmetic mean of the respective estimates for each of the OECD countries or sub-national entities included in the figure or table. In the calculation of the OECD average, England (United Kingdom) and Northern Ireland (United Kingdom) are treated as separate entities. Cyprus*, Jakarta (Indonesia), Lithuania, and the Russian Federation** and Singapore are not included in the OECD averages presented in any of the figures or tables.

Standard error (S.E.)

The statistical estimates presented in this report are based on samples of adults, rather than values that could be calculated if every person in the target population in every country had answered every question. Therefore, each estimate has a degree of uncertainty associated with sampling and measurement error, which can be expressed as a standard error. The use of confidence intervals provides a way to make inferences about the population means and proportions in a manner that reflects the uncertainty associated with the sample estimates. In this report, confidence intervals are stated at 95% confidence level. In other words, the result for the corresponding population would lie within the confidence interval in 95 out of 100 replications of the measurement on different samples drawn from the same population.

Statistical significance

Differences considered to be statistically significant from either zero or between estimates are based on the 5% level of significance, unless otherwise stated. In the figures, statistically significant estimates are denoted in a darker tone.

Symbols for missing data and abbreviations

a   Data are not applicable because the category does not apply.

c   There are too few observations or no observation to provide reliable estimates (i.e. there are fewer than 30 individuals). Also denotes unstable marginal probabilities which may occur when probabilities are very close to 0 or 1.

m   Data are not available. The data are not submitted by the country or were collected but subsequently removed from the publication for technical reasons.

w   Data have been withdrawn at the request of the country concerned.

S.E.   Standard Error

S.D.   Standard Deviation

Score dif.   Score-point difference between x and y

% dif.   Difference in percentage points between x and y

Marg. Prob.   Marginal probability

(L)   Literacy domain

(N)   Numeracy domain

(P)   Problem solving in technology-rich environments domain

GDP   Gross Domestic Product

ISCED   International Standard Classification of Education

ISCO   International Standard Classification of Occupations

Country coverage

This publication features data on 28 OECD countries (or regions within these countries): Australia, Austria, Belgium, Canada, Chile, the Czech Republic, Denmark, Estonia, Finland, France, Germany, Greece,*** Ireland, Israel, Italy, Japan, Korea, the Netherlands, New Zealand, Norway, Poland, the Slovak Republic, Slovenia, Spain, Sweden, Turkey, the United Kingdom and the United States. In Belgium, data was collected in the Flanders region only. In the United Kingdom, data was collected in England and Northern Ireland only. In addition, five countries that are not members of the OECD participated in the survey: Cyprus,* Jakarta (Indonesia), Lithuania, the Russian Federation** and Singapore. Data estimates for England (United Kingdom) and Northern Ireland (United Kingdom) are presented separately.

The names of the countries participating in Round 2 of the Survey of Adult Skills are presented in blue in all figures and tables.

Rounding

Data estimates, including mean scores, proportions and standard errors, are generally rounded to one decimal place. Therefore, even if the value (0.0) is shown for standard errors, this does not necessarily imply that the standard error is zero, but that it is smaller than 0.05.

Education levels

The classification of levels of education is based on the International Standard Classification of Education (ISCED 1997). A revised version of ISCED (ISCED 2011) was adopted by the UNESCO General Conference at its 36th session in November 2011 (UIS, 2012). Member States have applied ISCED 2011 in the reporting of their education statistics from 2014. Data on educational participation and attainment from Round 1 of the Survey of Adult Skills was coded using the ISECD 1997 classification. To maintain comparability with the data from Round 1, data from Round 2 has also been coded using ISCED 1997.

Further documentation and resources

The details of the technical standards guiding the design and implementation of the Survey of Adult Skills (PIAAC) can be found at (www.oecd.org/site/piaac/). Information regarding the design, methodology and implementation of the Survey of Adult Skills can be found in summary form in *The Survey of Adult Skills: Reader's Companion, Second Edition* (OECD, 2016) and, in detail, in the *Technical Report of the Survey of Adult Skills, Second Edition* (OECD, forthcoming).

*Note regarding Cyprus

Note by Turkey

The information in this document with reference to "Cyprus" relates to the southern part of the Island. There is no single authority representing both Turkish and Greek Cypriot people on the Island. Turkey recognises the Turkish Republic of Northern Cyprus (TRNC). Until a lasting and equitable solution is found within the context of the United Nations, Turkey shall preserve its position concerning the "Cyprus issue".

Note by all the European Union Member States of the OECD and the European Union

The Republic of Cyprus is recognised by all members of the United Nations with the exception of Turkey. The information in this document relates to the area under the effective control of the Government of the Republic of Cyprus.

Throughout this report, including the main body, boxes and annexes, Cyprus is accompanied by a symbol referring to this note.

**Note regarding the Russian Federation

The sample for the Russian Federation does not include the population of the Moscow municipal area. The data published, therefore, do not represent the entire resident population aged 16-65 in the Russian Federation but rather the population of the Russian Federation *excluding* the population residing in the Moscow municipal area. More detailed information regarding the data from the Russian Federation as well as that of other countries can be found in the *Technical Report of the Survey of Adult Skills, Second Edition* (OECD, forthcoming).

***Note regarding Greece

The data for Greece include a large number of cases (1 032) in which there are responses to the background questionnaire but where responses to the assessment are missing. Proficiency scores have been estimated for these respondents based on their responses to the background questionnaire and the population model used to estimate plausible values for responses missing by design derived from the remaining 3 893 cases. More details can be found in the *Technical Report of the Survey of Adult Skills, Second Edition* (OECD, forthcoming).

References

OECD (forthcoming), *Technical Report of the Survey of Adult Skills, Second Edition.*

OECD (2016), *The Survey of Adult Skills: Reader's Companion, Second Edition,* OECD Skills Studies, OECD Publishing, Paris, http://dx.doi.org/10.1787/9789264258075-en.

UNESCO Institute for Statistics (UIS) (2012), *International Standard Classification of Education ISCED 2011,* UNESCO Institute for Statistics.

Executive summary

The capacity to manage information and solve problems using computers is becoming a necessity as ICT applications permeate the workplace, the classroom and lecture hall, the home, and social interaction more generally. The Survey of Adult Skills, a product of the OECD Programme for the International Assessment of Adult Competencies (PIAAC), was designed to measure adults' proficiency in several key information-processing skills, namely literacy, numeracy and problem solving in technology-rich environments. Adults who are highly proficient in the skills measured by the survey are likely to be able to make the most of the opportunities created by the technological and structural changes modern societies are going through. Those who struggle to use new technologies are at greater risk of losing out.

The results from the first round of the survey, covering 24 countries and economies, were reported in the *OECD Skills Outlook 2013: First Results from the Survey of Adult Skills*. Another nine countries and economies collected data during 2014-15. This report presents the main findings for all 33 countries and economies that participated in the study over the two rounds. It finds substantial variation across countries/economies in adults' average proficiency in the three domains assessed. More than 80 score points separate the highest- and lowest-scoring countries in literacy and numeracy, although many countries and economies score within a relatively close range of each other. Within countries and economies, proficiency scores in literacy and numeracy vary considerably: on average, 62 score points separate the 25% of adults who attained the highest and lowest scores in literacy; in numeracy, 68 score points separate those two groups.

In almost all countries/economies, a sizeable proportion of adults (18.5% of adults, on average) has poor reading skills and poor numeracy skills (22.7% of adults, on average). Around one in four adults has no or only limited experience with computers or lacks confidence in their ability to use computers. In addition, nearly one in two adults is proficient only at or below Level 1 in problem solving in technology-rich environments. This adult can only use familiar applications to solve problems that involve few steps and explicit criteria, such as sorting e-mails into pre-existing folders.

SKILLS PROFICIENCY AND DEMOGRAPHICS

The survey finds that, in the cohorts examined, proficiency in literacy and numeracy peaks at around age 30, while proficiency in problem solving in technology-rich environments peaks at around age 25. On average, older adults (55-65 year-olds) score around 30 score points lower in literacy than 25-34 year-olds. A substantial share of age-related differences in proficiency is associated with other individual characteristics, particularly adults' level of educational attainment. This is likely because highly proficient adults are more likely to participate in higher levels of education, and because longer periods of study provide the opportunity to develop higher levels proficiency in information-processing skills.

Parents' educational background, a proxy for socio-economic status, exerts a significant influence on adults' proficiency in literacy. Having at least one parent with tertiary qualifications is associated with a 40 score-point advantage over adults with neither parent having attained an upper secondary degree. Gender gaps in proficiency – which are negligible in literacy and average around 10 score points, in favour of men, in numeracy – are more pronounced among older adults. This could reflect either the fact that gender gaps in educational attainment are wider among older adults, or that women's numeracy skills depreciate more over time, possibly because they participate less in the labour market.

PROFICIENCY AND THE LABOUR MARKET

Adults with higher proficiency in literacy, numeracy and problem solving in technology-rich environments tend to have better outcomes in the labour market than their less-proficient peers. They have greater chances of being employed and, if employed, of earning higher wages. Across the countries that participated in the Survey of Adult Skills, an adult who scores one standard deviation higher than another on the literacy scale (around 48 score points) is 0.8 percentage point more likely to be employed than unemployed, on average, after accounting for other factors, including educational attainment. And an increase of one standard deviation in literacy proficiency is associated with a 6% increase in wages, on average across the 33 participating countries and economies.

Workers who use information-processing skills more intensely in their jobs also tend to earn higher wages, even after accounting for differences in educational attainment and skills proficiency. Writing and problem solving are the skills most frequently used at work; reading skills follow close behind, while numeracy and ICT skills are least used.

On average across the countries/economies that participated in the survey, the intensity with which workers use their information-processing skills in their jobs is also related to the likelihood of being extremely satisfied at work, even after taking into account proficiency, educational attainment, gross hourly wages and a number of socio-demographic characteristics. The way work is organised – through implementing High-Performance Work Practices like team work, autonomy, task discretion, mentoring, job rotation and applying new learning – can increase the frequency with which skills are used at work.

SKILLS AND THE ENGAGED CITIZEN

Proficiency in information-processing skills is positively associated with many aspects of individual well-being, notably health, beliefs about one's impact on the political process, trust in others, and participation in volunteer or associative activities. In most countries, adults who scored at lower levels of proficiency in literacy were more likely than those who scored at high levels to have reported poor health, that they have little impact on the political process, and that they do not participate in associative or volunteer activities. Individuals with lower proficiency were also more likely than those with higher proficiency to have reported less trust in others.

Results from the survey show clearly that what people know and what they do with what they know have a major impact on their life chances. Skills have become the global currency of 21st-century economies; but this "currency" can depreciate as the requirements of labour markets evolve and individuals lose the skills they do not use. To ensure that people acquire the right skills and that economies and societies make good use of those skills, a concerted effort is needed by governments, which design financial incentives and favourable tax policies that are conducive to skills development; education systems, which foster entrepreneurship and offer vocational training; employers, who invest in learning and can motivate workers to put more of their skills to use; labour unions, which ensure that investments in training result in better-quality jobs and higher salaries; and individuals, who take advantage of learning opportunities and deploy their skills at work and in everyday life. The OECD is working with many of the countries who participated in the survey to develop national skills strategies that bring all of these players together to make this happen.

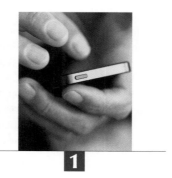

1

Overview:
Why skills matter

The Survey of Adult Skills, a product of the OECD Programme for the International Assessment of Adult Competencies (PIAAC), assesses adults' (16-65 year-olds) proficiency in three key information-processing skills: literacy, numeracy and problem solving in technology-rich environments. It provides a rich source of data for policy makers, analysts and researchers concerned with issues such as the development and maintenance of a population's skills, the relationships between the education system and the labour market, the efficiency of the labour market in matching workers and jobs, inequality, and the social and labour market integration of certain subgroups of the population, such as immigrants. Beyond offering an insight into the level and distribution of information-processing skills across the population as a whole and for key subgroups, it provides information on the benefits these skills provide in the labour market and in everyday life. Information about what the survey assesses and how it was carried out can be found in Box 1.1.

The results from the first round of the survey, covering 24 countries/economies, were released in October 2013 (OECD, 2013). Results are now available for a further nine countries/economies that collected data during 2014-15. This report presents the main findings for the 33 countries/economies that have participated in the study over the two rounds.

Box 1.1 **Key facts concerning the Survey of Adult Skills (PIAAC)**

What PIAAC assesses

The Survey of Adult Skills (PIAAC) assesses the proficiency of 16-65 year-olds in literacy, numeracy and problem solving in technology-rich environments. These are "key information-processing skills" that are relevant to adults in many social contexts and work situations, and necessary for fully integrating and participating in the labour market, education and training, and social and civic life.

In addition, the survey collects a range of information on the reading- and numeracy-related activities of respondents, the use of information and communication technologies at work and in everyday life, and on the practice of a range of other generic skills, such as collaborating with others and organising one's time, required of individuals in their work. Respondents are also asked whether their skills and qualifications match their work requirements and whether they have autonomy over key aspects of their work.

Methods

The Survey of Adults Skills was conducted over two rounds of data collection.

In the first round, around 166 000 adults aged 16-65 years in 24 countries/economies were surveyed. In 21 countries – Australia, Austria, Canada, Cyprus,[1] the Czech Republic, Denmark, Estonia, Finland, France, Germany, Ireland, Italy, Japan, Korea, the Netherlands, Norway, Poland, the Slovak Republic, Spain, Sweden and the United States – the entire national population was covered. In Belgium, data were collected in Flanders; in the United Kingdom, data were collected in England and Northern Ireland (data are reported separately for England and Northern Ireland in the report). In the Russian Federation, the data do not cover the Moscow municipal area.

Data collection for Round 1 of the Survey of Adult Skills took place from 1 August 2011 to 31 March 2012 in most participating countries/economies. In Canada, data were collected from November 2011 to June 2012; and France collected data from September to November 2012.

Nine countries took part in the second round of the assessment: Chile, Greece, Indonesia, Israel, Lithuania, New Zealand, Singapore, Slovenia and Turkey. A total of 50 250 adults were surveyed. In all countries except Indonesia the entire national population was covered. In Indonesia, data were collected in the Jakarta municipal area only.

Data collection for Round 2 of the Survey of Adult Skills took place from April 2014 to end-March 2015. The duration of fieldwork varied from around 100 to 330 days, depending on the country.

The language of assessment was the official language(s) of each participating country/economy. In some countries, the assessment was also conducted in widely spoken minority or regional languages.

Three domains of skills were assessed: literacy, numeracy and problem solving in technology-rich environments. In addition, a separate assessment of "reading components" that tested basic reading skills, such as vocabulary knowledge, understanding of the logic of sentences and fluency in the reading of passages of text, was also conducted.

...

Among Round-1 countries, four chose not to conduct the problem-solving assessment (Cyprus,[1] France, Italy and Spain), while four (France, Finland, Japan and the Russian Federation) chose not to conduct the assessment of reading components.

All countries/economies participating in Round 2 administered all components of the assessment, with the exception of Jakarta (Indonesia), where the assessment of problem solving in technology-rich environments was not conducted. This was because the problem-solving assessment existed only in a computer-based format, and Indonesia chose to administer all the components of the assessment exclusively in paper-and-pencil format.

The target population for the survey was the non-institutionalised population of 16-65 year-olds residing in the country or region at the time of the data collection, irrespective of nationality, citizenship or language status.

Sample sizes depended primarily on the number of cognitive domains assessed and the number of languages in which the assessment was administered. Some countries boosted sample sizes in order to have reliable estimates of proficiency for the residents of particular geographical regions and/or for certain subgroups of the population, such as indigenous inhabitants or immigrants. The achieved national samples ranged from a minimum of approximately 4 000 persons to a maximum of nearly 27 300 persons.

The survey was administered under the supervision of trained interviewers either in the respondent's home or in a location agreed between the respondent and the interviewer. The background questionnaire was delivered in Computer-Aided Personal Interview (CAPI) format by the interviewer. Depending on the situation of the respondent, the time taken to complete the questionnaire ranged between 30 and 45 minutes.

After having answered the background questionnaire, the respondent completed the assessment either on a laptop computer or by completing a paper version using printed test booklets, depending on the respondent's computer skills. Respondents could take as much or as little time as needed to complete the assessment. On average, respondents took 50 minutes to complete the cognitive assessment.

Identical instruments were used in Rounds 1 and 2 of the survey. The one exception was in Jakarta (Indonesia) where, since only paper-based instruments were used, additional test items were added to the paper-based instruments used in the other countries/economies. Specifically, the Indonesian instruments contained 49 literacy items and 49 numeracy items compared to the 20 items in both domains contained in the paper-based instruments used in other countries/economies.

Respondents with very low literacy skills bypassed the full literacy, numeracy and problem solving in technology-rich environments assessments and went directly to the test of basic "reading component" skills instead. As part of this test, the time taken by respondents to complete the tasks was recorded in addition to their answers. The reading components assessment was also taken by all respondents taking the paper version of the assessment.

Reporting the results

The results from the assessment are reported on a 500-point scale; a higher score indicates greater proficiency. To help interpret the scores, the scale is divided into proficiency levels. There are six levels for literacy and numeracy (from below Level 1 – the lowest – to Level 5 – the highest) and four in problem solving in technology-rich environments (from below Level 1 – the lowest – to Level 3 – the highest).

At each level, individuals can successfully complete certain types of tasks. For example, a person who scores at Level 1 in literacy can successfully complete reading tasks that require reading relatively short texts to locate a single piece of information, which is identical to or synonymous with the information given in the question or directive and in which there is little competing information. A person proficient at Level 5 in literacy can perform tasks that involve searching for and integrating information across multiple, dense texts, constructing syntheses of similar and contrasting ideas or points of view, or evaluating evidence and arguments. He or she can apply and evaluate logical and conceptual models, and evaluate the reliability of evidentiary sources and select key information. He or she is also aware of subtle, rhetorical cues and can make high-level inferences or use specialised background knowledge.

Results are reported in this publication for 33 countries/economies. In the case of the United Kingdom, results are presented separately for the two devolved administrations of England and Northern Ireland that implemented the Survey of Adult Skills.

...

Comparisons of the results of countries/economies in Round 1 and Round 2

Identical data-collection instruments and methodology were used in Rounds 1 and 2 of the survey. The one difference is that data collection for Rounds 1 and 2 occurred some three years apart. The difference in reference dates for the two rounds of the study is unlikely to have a major impact on the proficiency of the adult populations in Round-1 countries/economies compared to that of adults in Round-2 countries/economies. However, data were collected at different points in the economic cycle in the two rounds; this may have some effect on the relationships observed between proficiency and labour market outcomes and jobs characteristics, in particular, in the countries/economies in the two different rounds.

---

1. *Note by Turkey:* The information in this document with reference to "Cyprus" relates to the southern part of the Island. There is no single authority representing both Turkish and Greek Cypriot people on the Island. Turkey recognises the Turkish Republic of Northern Cyprus (TRNC). Until a lasting and equitable solution is found within the context of the United Nations, Turkey shall preserve its position concerning the "Cyprus issue".

Note by all the European Union Member States of the OECD and the European Union: The Republic of Cyprus is recognised by all members of the United Nations with the exception of Turkey. The information in this document relates to the area under the effective control of the Government of the Republic of Cyprus.

Figure 1.1 ■ **Snapshot of performance in literacy, numeracy and problem solving**

Mean proficiency scores of 16-65 year-olds in literacy and numeracy, and the percentage of 16-65 year-olds scoring at Level 2 or 3 in problem solving in technology-rich environments

■ Significantly **above** the average
□ Not significantly different from the average
■ Significantly **below** the average

	Literacy	Numeracy	Problem solving in technology-rich environments
	Mean score	Mean score	% at Level 2 or 3
OECD countries and economies			
Australia	280	268	38
Austria	269	275	32
Canada	273	265	37
Chile	220	206	15
Czech Republic	274	276	33
Denmark	271	278	39
England (UK)	273	262	35
Estonia	276	273	28
Finland	288	282	42
Flanders (Belgium)	275	280	35
France	262	254	m
Germany	270	272	36
Greece	254	252	14
Ireland	267	256	25
Israel	255	251	27
Italy	250	247	m
Japan	296	288	35
Korea	273	263	30
Netherlands	284	280	42
New Zealand	281	271	44
Northern Ireland (UK)	269	259	29
Norway	278	278	41
Poland	267	260	19
Slovak Republic	274	276	26
Slovenia	256	258	25
Spain	252	246	m
Sweden	279	279	44
Turkey	227	219	8
United States	270	253	31
OECD average	**268**	**263**	**31**
Partners			
Cyprus[1]	269	265	m
Jakarta (Indonesia)	200	210	m
Lithuania	267	267	18
Russian Federation[2]	275	270	26
Singapore	258	257	37

Notes: Cyprus,[1] France, Italy, Jakarta (Indonesia) and Spain did not participate in the problem solving in technology-rich environments assessment.
1. See note 1 in Box 1.1.
2. See note at the end of this chapter.
Countries and economies are listed in alphabetical order.
Source: Survey of Adult Skills (PIAAC) (2012, 2015), Tables A2.3, A2.5 and A2.6.
StatLink ⟹ http://dx.doi.org/10.1787/888933365695

PROFICIENCY IN INFORMATION-PROCESSING SKILLS AMONG ADULTS

Average adult proficiency in information-processing skills varies considerably among the 33 countries/economies covered by the Survey of Adult Skills, although many countries/economies have average scores that fall within a relatively limited range. Some 97 score points[2] separate the average adult proficiency in literacy in Japan and Jakarta (Indonesia) – the highest- and lowest-scoring countries/economies, respectively. The differences between countries/economies reflect, in part, the different starting points and pathways of economic, educational and social development that the countries/economies in the study have followed over the past half century, as well as current institutional arrangements and policies. For example, the rapid economic development and educational expansion over the post-war period in Korea and Singapore are reflected in low levels of educational attainment and proficiency among older generations and high attainment and proficiency among younger adults. In some countries/economies, high average proficiency in literacy and numeracy is not necessarily accompanied by high proficiency in problem solving in technology-rich environments. This could reflect historical differences across countries in how access to ICT was expanded among the population.

There are also considerable differences in the extent of the variation or dispersion of proficiency across countries/economies. Furthermore, the extent of the score variation within countries/economies is inversely related to their average level of proficiency. In other words, good average performance is usually associated with less variation in performance within a country/economy. Nevertheless, it is important to be cautious when interpreting this correlation as it is relatively weak and overwhelmingly relies on the few (outlier) countries.

In almost all countries/economies, a sizeable proportion of adults has poor reading skills (18.9% of adults, on average) and poor numeracy skills (22.7% of adults, on average). The share of adults proficient at or below Level 1 in literacy ranges from 69.3% in Jakarta (Indonesia) to 4.9% in Japan and, in numeracy, from 61.9% in Chile to 8.1% in Japan. These are adults who can successfully complete reading tasks that involve only short and simple texts, and mathematics tasks involving only basic operations.

Figure 1.2 ■ **Average and variability of numeracy scores**
Relationship between mean numeracy proficiency score and variability

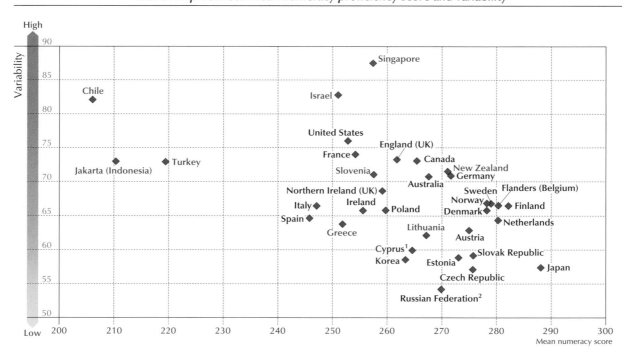

Note: The measure of variability used is the interquartile range (difference between the third quartile and the first quartile).
1. See note 1 in Box 1.1.
2. See note at the end of this chapter.
Source: Survey of Adult Skills (PIAAC) (2012, 2015), Table A2.5.
StatLink ⎙ http://dx.doi.org/10.1787/888933365704

Yet there are very few adults in any of the participating countries/economies who can be described as illiterate in the language of the test. As part of the assessment, information was collected on the vocabulary knowledge, the level of understanding of the logic of sentences, and fluency in reading paragraphs of text of adults with poor reading skills. In most cases, adults with poor reading skills displayed a good knowledge of basic print vocabulary, but they had somewhat limited understanding of sentence logic and had some difficulty reading passages of text fluently. They also took considerably more time to complete the vocabulary, sentence-processing and fluency tasks than adults with better reading skills. In other words, they had not reached the level of automaticity that characterises efficient reading.

Many adults in all countries/economies have no experience using computers, or extremely limited ICT skills, or have low proficiency in problem solving in technology-rich environments. Around one in four adults has no or only limited experience with computers or lacks confidence in their ability to use computers. In addition, nearly one in two adults is proficient only at or below Level 1 in problem solving in technology-rich environments, which translates into being able to use only familiar applications to solve problems that involve few steps and explicit criteria, such as sorting e-mails into pre-existing folders.

A close relationship is found among low proficiency in literacy and numeracy, low proficiency in problem solving in technology-rich environments, and limited familiarity with computers. Low proficiency in literacy and numeracy can be a significant barrier to using ICT applications to manage information. First, poor literacy may hinder the acquisition of basic ICT skills. Second, even if adults have some computer skills, those with poor literacy and numeracy skills will find it difficult to handle many of the information-management and information-processing tasks encountered in online environments. This implies that, in some countries/economies, adults with poor proficiency in literacy and numeracy may be slow to adopt and use information technologies, which could undermine their labour market outcomes. Given these findings, policies to improve adults' ICT competence should focus as much on improving literacy and numeracy skills as on improving access to technology (OECD, 2015).

PROFICIENCY AND SOCIO-DEMOGRAPHIC CHARACTERISTICS

Within countries/economies there is considerable variation in proficiency in information-processing skills across adults with different socio-demographic characteristics. In particular, proficiency is closely associated with age, educational attainment, parents' level of education and immigrant background, but only weakly associated with gender.

In general, proficiency in literacy and numeracy peaks at around age 30, while proficiency in problem solving in technology-rich environments peaks at around age 25. On average, older adults (55-65 year-olds) score around 30 score points lower in literacy than 25-34 year-olds. A substantial share of the age-related differences in proficiency is associated with other individual characteristics, particularly adults' level of educational attainment. Accounting for other background characteristics strongly reduces observed age-related differences in proficiency, especially in countries/ economies that expanded access to higher education over the past three decades; however, in the majority of countries, those differences are not completely eradicated. Still, variations in age-related proficiency across countries/economies suggest that the evolution of proficiency over a lifetime is not determined solely by biological factors; policy, too, can influence the maintenance or loss of proficiency among older adults.

As expected, in all countries/economies there is a close association between the educational attainment of adults and their proficiency in information-processing skills. This is likely because, on the one hand, adults with higher proficiency are more likely to participate in higher levels of education and, on the other, longer periods of study provide the opportunity to develop higher levels proficiency in information-processing skills. Among 25-65 year-olds (i.e. adults who have generally completed formal education), proficiency is highest among those with tertiary qualifications and lowest among those whose highest qualification is less than secondary education. On average, some 61 score points separate the estimated literacy proficiency of a 25-65 year-old with a tertiary qualification from someone whose highest qualification is less than secondary education.

Parents' educational background exerts a significant influence on adults' proficiency in literacy. Having at least one parent with tertiary qualifications is associated with a 40 score-point advantage over adults with neither parent having attained an upper secondary degree. A significant portion of this difference (about half) is explained by other socio-demographic characteristics, most notably the fact that children of high-educated parents are themselves more likely to attain higher levels of education.

Immigrants who were brought up speaking a different language from that of the assessment have significantly lower average proficiency. Native-born adults whose first or second language learned as a child is the same as that of the assessment scored 30 points higher than foreign-born adults whose native language is different from that of the assessment, on average.

Immigrants whose native language is the same as that of the host country tend to score significantly better than other immigrants, and are often nearly as proficient as native-born adults. The magnitude of the differences, and the extent to which other background characteristics might account for them, varies enormously across countries/economies, reflecting countries' vastly different migration histories and policies.

There are a number of countries/economies in which immigrants' reading proficiency in the language of the host country is extremely low in absolute terms as well as relative to that of adults who were born in the country and have spoken the local language from birth. While this is partly related to the age at arrival in the country, it is also an indication of possible difficulties in integrating into the host country's labour market.

The difference in literacy proficiency between men and women is negligible. In numeracy, men have a more substantial advantage, scoring about 10 score points higher than women, on average. Gender gaps in proficiency are more pronounced among older adults. This could reflect either the fact that gender gaps in educational attainment are wider among older adults, or that women's skills depreciate more over time, possibly because they participate less in the labour market.

Figure 1.3 ■ Literacy proficiency, by educational attainment

Mean literacy proficiency scores, by educational attainment (adults aged 25-65)

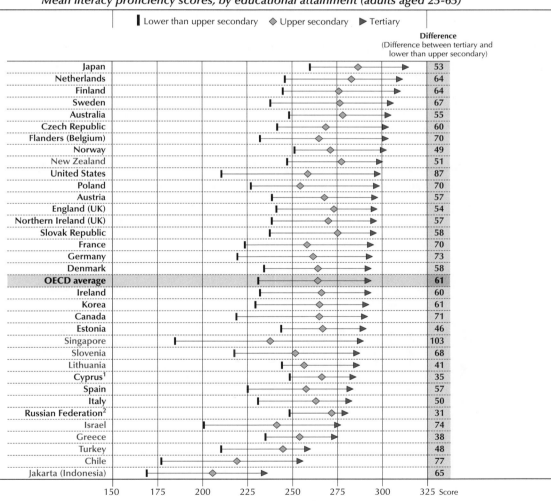

■ Lower than upper secondary ◆ Upper secondary ▶ Tertiary

Difference
(Difference between tertiary and lower than upper secondary)

Country	Difference
Japan	53
Netherlands	64
Finland	64
Sweden	67
Australia	55
Czech Republic	60
Flanders (Belgium)	70
Norway	49
New Zealand	51
United States	87
Poland	70
Austria	57
England (UK)	54
Northern Ireland (UK)	57
Slovak Republic	58
France	70
Germany	73
Denmark	58
OECD average	**61**
Ireland	60
Korea	61
Canada	71
Estonia	46
Singapore	103
Slovenia	68
Lithuania	41
Cyprus[1]	35
Spain	57
Italy	50
Russian Federation[2]	31
Israel	74
Greece	38
Turkey	48
Chile	77
Jakarta (Indonesia)	65

150   175   200   225   250   275   300   325 Score

Notes: All differences are statistically significant. Lower than upper secondary education includes ISCED 1, 2 and 3C short. Upper secondary education includes ISCED 3A, 3B, 3C long and 4. Tertiary education includes ISCED 5A, 5B and 6. Where possible, foreign qualifications are included as per their closest correspondance to the respective national education systems.

1. See note 1 in Box 1.1.

2. See note at the end of this chapter.

Countries and economies are ranked in descending order of the mean score in literacy for adults aged 25-65 who have attained tertiary education.

Source: Survey of Adult Skills (PIAAC) (2012, 2015), Table A3.2 (L).

StatLink ᐅᐸᖗ http://dx.doi.org/10.1787/888933365719

INFORMATION-PROCESSING SKILLS AND WELL-BEING

Proficiency in information-processing skills is positively associated with many aspects of individual well-being, notably health, beliefs about one's impact on the political process, trust in others, and participation in volunteer activities. This is true both on average across the countries/economies that participated in the Survey of Adult Skills and in most countries/economies. In most countries/economies, adults who scored at lower levels of proficiency in literacy were more likely than those who scored at high levels to have reported poor health, that they have little impact on the political process, and that they do not participate in associative or volunteer activities. Individuals with lower proficiency were also more likely than those with higher proficiency to have reported less trust in others. These relationships hold even after accounting for educational attainment and other socio-demographic characteristics, such as age, gender and family background. As is discussed in more detail in the next section, adults with higher proficiency in these skills also tend to have better outcomes in the labour market.

INFORMATION-PROCESSING SKILLS AND THE LABOUR MARKET

The Survey of Adult Skills provides a rich source of data for analysing a number of labour market issues, such as the relationship of proficiency in information-processing skills and other components of human capital to employment and wages; the extent to which workers use information-processing skills in their jobs and the factors that encourage more or less frequent use of such skills; and the effectiveness of the labour market in ensuring a good match between workers' qualifications and skills and the demands of their jobs.

Proficiency in information-processing skills and labour market outcomes

Adults with higher proficiency in literacy, numeracy and problem solving in technology-rich environments tend to have better outcomes in the labour market than their less-proficient peers. They have somewhat greater chances of being employed and, if employed, of earning higher wages. This holds true also when accounting for other factors commonly associated with better outcomes in the labour market, such as educational attainment, work experience, occupation and field of study.

Figure 1.4 ■ **Impact of education, literacy proficiency and use of reading at work on wages**

Percentage change in wages associated with a change of one standard deviation in years of education, proficiency in literacy and use of reading at work

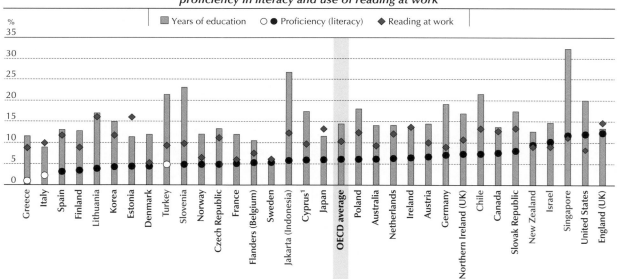

Notes: Hourly wages, including bonuses, in PPP-adjusted USD (2012). Coefficients from the OLS regression of log hourly wages on years of education, proficiency and use of reading skills at work, directly interpreted as percentage effects on wages. Coefficients adjusted for age, gender, foreign-born status and tenure. The wage distribution was trimmed to eliminate the 1st and 99th percentiles. One standard deviation in proficiency in literacy is 48 points. One standard deviation in years of education is 3.2 years. The analysis excludes the Russian Federation because wage data obtained through the survey do not compare well with those available from other sources. Hence further checks are required before wage data for this country can be considered reliable. Statistically significant values (at the 10% level) are shown in a darker tone.

1. See note 1 in Box 1.1.

Countries and economies are ranked in ascending order of the effect of literacy proficiency on wages.

Source: Survey of Adult Skills (PIAAC) (2012, 2015), Table A5.4.

StatLink ᴍᴤ᠍ᴾ http://dx.doi.org/10.1787/888933365726

Across the countries/economies that participated in the Survey of Adult Skills, an adult who scores 48 points higher than another on the literacy scale (the equivalent of one standard deviation) is 0.8 percentage point more likely to be employed than unemployed, on average, after accounting for other factors, including educational attainment. The relationship between literacy proficiency and employment varies considerably among countries/economies. While in most countries/economies the relationship between literacy proficiency and the chances of being employed is strong and positive, it is weak or even negative in a few countries/economies. This may reflect differences in the support and incentives available to unemployed workers with different skill levels across countries/economies. In countries/economies with weak support schemes for the unemployed, the low skilled may need to find a job – any job – to maintain certain income security; in these countries only the high skilled with capacity to save may be able to spend time in unemployment. In countries/economies with more comprehensive income support for the unemployed, the low- and high- skilled may be able to take time to find a well-matched job.

The relationship between literacy proficiency and employment is not as strong as that between educational attainment[3] and employment. An increase of 3.4 years of completed formal education (the equivalent of one standard deviation) is related to a 3.1 percentage point increase in the likelihood of being employed. This is not surprising, given the breadth and variety of skills that are developed in education and training, and the role of education qualifications as a signal of an individual's level of skills.

The importance of literacy proficiency relative to education qualifications for employment increases with age. This is consistent with the phenomenon known as "employer learning" (OECD, 2014). In the case of young people with little work experience, employers are likely to rely on the available, albeit imperfect, signals of skills, such as education qualifications, when hiring or firing. For adults who have worked more years and whose performance has been observed over time, actual proficiency is a stronger predictor of labour market outcomes than qualifications.

Figure 1.5 ▪ **Contribution of education, literacy and numeracy to the variation in wages**
Contribution of each factor to the percentage of the explained variance (R-squared) in hourly wages

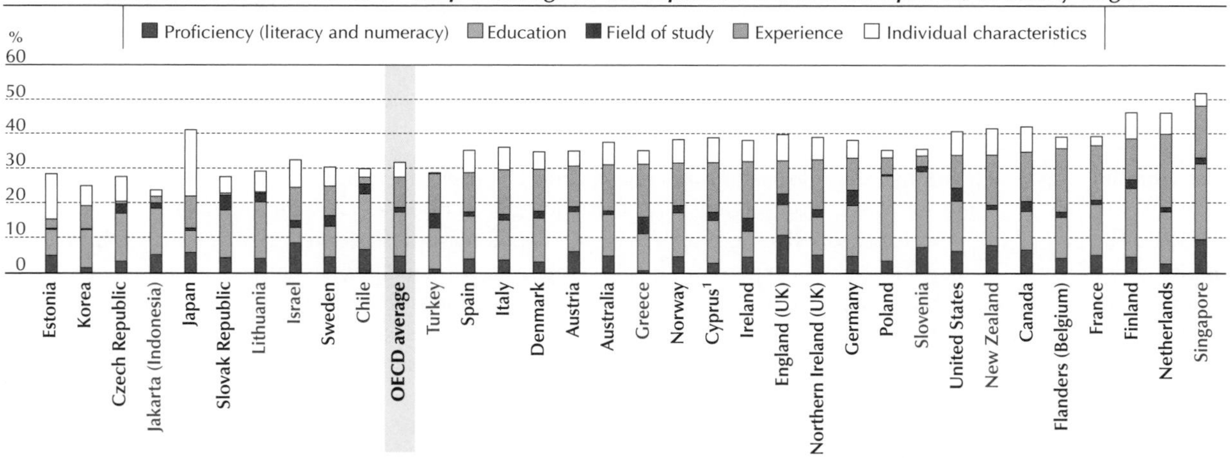

Notes: Results obtained using a regression-based decomposition following the methods in Fields (2004). Each bar summarises the results from one regression and its height represents the R-squared of that regression. The sub-components of each bar show the contribution of each factor (or set of regressors) to the total R-squared. The Fields decomposition is explained in more detail in Box 5.4 of the *OECD Employment Outlook 2014* (OECD, 2014).

The dependent variable in the regression model is the log of hourly wages, including bonuses in PPP-adjusted USD (2012). The regressors for each factor are: years of working experience and its squared term for "Experience"; proficiency in literacy and numeracy for "Proficiency"; years of education for "Education"; and gender, marital status, migration status and language spoken at home for "Individual characteristics".

The analysis excludes the Russian Federation because wage data obtained through the survey do not compare well with those available from other sources. Hence, further checks are required before wage data for this country can be considered reliable.

1. See note 1 in Box 1.1.

Countries and economies are ranked in ascending order of the sum of the contributions of education, proficiency, field of study and experience.

Source: Survey of Adult Skills (PIAAC) (2012, 2015), Table A5.5.

StatLink ⌨📊 http://dx.doi.org/10.1787/888933365732

Higher literacy proficiency is also associated with higher wages. The increase in wages associated with a one standard deviation increase in literacy proficiency is 6%, on average across the 33 participating countries/economies. It varies from 4% or less in Finland, Greece, Italy, Lithuania, Slovenia and Spain, to 10% or more in England (United Kingdom), Israel, Singapore and the United States. As with employment, other factors, particularly educational attainment and length of work experience, also have an impact on wages. The increase in wages associated with a one standard deviation rise in years of education (around 3.2 years) is larger (14%), ranging from less than 7% in Sweden to more than 20% in Chile, Jakarta (Indonesia), Slovenia, Turkey and the United States, and more than 30% in Singapore.

A different way to assess the relative influence of proficiency and other factors on wages is to look at the share of explained variation by each factor. According to the survey, some 32% of the variation observed in wages on average across countries/economies is explained by factors such as age, skills use, experience and job characteristics, years of education and skills proficiency. Proficiency in information-processing skills accounts for 5% of the variation, compared to 13% for educational attainment, 1% for field of study, and 9% for work experience. Individual characteristics, such as gender, immigrant background, marital status and language spoken at home, account for a further 4% of the variation. In summary, proficiency in literacy and numeracy, educational attainment, field of study and work experience can all be considered different aspects of workers' human capital that contribute independently to adults' productivity and wages.

THE USE OF INFORMATION-PROCESSING SKILLS AT WORK

As noted above, workers who use information-processing skills more intensely in their jobs also tend to earn higher wages, even after accounting for differences in educational attainment, skills proficiency and occupation. Writing and problem solving are the skills most frequently used at work; reading skills follow close behind, while numeracy and ICT skills are least used. The use of ICT and reading skills are the most closely related to hourly wages. In contrast, while using numeracy and problem-solving skills at work matters as much as proficiency, its correlation with wages is much weaker than using ICT and reading skills.

The tasks involved in a job are also linked to greater job satisfaction and employee well-being. This is in line with other research in which skills use has sometimes been associated with concepts of job quality (e.g. Green et al. 2013), with possible spill-over effects into life satisfaction, more generally, and better health. Across the countries/economies that participated in the survey, on average, the intensity of the use of information-processing skills is related to the likelihood of being extremely satisfied at work, even after taking into account proficiency, educational attainment, gross hourly wages and a number of socio-demographic characteristics. In fact, the use of information-processing skills has a stronger impact on job satisfaction than the level of proficiency or years of education. Although magnitudes vary, patterns across countries/economies are strikingly similar. The relationships between the use of reading, writing and ICT skills at work and job satisfaction are statistically significant in nearly all countries/economies, while this is rarely the case for the use of numeracy and problem-solving skills.

The intensity with which workers use information-processing skills is closely and positively related to the presence of management practices and forms of work organisation that can be described as High-Performance Work Practices (HPWP). HPWP include aspects of work organisation – team work, autonomy, task discretion, mentoring, job rotation, applying new learning – as well as management practices – employee participation, incentive pay, training practices and flexibility in working hours (Johnston and Hawke, 2002). Workers in jobs that benefit from these practices make greater use of reading, writing, numeracy, ICT and problem-solving skills. The extent to which workers are engaged in these practices accounts for between 14% and 27% of the variation in the intensity with which workers use information-processing skills. The way work is organised – the extent of team work, autonomy, task discretion, mentoring, job rotation and applying new learning – influences the degree of a firm's flexibility to adapt job tasks to the skills of new hires. Some management practices, such as offering bonus pay, training and/or flexible working hours, may provide incentives for workers to shape their own jobs or to adapt job tasks to their own skills and interests.

Some studies have shown a link between greater intensity of skills use and higher productivity (UKCES, 2014) and lower staff turnover at the firm level. Some have argued that intensive skills use stimulates investment, employees' engagement and innovation (Wright and Sissons, 2012). In the Survey of Adult Skills, the intensity of use of reading skills at work is found to correlate strongly with output per hour worked. This is also the case for writing skills. One possible explanation for this is that skills use simply reflects workers' proficiency in those skills. If so, the link between the use of reading skills at work and productivity could actually reflect a relationship between literacy proficiency and productivity.

But this is not what the data show. The positive link between labour productivity and reading at work remains strong even after accounting for average proficiency scores in literacy and numeracy.[4] Once these adjustments are made, the average use of reading skills explains less of the variation in labour productivity across countries/economies (26% compared to 32% before the adjustment), but the variation remains statistically significant. Put simply, the intensity with which workers use information-processing skills is important, in itself, in accounting for differences in labour productivity, beyond workers' level of proficiency.

Figure 1.6 ■ **Correlation between labour productivity and the use of reading skills at work**

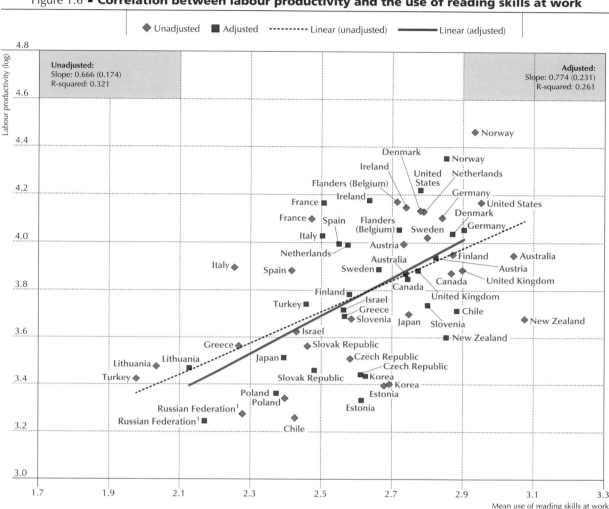

◆ Unadjusted　■ Adjusted　- - - - - Linear (unadjusted)　—— Linear (adjusted)

Unadjusted:
Slope: 0.666 (0.174)
R-squared: 0.321

Adjusted:
Slope: 0.774 (0.231)
R-squared: 0.261

Notes: Lines are best linear predictions. Labour productivity is equal to the GDP per hour worked, in USD current prices 2012 for Round-1 and 2014 for Round-2 countries/economies. Adjusted estimates are based on OLS regressions including controls for literacy and numeracy proficiency scores. Standard errors in parentheses.

1. See note at the end of this chapter.

Source: Survey of Adult Skills (PIAAC) (2012, 2015), Table A4.3.

StatLink ⏩ http://dx.doi.org/10.1787/888933365746

Mismatches of qualifications and skills

While it is important to have an education and training system that ensures that adults develop the skills needed in the labour market, it is also important that the labour market matches workers to jobs in which they can put their human capital to the best use. This is crucial if countries are to make the most of their investments in human capital and promote strong and inclusive growth. This is also a desirable outcome for individuals. A mismatch between workers' skills and the demands of their job has potentially significant economic implications. At the individual level, it affects job satisfaction and wages. At the firm level, it increases the rate of turnover and may reduce productivity. At the macro-economic level, it increases unemployment and reduces GDP growth through the waste of human capital and the implied reduction in productivity.

The Survey of Adult Skills provides a unique source of information on the match between workers and the skills demands of their jobs, in terms of qualifications, field of study, and proficiency in literacy, numeracy and problem solving. Mismatches between adults' skills and what is required or expected of them at work are found to be pervasive, but generate negative outcomes for workers when related to overqualification (Montt, 2015) or negative outcomes for economies when related to over- or underskilling (Adalet McGowan and Andrews, 2015).

On average, about 22% of workers reported that they are overqualified (i.e. that they have higher qualifications than those required to get their jobs) and 13% reported that they are underqualified for their jobs (i.e. that their qualifications are lower than those required to get their jobs). Moreover, 11% have higher literacy skills than those typically required in their job (overskilled), and 4% are underskilled. Finally, some 40% of workers are employed in an occupation that is unrelated to their field of study.

Some level of mismatch is inevitable in a dynamic economy. Requirements regarding skills and qualifications are never fixed. The task content of jobs changes over time in response to technological and organisational change, the demands of customers, and in response to the evolution of the supply of labour. Young people leaving education and people moving from unemployment into employment, for example, may take jobs that do not necessarily fully match their qualifications and skills. Thus, for a number of reasons, some workers are likely to be employed in jobs for which they are too qualified while others may be in jobs, at least temporarily, for which they lack adequate schooling.

Qualifications mismatch is found to have a greater impact on wages than other forms of mismatch. On average across countries/economies, overqualified workers earn about 14% less than well-matched workers with the same qualifications and skills proficiency. When compared to workers in the same job, overqualified workers earn 4% higher wages. At the firm level, there may be incentives to hire overqualified workers: they are more productive, as indicated by their wages. But, on aggregate, these workers and the economy would be better off if they were working at their adequate qualifications level (Montt, 2015). The effect of overskilling on wages is small and often not statistically significant. Mismatch by field of study does not have a strong impact on wages; in many countries/economies, such mismatch is not necessarily negative. Only when workers are employed outside their field and become overqualified do field-mismatched workers suffer a significant wage penalty.

Notes

1. See note regarding Cyprus in Box 1.1.

2. Approximately 1.6 of a standard deviation.

3. It should be acknowledged here that separating the effects of proficiency and educational attainment is difficult due to the fact that they are mutually reinforcing. Adults with higher proficiency will be more likely to undertake higher levels of education which, in turn, facilitates the development of higher proficiency.

4. The adjustment is based on multivariate regression analysis. First, both labour productivity and the average use of reading skills at work are separately regressed on average proficiency scores in literacy and numeracy, i.e. they are adjusted to control for the effect of literacy and numeracy proficiency. Then, the residuals of the two regressions are, in turn, regressed on one another. The adjusted results displayed in Figure 1.6 come from such a regression. This is a standard econometric procedure, commonly known as *partitioned regression*.

A note regarding the Russian Federation

The sample for the Russian Federation does not include the population of the Moscow municipal area. The data published, therefore, do not represent the entire resident population aged 16-65 in the Russian Federation but rather the population of the Russian Federation *excluding* the population residing in the Moscow municipal area.

More detailed information regarding the data from the Russian Federation as well as that of other countries can be found in the *Technical Report of the Survey of Adult Skills, Second Edition* (OECD, forthcoming).

References and further reading

Adalet McGowan, M. and **D. Andrews** (2015), "Labour market mismatch and labour productivity: Evidence from PIAAC data", *OECD Economics Department Working Papers*, No. 1209, OECD Publishing, Paris, http://dx.doi.org/10.1787/5js1pzx1r2kb-en.

Fields, G.S. (2004), *Regression-based Decompositions: A New Tool for Managerial Decision-making,* Department of Labor Economics, Cornell University, pp. 1-41.

Green, F., A. Felstead, D. Gallie and **H. Inanc** (2013), *Job-related Well-being in Britain, First Findings from the Skills and Employment Survey 2012,* Centre for Learning and Life Chances in Knowledge Economies and Societies, Institute of Education, London, www.cardiff.ac.uk/__data/assets/pdf_file/0003/118659/6.-Job-related-Well-being-in-Britain-mini-report.pdf.

Johnston, R. and **G. Hawke** (2002), *Case Studies of Organisations with Established Learning Cultures*, NCVER, Adelaide.

Montt, G. (2015), "The causes and consequences of field-of-study mismatch: An analysis using PIAAC", *OECD Social, Employment and Migration Working Papers*, No. 167, OECD Publishing, Paris, http://dx.doi.org/10.1787/5jrxm4dhv9r2-en.

OECD (forthcoming), *Technical Report of the Survey of Adult Skills, Second Edition*.

OECD (2016), *Survey of Adult Skills (PIAAC)* (Database 2012, 2015), www.oecd.org/site/piaac/publicdataandanalysis.htm.

OECD (2015), *Adults, Computers and Problem Solving: What's the Problem?*, OECD Skills Studies, OECD Publishing, Paris, http://dx.doi.org/10.1787/9789264236844-en.

OECD (2014), *OECD Employment Outlook 2014*, OECD Publishing, Paris, http://dx.doi.org/10.1787/empl_outlook-2014-en.

OECD (2013), *OECD Skills Outlook 2013: First Results from the Survey of Adult Skills*, OECD Publishing, Paris, http://dx.doi.org/10.1787/9789264204256-en.

UKCES (2014), *The Labour Market Story: Skills Use at Work, Briefing Paper*, UK Commission for Employment and Skills, www.gov.uk/government/uploads/system/uploads/attachment_data/file/343457/The_Labour_Market_Story-_Skills_Use_at_Work.pdf.

Wright J. and **P. Sissons** (2012), *The Skills Dilemma - Skills Under-Utilisation and Low-Wage Work - A Bottom Ten Million Research Paper,* The Work Foundation, Lancaster University, www.theworkfoundation.com/DownloadPublication/Report/307_Skills%20Dilemma.pdf.

2

Adults' proficiency in key information-processing skills

This chapter describes the level and distribution of proficiency in the three information-processing skills assessed – literacy, numeracy and problem solving in technology-rich environments – among adults in the participating countries and economies. To help readers interpret the findings, the results are linked to descriptions of what particular scores mean in concrete terms. In addition to presenting the distribution of scores across countries/economies, the chapter also shows the variation in scores among adults in individual countries/economies, and the relationship between the average proficiency level and the degree of variation in scores within a given country. The chapter describes the relationship among the three proficiencies and compares results from this survey with the two previous surveys of adult skills: the International Adult Literacy Survey (IALS) and the Adult Literacy and Life Skills Survey (ALL).

A note regarding Israel

The statistical data for Israel are supplied by and under the responsibility of the relevant Israeli authorities. The use of such data by the OECD is without prejudice to the status of the Golan Heights, East Jerusalem and Israeli settlements in the West Bank under the terms of international law.

The Survey of Adult Skills, a product of the OECD Programme for the International Assessment of Adult Competencies (PIAAC), assesses the proficiency of adults in literacy, numeracy and problem solving in technology-rich environments. These are considered to be "key information-processing skills" (OECD, 2013a, p.94) in that they are:

- Necessary for fully integrating and participating in the labour market, education and training, and in social and civic life
- Highly transferable, in that they are relevant to many social contexts and work situations
- "Learnable" and, therefore, subject to the influence of policy.

Literacy and numeracy skills constitute a foundation for developing higher-order cognitive skills, such as analytic reasoning, and are essential for gaining access to and understanding specific domains of knowledge. In addition, these skills are relevant across the range of life contexts, from education through work to home and social life and interaction with public authorities. The capacity to manage information and solve problems in technology-rich environments is becoming a necessity as information and communication technology (ICT) applications permeate the workplace, the classroom and lecture hall, the home, and social interaction more generally. Adults who are highly proficient in the skills measured by the Survey of Adult Skills are likely to be able to make the most of the opportunities created by the technological and structural changes modern societies are going through. Those who struggle to use new technologies are at greater risk of losing out.

The skills assessed in the Survey of Adult Skills are each defined by a framework that guided the development of the assessment and that provides a reference point for interpreting results. Each framework defines the skills assessed in terms of:

- **Content** – the texts, artefacts, tools, knowledge, representations and cognitive challenges that constitute the corpus to which adults must respond or use when they read, act in a numerate way or solve problems in technology-rich environments.
- **Cognitive strategies** – the processes that adults must bring into play to respond to or use a given content in an appropriate manner.
- **Context** – the different situations in which adults have to read, display numerate behaviour, and solve problems.

For an overview of the conceptual frameworks of each of the three domains, please consult the *Reader's Companion* (OECD, 2016a).

Among the main findings discussed in this chapter:

- Variation across countries/economies in adults' average proficiency in the three domains assessed in the Survey of Adult Skills is substantial: some 97 and 82 score points separate the highest- and lowest-scoring countries in literacy and numeracy proficiency, respectively, although many countries score within a relatively close range of each other.
- While the proficiency of adults differs across countries/economies, it varies to an even larger degree within countries, with a difference of 62 and 68 score points between the 25% of adults who attained the highest and lowest scores in literacy and numeracy, respectively. Countries with higher mean scores tend to have less variation in scores, with negative correlations at the country level ranging between r=-0.44 in literacy and r=-0.52 in numeracy.
- Among the countries/economies participating in Round 2 of the study, adults in New Zealand performed the best, scoring significantly above average in all three domains. Adults in Lithuania and Singapore performed better than average in some domains (numeracy and problem solving, respectively) and at around the average or slightly below in others. Adults in Greece, Israel and Slovenia performed below average in all three domains but, with the exception of problem solving in technology-rich environments in Greece, scored relatively close to the OECD average. Mean scores in all three domains in Chile and Turkey were substantially below the OECD average. In addition, Chile, Israel and Singapore showed the widest dispersion of scores among adults, indicating the need for policies to focus specifically on adults with low proficiency.
- As expected, proficiency in literacy and numeracy is closely related. Adults who are highly proficient in one domain are likely to be highly proficient in the other. There is also a strong positive relationship between literacy and numeracy, on the one hand, and problem solving in technology-rich environments on the other.
- Low-skilled adults represent a significant proportion of the population in all countries/economies. At least one in ten adults is proficient at or below Level 1 in literacy or numeracy in all countries in the study except Japan; more than one in two adults in Chile and Jakarta (Indonesia) score at these levels in literacy. At these levels, individuals can usually complete simple reading and numeracy tasks, such as locating information in a short text or performing simple one-step

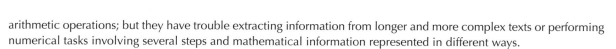

arithmetic operations; but they have trouble extracting information from longer and more complex texts or performing numerical tasks involving several steps and mathematical information represented in different ways.

- Around one in four adults has no or only limited experience with computers or lacks confidence in their ability to use computers. In addition, nearly one in two adults is proficient only at or below Level 1 in problem solving in technology-rich environments. This means they are able to use only familiar applications to solve problems that involve few steps and explicit criteria, such as sorting e-mails into pre-existing folders.

Box 2.1 **A context for cross-national comparisons of adult proficiency**

The Survey of Adult Skills is conducted in rounds within the same cycle, using the same survey protocols and survey instruments. Round 1, which involved 24 countries/economies, took place in 2011-2012; nine additional countries/economies participated in Round 2, which was conducted during 2014-15; and six other countries will participate in Round 3 (2017-18).

The survey was designed to ensure that the cross-national comparisons of proficiency in literacy, numeracy and problem solving in technology-rich environments are as robust as possible and that the content of the assessment was equivalent in difficulty in each of the 28 language versions. Care was taken to standardise implementation, including sample design and field operations, in the 33 participating countries/economies. The quality-assurance and quality-control procedures put in place are among the most comprehensive and stringent ever implemented for an international household survey. The details of the technical standards guiding the design and implementation of the survey can be found in the Reader's Companion to the previous and this report (OECD, 2013a; OECD, 2016a) and in the *Technical Report of the Survey of Adult Skills, Second Edition* (OECD, forthcoming).

Interpreting differences in results among countries is nonetheless a challenging task, particularly as the Survey of Adult Skills covers adults born between 1946 and 1996 (countries included in Round 1) and between 1948 and 1998 (countries included in Round 2). These adults started their schooling from the early 1950s to the early 2000s and entered the labour market from the early 1960s to the present day. The results observed for each participating country, at least at the aggregate level reported in this chapter, represent the outcomes of a period of history that extends as far back as the immediate post-war era, which has been marked by significant social, political and economic change. For this reason, the results of the Survey of Adult Skills should not be interpreted only, or even primarily, in light of current policy settings or those of the recent past, important as these may be. The opportunities to develop, maintain and enhance the skills assessed will have varied significantly among countries over this period, and among different age cohorts within countries, depending on the evolution of education and training systems and policies, the path of national economic development, and changes in social norms and expectations.

The diversity of the countries/economies in the Survey of Adult Skills is evident in the timing and extent of economic development and educational expansion, and the growth of the countries' immigrant population. As Figure 2.1 illustrates, while there has been an overall increase in per capita GDP from 1970, through 1995, to 2014 in all of the participating countries/economies, Ireland, Korea, Norway and Singapore have seen particularly large increases during the period. Chile, Estonia, Lithuania and the Russian Federation have also seen a rapid expansion of per capita GDP in the past two decades or so.

At the same time, some participating countries, such as Korea, Poland and Singapore, have seen rapid expansion in higher education (Figure 2.2) from a relatively low starting point, reflected in larger differences in the rates of tertiary attainment between older and younger age groups. Other countries, such as Canada, Estonia, Israel, New Zealand, the Russian Federation and the United States, have had high levels of participation in tertiary education throughout the post-war period. By contrast, in some participating countries, large proportions of older adults have not completed upper secondary education (Figure 2.3). While some of these countries, such as Greece, Ireland, Korea and Singapore, have seen substantial decreases in the proportion of young adults without upper secondary education, more than half of young adults in Turkey, and one-quarter of young adults in Italy and Spain have not attained upper secondary education.

The proportion of the population that is foreign-born adds to the diversity of country contexts. As shown in Figure 2.4, the proportion of the population that was foreign-born in 2011 varied from less than 1% in Korea to more than 25% in Australia. During the period from 1995 or 2000 to 2011, the proportion of the population in Spain, Norway and Ireland that was foreign-born more than doubled, while the proportion of foreign-born persons shrank in Israel and, to a lesser extent, in Estonia.

...

Figure 2.1 ▪ **Per capita GDP, USD**
Constant 2005 prices, using PPP

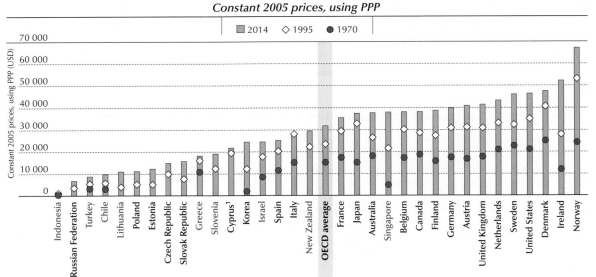

1. *Note by Turkey:* The information in this document with reference to "Cyprus" relates to the southern part of the Island. There is no single authority representing both Turkish and Greek Cypriot people on the Island. Turkey recognises the Turkish Republic of Northern Cyprus (TRNC). Until a lasting and equitable solution is found within the context of the United Nations, Turkey shall preserve its position concerning the "Cyprus issue".

Note by all the European Union Member States of the OECD and the European Union: The Republic of Cyprus is recognised by all members of the United Nations with the exception of Turkey. The information in this document relates to the area under the effective control of the Government of the Republic of Cyprus.

Countries are ranked in ascending order of per capita GDP in 2014.

Source: World Bank, World Development Indicators; Table B2.1.

StatLink ⬛⬛ http://dx.doi.org/10.1787/888933365757

Figure 2.2 ▪ **Population with tertiary education**
Percentage, by age group

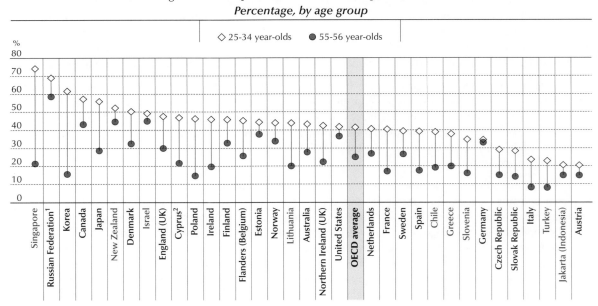

1. See note at the end of this chapter.
2. See note 1 under Figure 2.1.

Countries and economies are ranked in descending order of the percentage of 25-34 year-olds with tertiary education.

Source: Survey of Adult Skills (PIAAC) (2012, 2015), Table B2.2.

StatLink ⬛⬛ http://dx.doi.org/10.1787/888933365761

...

Figure 2.3 ■ **Population without upper secondary education**

Percentage, by age group

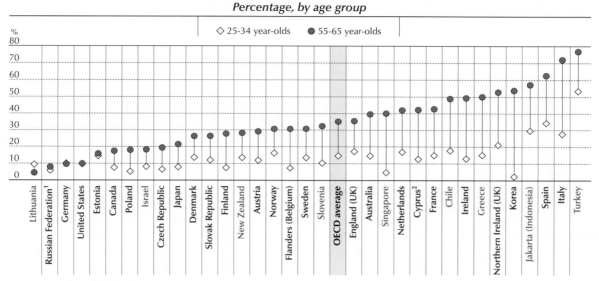

1. See note at the end of this chapter.
2. See note 1 under Figure 2.1.
Countries and economies are ranked in ascending order of the percentage of 55-65 year-olds without upper secondary education.
Source: Survey of Adult Skills (PIAAC) (2012, 2015), Table B2.2.
StatLink ⧉ http://dx.doi.org/10.1787/888933365773

Figure 2.4 ■ **Foreign-born population as a percentage of total population**

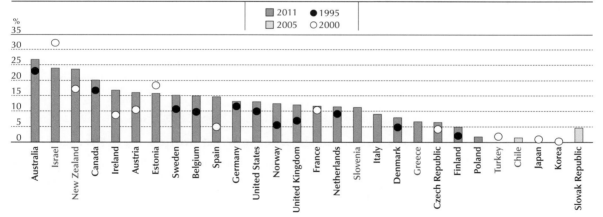

Countries are ranked in descending order of the percentage of total population that was foreign-born in 2011.
Source: OECD.Stat, Country profiles database; Table B2.3.
StatLink ⧉ http://dx.doi.org/10.1787/888933365785

REPORTING THE RESULTS

In each of the three domains assessed, proficiency is considered as a continuum of ability involving the mastery of information-processing tasks of increasing complexity. The results are represented on a 500-point scale, ranging from 0 to 500.

Each of the three proficiency scales was divided into "proficiency levels", defined by particular score-point ranges and the level of difficulty of the tasks within these ranges. The descriptors provide a summary of the types of tasks that can be successfully completed by adults with proficiency scores in a particular range. In other words, they suggest what adults with particular proficiency scores in a particular skills domain can do. Six proficiency levels are defined for literacy and numeracy (Levels 1 through 5 plus below Level 1) and four for problem solving in technology-rich environments (Levels 1 through 3 plus below Level 1).[1] The value ranges defining the levels and their respective descriptors are presented in Tables 2.1, 2.2 and 2.3 in this chapter, and in Chapter 4 of the Reader's Companion to this report[2] (OECD, 2016a).

Tasks (test items) vary in difficulty and as such are located at different points on the proficiency scales. For example, some tasks are easy and can be correctly solved by most of the respondents with low proficiency while others are difficult and can be successfully completed only by those with high proficiency. A person with a score at the middle of a certain proficiency level can successfully complete tasks located at this level around two-thirds of the time; a person with a score at the bottom of the level would successfully complete tasks at that level only about half the time; and someone with a score at the top of the level would successfully complete tasks at that level about 80% of the time.

The proficiency levels have a descriptive purpose. They are intended to aid in the interpretation and understanding of the reporting scales by describing the attributes of the tasks that adults with particular proficiency scores can successfully complete. In particular, they have no normative element and should not be understood as "standards" or "benchmarks" in the sense of defining levels of proficiency appropriate for particular purposes (e.g. access to post-secondary education or fully participating in a modern economy) or for particular population groups. The division between Level 2 and below and Level 3 and above in literacy and numeracy and Level 2 and above and Level 1 or below in problem solving in technology-rich environments in the figures showing the distribution of the population by proficiency level has been made for ease of presentation. It does not reflect a judgement that Level 3 in literacy or Level 2 in problem solving represents a performance benchmark in any sense.

PROFICIENCY IN LITERACY

The Survey of Adult Skills defines literacy as the ability to understand, evaluate, use and engage with written texts in order to participate in society, achieve one's goals, and develop one's knowledge and potential. In the survey, the term "literacy" refers to reading written texts; it does not involve either comprehending or producing spoken language or producing text (writing). In addition, given the growing importance of digital devices and applications as a means of generating, accessing and storing written text, reading digital texts is an integral part of literacy measured in the Survey of Adult Skills (Box 2.2).

Digital texts are texts that are stored as digital information and accessed in the form of screen-based displays on devices such as computers and smart phones. Digital texts have a range of features that distinguish them from print-based texts: in addition to being displayed on screens, they include hypertext links to other documents, specific navigation features (e.g. scroll bars, use of menus) and interactivity. The Survey of Adult Skills is the first international assessment of adult literacy to cover this dimension of reading.

Box 2.2 **Reading on a screen or on paper: Does it affect proficiency in literacy?**

The assessment component of the Survey of Adult Skills was delivered in both a computer-based and a paper-based version. On average across OECD countries and economies 72% of respondents took the computer-based assessment and some 24% took the paper-based assessment as they had no or poor computer skills or expressed a preference to do so (Figure 2.5).

The computer-based and paper-based assessments of literacy differ in two main ways. First, the paper-based assessment tests the reading of print texts exclusively whereas the computer-based version covers the reading of digital texts, such as simulated websites, results pages from search engines and blog posts, in addition to the reading of print texts presented on a screen. Thus, while a set of items that contains print text is common to both modes, a subset of items with digital text is used only in the computer-based assessment.

Second, the response modes differ. In the paper-based test, respondents provide written answers in paper test booklets. In the computer-based test, responding to the assessment tasks involves interacting with text and visual displays on a computer screen using devices, such as a keyboard and a mouse, and functions, such as highlighting and drag-and-drop.

In spite of these differences, most of the test items that are common to both versions are found to have equal difficulty and discrimination properties (for details, see OECD, 2013b). In other words, their measurement properties are unaffected by the mode in which the test was taken and as such can be placed on the same scale.

...

This means that the processes of understanding the meaning of text are fundamentally the same for all types of text.

Analyses of the results from the Survey of Adult Skills show that once socio-demographic factors (age, educational attainment, immigrant background and gender) are taken into account, there are no systematic differences between the scores of adults who took the paper-based assessment and those who took the computer-based assessment (differences across several variables between adults who took the paper-based assessment and those who took the computer-based assessment are shown in Tables B2.4, B2.5, B2.6, B2.7 and B2.8 in Annex B).

Figure 2.5 ▪ **Percentage of respondents taking different pathways in the Survey of Adult Skills (PIAAC)**

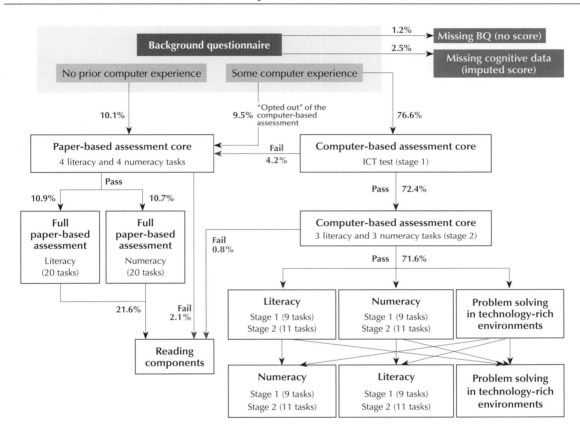

Note: The figures presented in this diagram are based on the average of OECD countries/economies participating in the Survey of Adult Skills (PIAAC).
StatLink ⛁ http://dx.doi.org/10.1787/888933365791

Levels of literacy proficiency across countries and economies

The literacy proficiency scale is divided into six levels of proficiency: Levels 1 through 5 and below Level 1. The features of the tasks at these levels are described in detail in Table 2.1 (examples of literacy items are available in OECD, 2013c) and the Reader's Companion to this report (OECD, 2016a).

Figure 2.6 presents the percentage of adults in each participating country who scored at each of the six levels of proficiency on the literacy scale.

On average, one in ten adults (10.6%) scored at Level 4 or higher and one in three (35.4%) scored at Level 3. Overall, almost half of all adults (46.0%) scored at the three highest levels (Level 3, 4 or 5). The largest proportions of adults who scored at Level 3 or higher are found in Japan (71.1%), Finland (62.9%) and the Netherlands (59.6%). Fewer than one in six adults in Turkey (12.0%) and Chile (14.5%) attained these levels of proficiency in literacy. In Jakarta (Indonesia), only 6% of adults scored at the three highest proficiency levels in literacy.

Table 2.1 **Description of proficiency levels in literacy**

Level	Score range	Percentage of adults scoring at each level (average)	Types of tasks completed successfully at each level of proficiency
Below Level 1	Below 176 points	4.5%	The tasks at this level require the respondent to read brief texts on familiar topics to locate a single piece of specific information. There is seldom any competing information in the text and the requested information is identical in form to information in the question or directive. The respondent may be required to locate information in short continuous texts. However, in this case, the information can be located as if the text were non-continuous in format. Only basic vocabulary knowledge is required, and the reader is not required to understand the structure of sentences or paragraphs or make use of other text features. Tasks below Level 1 do not make use of any features specific to digital texts.
1	176 to less than 226 points	14.4%	Most of the tasks at this level require the respondent to read relatively short digital or print continuous, non-continuous, or mixed texts to locate a single piece of information that is identical to or synonymous with the information given in the question or directive. Some tasks, such as those involving non-continuous texts, may require the respondent to enter personal information onto a document. Little, if any, competing information is present. Some tasks may require simple cycling through more than one piece of information. Knowledge and skill in recognising basic vocabulary determining the meaning of sentences, and reading paragraphs of text is expected.
2	226 to less than 276 points	33.9%	At this level, the medium of texts may be digital or printed, and texts may comprise continuous, non-continuous, or mixed types. Tasks at this level require respondents to make matches between the text and information, and may require paraphrasing or low-level inferences. Some competing pieces of information may be present. Some tasks require the respondent to: • Cycle through or integrate two or more pieces of information based on criteria • Compare and contrast or reason about information requested in the question • Navigate within digital texts to access and identify information from various parts of a document.
3	276 to less than 326 points	35.4%	Texts at this level are often dense or lengthy, and include continuous, non-continuous, mixed or multiple pages of text. Understanding text and rhetorical structures become more central to successfully completing tasks, especially navigating complex digital texts. Tasks require the respondent to identify, interpret or evaluate one or more pieces of information, and often require varying levels of inference. Many tasks require the respondent to construct meaning across larger chunks of text or perform multi-step operations in order to identify and formulate responses. Often tasks also demand that the respondent disregard irrelevant or inappropriate content to answer accurately. Competing information is often present, but it is not more prominent than the correct information.
4	326 to less than 376 points	10.0%	Tasks at this level often require respondents to perform multiple-step operations to integrate, interpret or synthesise information from complex or lengthy continuous, non-continuous, mixed, or multiple type texts. Complex inferences and application of background knowledge may be needed to perform the task successfully. Many tasks require identifying and understanding one or more specific, non-central idea(s) in the text in order to interpret or evaluate subtle evidence-claim or persuasive discourse relationships. Conditional information is frequently present in tasks at this level and must be taken into consideration by the respondent. Competing information is present and sometimes seemingly as prominent as correct information.
5	Equal or higher than 376 points	0.7%	At this level, tasks may require the respondent to search for and integrate information across multiple, dense texts; construct syntheses of similar and contrasting ideas or points of view; or evaluate evidence-based arguments. Application and evaluation of logical and conceptual models of ideas may be required to accomplish tasks. Evaluating the reliability of evidentiary sources and selecting key information is frequently a requirement. Tasks often require respondents to be aware of subtle, rhetorical cues and to make high-level inferences or use specialised background knowledge.

Note: The percentage of adults scoring at different levels of proficiency adds up to 100% when 1.4% of literacy-related non-respondents across countries/economies are taken into account. Adults in this category were not able to complete the background questionnaire due to language difficulties or learning and mental disabilities (see section on literacy-related non-response).

Figure 2.6 ▪ **Literacy proficiency among adults**
Percentage of adults scoring at each proficiency level in literacy

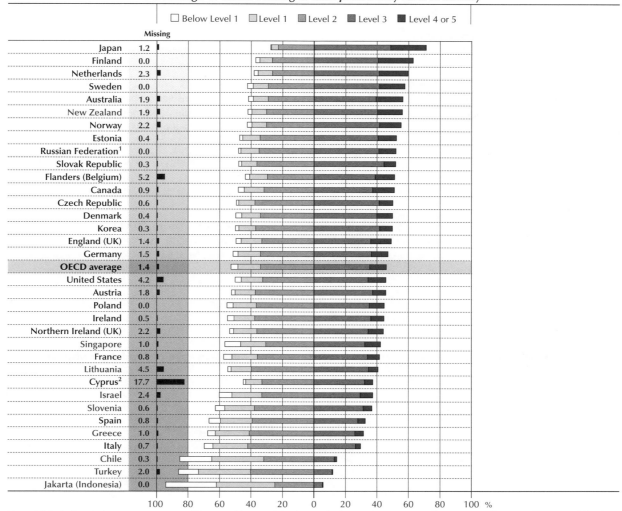

Legend: □ Below Level 1 □ Level 1 ▨ Level 2 ▨ Level 3 ■ Level 4 or 5

Country	Missing
Japan	1.2
Finland	0.0
Netherlands	2.3
Sweden	0.0
Australia	1.9
New Zealand	1.9
Norway	2.2
Estonia	0.4
Russian Federation[1]	0.0
Slovak Republic	0.3
Flanders (Belgium)	5.2
Canada	0.9
Czech Republic	0.6
Denmark	0.4
Korea	0.3
England (UK)	1.4
Germany	1.5
OECD average	1.4
United States	4.2
Austria	1.8
Poland	0.0
Ireland	0.5
Northern Ireland (UK)	2.2
Singapore	1.0
France	0.8
Lithuania	4.5
Cyprus[2]	17.7
Israel	2.4
Slovenia	0.6
Spain	0.8
Greece	1.0
Italy	0.7
Chile	0.3
Turkey	2.0
Jakarta (Indonesia)	0.0

100 80 60 40 20 0 20 40 60 80 100 %

Note: Adults in the missing category were not able to provide enough background information to impute proficiency scores because of language difficulties, or learning or mental disabilities (referred to as literacy-related non-response).
1. See note at the end of this chapter.
2. See note 1 under Figure 2.1.
Countries and economies are ranked in descending order of the combined percentages of adults scoring at Level 3 and at Level 4 or 5.
Source: Survey of Adult Skills (PIAAC) (2012, 2015), Table A2.1.
StatLink ⟨⟩ http://dx.doi.org/10.1787/888933365800

Overall, less than 1% (0.7%) of adults performed at the highest proficiency, Level 5. Apart from Finland (2.2%), no other country/economy, had more than 1.3% of adults performing at this level. In a number of countries, such as Chile, Italy and Turkey, very few adults scored at this proficiency level in literacy (see Table A2.1 in Annex A). Given the growing demand for complex information-processing skills in the labour market (Autor, Levy and Murnane, 2003; Levy and Murnane, 2006), these proportions are worryingly small.

On average, around one in three adults (33.9%) performed at Level 2. Italy (42.0%), Turkey (40.2%) and Greece (41%) have the largest proportions of adults scoring at this level. In contrast, Japan (22.8%), the Netherlands (26.4%) and Finland (26.5%) have the smallest proportions of adults scoring at Level 2.

Overall, around one in five adults scored at Level 1 (14.4%) or below Level 1 (4.5%). Countries/economies with the largest proportions of adults who scored at Level 1 or below include Chile (53.4%), Turkey (45.7%), Italy (27.7%), Spain (27.5%) and Israel (27.1%). In Jakarta (Indonesia), this proportion is even higher, with 69.3% of adults scoring at the two lowest proficiency levels in literacy. Japan (4.9%), Finland (10.6%), the Slovak Republic (11.6%), the Netherlands (11.7%),

New Zealand (11.8%) and the Czech Republic (11.8%) recorded the smallest proportions of adults who scored at or below Level 1. More information about the skills of readers with low literacy proficiency is provided through the reading components assessment (see below).

Literacy-related non-response

In all of the participating countries/economies, some adults were unable to complete the background questionnaire as they were unable to understand or read the language of the assessment, have difficulty reading or writing, or have learning or mental disabilities. In the case of the background questionnaire, there was no one present (either the interviewer or another person) to translate into the language of the respondent or answer on behalf of the respondent. In the case of these respondents, only their age, sex, and, in some cases, educational attainment is known. In most countries, non-respondents represented less than 5% of the total population. This category is identified separately in Figure 2.6 as a black bar in each country (categorised as "missing"). While the proficiency of this group is likely to vary among countries, in most cases, these persons are likely to have low levels of proficiency (Level 1 or below) in the test language(s) of the country concerned.

READING COMPONENTS

The Survey of Adult Skills included an assessment of reading components designed to provide information about adults with very low levels of proficiency in reading. This module was implemented in 29 of the 33 participating countries/economies (Finland, France, Japan and the Russian Federation did not participate in this assessment). The reading components assessment was designed to assess three skills considered as essential for understanding the meaning of written texts: knowledge of print vocabulary (word recognition), the ability to evaluate the logic of sentences (sentence processing), and fluency in reading passages of text (passage comprehension). Skilled readers are able to undertake these types of operations automatically.

Figure 2.7 ■ **Relationship between literacy proficiency and performance in reading components**

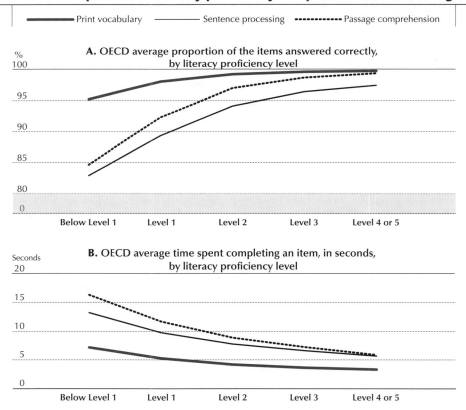

Notes: The results for each country/economy can be found in the table mentioned in the source below. Finland, France and Japan did not participate in the reading components assessment.

Source: Survey of Adult Skills (PIAAC) (2012, 2015), Table A2.2.

StatLink ⇒ http://dx.doi.org/10.1787/888933365810

The print-vocabulary tasks required test takers to select the word corresponding to a picture of an object from a selection of four alternative words. The sentence-processing tasks required test takers to identify whether a sentence made logical sense in the properties of the real world. The passage-comprehension tasks entailed reading a prose text. At certain points in the text, test takers were given a choice of two words and required to select the word that made the most sense in the context of the passage. Chapter 1 in the Reader's Companion to this report presents samples of the reading-components tasks (OECD, 2016a).

The assessment of reading components was completed by respondents who failed the literacy and numeracy core assessment in the computer-based version of the assessment, and by all respondents taking the paper version of the assessment in order to obtain comparative results (Box 2.2, Figure 2.5).

Figure 2.7 shows the relationship between literacy proficiency and the average performance in the three components of this assessment across the OECD countries/economies that participated in the reading components assessment. Information is available about two dimensions of performance in reading components: the proportion of items that were correctly answered by respondents and the time taken to complete the assessment. Figure 2.7a shows the relationship between literacy proficiency and the percentage of items answered correctly (accuracy); Figure 2.7b shows the relationship between literacy proficiency and the time taken (in seconds) to complete an item (speed). Both accuracy and speed increase with higher proficiency in all three of the components, with the gains in both accuracy and speed tapering off markedly among adults who are proficient at Level 2 or higher.

Figure 2.8 presents the average proportions of correctly answered items across countries/economies and in each of the three reading components. Since adults with higher literacy proficiency (Level 2 or above) correctly perform almost all tasks, results are presented only for adults proficient at or below Level 1 in literacy. Their scores in the reading components assessment vary much more.

Figure 2.8 ▪ **Performance in reading components**

Average proportion of items answered correctly, adults who score at or below Level 1 in literacy proficiency

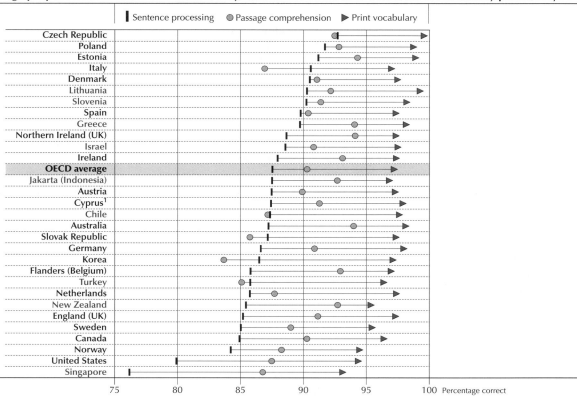

Note: Finland, France, Japan and the Russian Federation did not participate in the reading components assessment.

1. See note 1 under Figure 2.1.

Countries and economies are ranked in descending order of the mean proportion of items answered correctly in sentence processing.

Source: Survey of Adult Skills (PIAAC) (2012, 2015), Table A2.2.

StatLink ⟲ http://dx.doi.org/10.1787/888933365824

There is little difference across countries/economies in the average proportion of correct answers in the print-vocabulary component, with the proportion varying between 93% in Singapore and 99.6% in the Czech Republic. More variability is observed in the case of passage comprehension. The largest variation occurs in the sentence-processing component, where the proportion of correct answers varies between 76% in Singapore and 92.7% in the Czech Republic.

Although the passage-comprehension tasks took longer to complete, on average in the majority of countries/economies, adults with low literacy found the sentence-processing tasks to be the most difficult to answer correctly. Adults with low proficiency in Singapore and the United States struggled much more with tasks in all three reading components than their peers in other participating countries did. These results may be related to the language background of the immigrant population in the United States and, in the case of Singapore, to both the considerably lower levels of educational attainment and poorer English-language skills among older cohorts (see Figures 2.2 and 2.3 in Box 2.1).[3] A more detailed analysis of reading components results is presented in a newly published report on adults with low proficiency in literacy and numeracy (Grotlüschen et al., 2016).

DISTRIBUTION OF PROFICIENCY SCORES ACROSS COUNTRIES AND ECONOMIES
Mean proficiency scores in literacy

Mean literacy scores among adults in the countries/economies participating in the Survey of Adult Skills are presented in Figure 2.9. Countries with mean scores that are not statistically different from those of other countries are identified (Box 2.3). For example, the mean score of adults in Israel (255 points) is similar to that of adults in Slovenia (256 points) and Greece (254 points), but is lower than that of adults in Singapore (258 points) and France (262 points), and higher than that of adults in Spain (252 points) and the countries whose mean scores are lower than that of Spain. For each country, a list of countries whose adults' average score is statistically similar is also shown.

Box 2.3 **Comparing results among countries/economies and population subgroups**

The statistics in this report are estimates of national performance based on samples of adults from each country, rather than values that would be obtained if every person in the target population in every country had answered every question. Consequently, in the Survey of Adult Skills, each estimate has an associated degree of uncertainty, which is expressed through a standard error. The use of confidence intervals provides a way to make inferences about the population means and proportions in a manner that reflects the uncertainty associated with the sample estimates. From an observed sample statistic, and assuming a normal distribution, it can be inferred that the result for the corresponding population would lie within the confidence interval in 95 out of 100 replications of the measurement on different samples drawn from the same population.

In many cases, readers are primarily interested in whether a given value in a particular country is different from a second value in the same or another country, e.g. whether women in a country perform better than men in the same country or whether adults in one country have higher average scores than adults in another country. In the tables and figures used in this report, differences are labelled as statistically significant when there is less than a 5% chance that an observed difference between two representative samples reflects random sample variation, rather than actual differences between these populations.

In addition to error associated with sampling, there is a range of other possible sources of error in sample surveys such as the Survey of Adult Skills, including error associated with survey non-response (see Chapter 3 of the Reader's Companion to this report for a discussion of response rates and non-response bias [OECD, 2016a]). While the likely level of bias associated with non-response is assessed as minimal to low for most countries/economies that participated in the study, the possibility of biases associated with non-response cannot be ruled out. Readers should, therefore, exercise caution in drawing conclusions from small score-point differences between countries or population groups, even if the differences concerned are statistically significant.

The average literacy score across the OECD countries/economies that participated in the assessment is 268 points. Japan had the highest average level of proficiency in literacy (296 points) followed by Finland (288 points) and the Netherlands (284 points). Chile (220 points) and Turkey (227 points) recorded the lowest average scores among countries. Jakarta (Indonesia) had an even lower average score (200 points). Given that Level 2 ranges between 226 and 275 points and Level 3 ranges between 276 and 325 points, adults in the eight best-performing countries scored, on average, towards the lower end of Level 3. This implies that an average adult in these countries could successfully complete almost all of the tasks at Level 2 difficulty and below, and more than half of the tasks at Level 3 difficulty.

Figure 2.9 ■ **Comparison of average literacy proficiency**

Mean literacy proficiency scores of 16-65 year-olds

Significantly **above** the average
Not significantly different from the average
Significantly **below** the average

Mean	Comparison country/economy	Countries/economies whose mean score is NOT significantly different from the comparison country/economy
296	Japan	
288	Finland	
284	Netherlands	
281	New Zealand	Australia, Sweden, Russian Federation[1]
280	Australia	New Zealand, Norway, Sweden, Russian Federation[1]
279	Sweden	Australia, New Zealand, Norway, Russian Federation[1]
278	Norway	Australia, Sweden, Russian Federation[1]
276	Estonia	Czech Republic, Flanders (Belgium), Russian Federation[1]
275	Flanders (Belgium)	Czech Republic, Estonia, Slovak Republic, Russian Federation[1]
275	Russian Federation[1]	Australia, Canada, Czech Republic, Denmark, England (UK), Estonia, Flanders (Belgium), Germany, Korea, New Zealand, Northern Ireland (UK), Norway, Slovak Republic, Sweden, United States
274	Czech Republic	Canada, England (UK), Estonia, Flanders (Belgium), Korea, Slovak Republic, Russian Federation[1]
274	Slovak Republic	Canada, Czech Republic, England (UK), Flanders (Belgium), Korea, Russian Federation[1]
273	Canada	Czech Republic, England (UK), Korea, Slovak Republic, Russian Federation[1]
273	England (UK)	Canada, Czech Republic, Denmark, Korea, Northern Ireland (UK), Slovak Republic, United States, Russian Federation[1]
273	Korea	Canada, Czech Republic, England (UK), Northern Ireland (UK), Slovak Republic, Russian Federation[1]
271	Denmark	Austria, England (UK), Germany, Northern Ireland (UK), United States, Russian Federation[1]
270	Germany	Austria, Denmark, Northern Ireland (UK), United States, Cyprus,[2] Russian Federation[1]
270	United States	Austria, Denmark, England (UK), Germany, Northern Ireland (UK), Cyprus,[2] Russian Federation[1]
269	Austria	Denmark, Germany, Northern Ireland (UK), United States, Cyprus[2]
269	Cyprus[2]	Austria, Germany, Ireland, Northern Ireland (UK), United States, Lithuania
269	Northern Ireland (UK)	Austria, Denmark, England (UK), Germany, Ireland, Korea, Poland, United States, Cyprus,[2] Lithuania, Russian Federation[1]
268	**OECD average**	**Ireland, Northern Ireland (UK), Poland, Cyprus,[2] Lithuania**
267	Poland	Ireland, Northern Ireland (UK), Lithuania
267	Lithuania	Ireland, Northern Ireland (UK), Poland, Cyprus[2]
267	Ireland	Northern Ireland (UK), Poland, Cyprus,[2] Lithuania
262	France	
258	Singapore	Slovenia
256	Slovenia	Greece, Israel, Singapore
255	Israel	Greece, Slovenia
254	Greece	Israel, Slovenia, Spain
252	Spain	Greece, Italy
250	Italy	Spain
227	Turkey	
220	Chile	
200	Jakarta (Indonesia)	

Notes: Statistical significance is at the 5% level. Literacy-related non-response (missing) is excluded from the calculation of mean scores.

1. See note at the end of this chapter.

2. See note 1 under Figure 2.1.

Countries and economies are ranked in descending order of the mean score.

Source: Survey of Adult Skills (PIAAC) (2012, 2015), Table A2.3.

StatLink ⊟⊡ http://dx.doi.org/10.1787/888933365839

The average proficiency of most countries, and the international average, rests at the upper part of Level 2. An average adult in these countries could successfully complete almost all of the tasks at Level 2 difficulty and some tasks at Level 3. By contrast, the average score in Chile is below Level 2 (the upper part of Level 1), indicating that the average adult in Chile could complete almost all tasks at Level 1 difficulty but only a few tasks at Level 2. The average adult in Jakarta (Indonesia) can complete even fewer tasks at Level 1 (around two-thirds), and very few if any at Level 2.

Overall, the variation in literacy proficiency among participating countries/economies is considerable. Some 76 score points separate the countries/economies with the highest and lowest mean score (96 points when Jakarta [Indonesia] is included). However, around two-third of countries/economies (22 of 33) differ by 21 points or less (they have mean scores within the range of 267 to 288 points) and around half of countries/economies (16) differ by 9 score points or less (they have mean scores within the range of 267 to 276 points). By way of comparison, the average score-point gap between the highest- and lowest-performing 25% of adults (first and third quartiles) in literacy is 62 score points across all countries/economies (see Table A2.3 in Annex A).

Variation of proficiency scores within countries/economies

In addition to examining differences in national averages in literacy proficiency, it is also useful to explore the distribution of proficiency scores within each country/economy. This can be done by identifying the score below which 5%, 25%, 75% and 95% of adults perform. Comparing score-point differences among adults at different points in the distribution of proficiency measures the extent of variation in that distribution in each participating country or economy. Figure 2.10 presents the distribution of scores within countries/economies in addition to the mean score. A longer bar indicates greater variations in literacy proficiency within a country; a shorter bar indicates smaller variations.

On average, 62 score points separate the 25% of adults who attained the highest and lowest scores in literacy (a measure known as the interquartile range). In a number of countries, comparatively small variations in literacy proficiency are observed. These include Japan (51 score points), the Slovak Republic (51 points), Cyprus[4] (52 points) and the Czech Republic (53 points). Countries with comparatively large variations in scores between the top- and bottom-performing 25% of adults include Singapore (77 points), Israel (74 points) and Chile (73 points).

Figure 2.10 ▪ **Distribution of literacy proficiency scores**

Mean literacy proficiency and distribution of literacy scores, by percentile

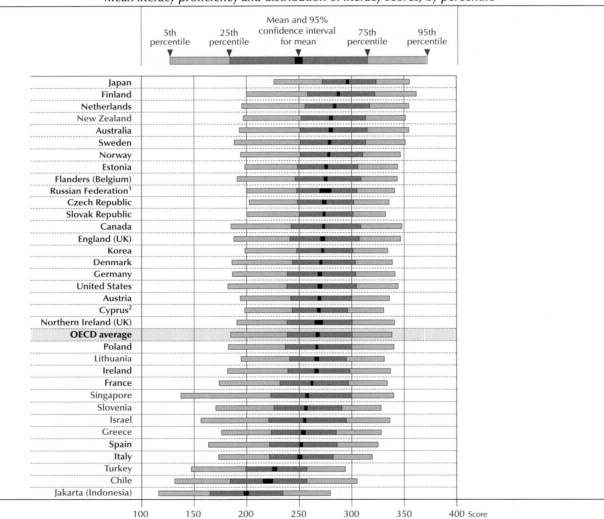

Notes: Mean scores are shown with a 95% confidence interval. Literacy-related non-response (missing) is excluded from the calculation of mean scores.

1. See note at the end of this chapter.

2. See note 1 under Figure 2.1.

Countries and economies are ranked in descending order of the mean score.

Source: Survey of Adult Skills (PIAAC) (2012, 2015), Table A2.3.

StatLink ⚓ http://dx.doi.org/10.1787/888933365842

Interestingly, there is a moderate inverse relationship (r=-0.44) between the overall level of adults' proficiency in literacy and the variation in scores: the higher the average level of proficiency, the smaller the variation in scores. Figure 2.11 presents this relationship between average scores and variation in scores, expressed through the interquartile range, across countries/economies. This suggests that there might not be a trade-off between achieving higher average skills proficiency and less inequality in skills distribution. Nevertheless, it is important to be cautious when interpreting this correlation as it is relatively weak and overwhelmingly relies on few (outlier) countries/economies.

Figure 2.11 ▪ **Average and distribution of literacy scores**
Relationship between mean literacy proficiency score and variability

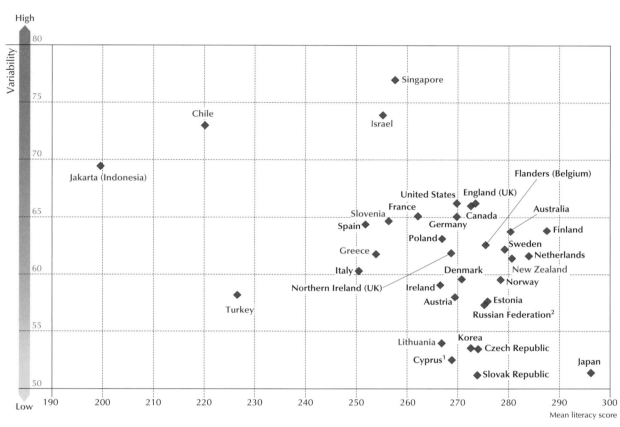

Note: The measure of variability used is the interquartile range (difference between the third quartile and the first quartile).
1. See note 1 under Figure 2.1.
2. See note at the end of this chapter.
Source: Survey of Adult Skills (PIAAC) (2012, 2015), Table A2.3.

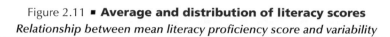
StatLink ⫴ http://dx.doi.org/10.1787/888933365856

Small variations in scores are found in countries/economies with high (Japan) or middle (the Slovak Republic and the Czech Republic) levels of literacy proficiency among adults, while large variations are found in countries/economies with low proficiency in literacy (Chile, Israel and Singapore). Relatively large variation is observed in Jakarta (Indonesia) as well. One exception to this trend is Turkey, which shows low overall literacy proficiency among adults, but smaller variations in scores. This might be because few adults score at the high end of the literacy proficiency scale.

The reasons underlying the differences in the distribution of scores are undoubtedly complex and likely to be affected by such factors as the historical patterns of participation in education, support for adult learning and practicing skills at and outside the workplace, and patterns of immigration. In Singapore, for example, a wide gap in average performance between different age cohorts contributed to both a wider dispersion of scores and a lower average proficiency level (see Chapter 3).

PROFICIENCY IN NUMERACY

The Survey of Adult Skills defines numeracy as the ability to access, use, interpret and communicate mathematical information and ideas in order to engage in and manage the mathematical demands of a range of situations in adult life. A numerate adult is one who responds appropriately to mathematical content, information and ideas represented in various ways in order to manage situations and solve problems in a real-life context. While performance on numeracy tasks is, in part, dependent on the ability to read and understand text, numeracy involves more than applying arithmetical skills to information embedded in text.

Levels of numeracy proficiency across countries/economies

Like the literacy scale, the numeracy proficiency scale is divided into six proficiency levels: Levels 1 through 5 and below Level 1. The features of the tasks located at these levels are described in detail in Table 2.2 (examples of numeracy items are available in OECD, 2013c).

Table 2.2 **Description of proficiency levels in numeracy**

Level	Score range	Percentage of adults scoring at each level (average)	The types of tasks completed successfully at each level of proficiency
Below Level 1	Below 176 points	6.7%	Tasks at this level require the respondents to carry out simple processes, such as counting, sorting, performing basic arithmetic operations with whole numbers or money, or recognising common spatial representations in concrete, familiar contexts where the mathematics content is explicit with little or no text or distractors.
1	176 to less than 226 points	16.0%	Tasks at this level require the respondent to carry out basic mathematical processes in common, concrete contexts where the mathematical content is explicit, with little text and minimal distractors. Tasks usually require one-step or simple processes involving counting, sorting, performing basic arithmetic operations, understanding simple percentages, such as 50%, and locating and identifying elements of simple or common graphical or spatial representations.
2	226 to less than 276 points	33.0%	Tasks at this level require the respondent to identify and act on mathematical information and ideas embedded in a range of common contexts where the mathematics content is fairly explicit or visual with relatively few distractors. Tasks tend to require the application of two or more steps or processes involving calculation with whole numbers and common decimals, percentages and fractions; simple measurement and spatial representation; estimation; and interpretation of relatively simple data and statistics in texts, tables and graphs.
3	276 to less than 326 points	31.8%	Tasks at this level require the respondent to understand mathematical information that may be less explicit, embedded in contexts that are not always familiar and represented in more complex ways. Tasks require several steps and may involve the choice of problem-solving strategies and relevant processes. Tasks tend to require the application of number sense and spatial sense; recognising and working with mathematical relationships, patterns and proportions expressed in verbal or numerical form; and interpretation and basic analysis of data and statistics in texts, tables and graphs.
4	326 to less than 376 points	10.2%	Tasks at this level require the respondent to understand a broad range of mathematical information that may be complex, abstract or embedded in unfamiliar contexts. These tasks involve undertaking multiple steps and choosing relevant problem-solving strategies and processes. Tasks tend to require analysis and more complex reasoning about quantities and data; statistics and chance; spatial relationships; and change, proportions and formulas. Tasks at this level may also require understanding arguments or communicating well-reasoned explanations for answers or choices.
5	Equal or higher than 376 points	1.0%	Tasks at this level require the respondent to understand complex representations and abstract and formal mathematical and statistical ideas, possibly embedded in complex texts. Respondents may have to integrate multiple types of mathematical information where considerable translation or interpretation is required; draw inferences; develop or work with mathematical arguments or models; and justify, evaluate and critically reflect upon solutions or choices.

Note: The proportion of adults scoring at different levels of proficiency adds up to 100% when the 1.4% of numeracy-related non-respondents across countries/economies are taken into account. Adults in the missing category were not able to provide enough background information to impute proficiency scores because of language difficulties, or learning or mental disabilities (see section on literacy-related non-response above).

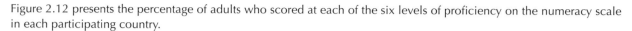

Figure 2.12 presents the percentage of adults who scored at each of the six levels of proficiency on the numeracy scale in each participating country.

On average across participating OECD countries/economies, only 1.0% of adults scored at Level 5 and an additional 10.2% of adults scored at Level 4 in numeracy (see Table A2.4 in Annex A). Finland (19.4%), Japan (18.8%) and Sweden (18.6%) had the largest proportions of adults scoring at the two highest numeracy levels (Level 4 or 5). In contrast, Jakarta (Indonesia) (1.4%), Turkey (1.5%) and Chile (1.9%) had the smallest proportions of adults scoring at Level 4 or higher.

On average, around one in three adults scored at Level 3 (31.8%) and another one in three scored at Level 2 (33.0%). Japan had the largest proportion of adults scoring at Level 3 (43.7%), while the smallest proportions of adults at this level were observed in Jakarta (Indonesia) and Chile, where only around one in ten adults scored at Level 3 (9.1% and 10.0%, respectively), followed by Turkey (13.0%).

Around four in ten adults in Spain (40.1%), Greece (39.8%), the Russian Federation (39.7%), Korea (39.4%) and Italy (38.8%) scored at Level 2, while Chile (25.9%), Singapore (26.6%) and Flanders (Belgium) (27.7%) had the smallest proportions of adults who scored at this level.

Around one in four adults (22.7%) across OECD countries/economies scored at the two lowest levels of numeracy proficiency (16% at Level 1 and 6.7% below Level 1). Almost two in three adults in Chile (61.9%) and around half of adults in Turkey (50.2%) scored at these two levels. By contrast, only around one in ten adults in Japan (8.1%), Finland (12.8%) and the Czech Republic (12.9%) scored at or below Level 1.

Figure 2.12 ▪ **Numeracy proficiency among adults**

Percentage of 16-65 year-olds scoring at each proficiency level in numeracy

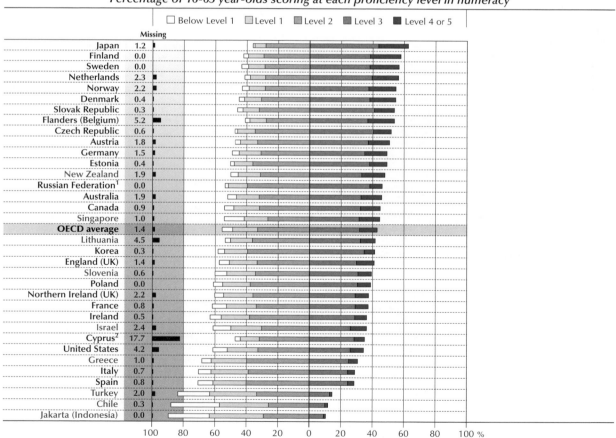

Note: Adults in the missing category were not able to provide enough background information to impute proficiency scores because of language difficulties, or learning or mental disabilities (referred to as literacy-related non-response).
1. See note at the end of this chapter.
2. See note 1 under Figure 2.1.
Countries and economies are ranked in descending order of the combined percentage of adults scoring at Level 3 and at Level 4 or 5.
Source: Survey of Adult Skills (PIAAC) (2012, 2015), Table A2.4.
StatLink ᵐˢᵖ http://dx.doi.org/10.1787/888933365863

Literacy-related non-response

As noted above, in all countries/economies some adults were unable to complete the background questionnaire as they are unable to understand or read the language of the assessment, have difficulty reading or writing, or have a learning or mental disability. This category is identified separately in Figure 2.12 as a black bar in each country (categorised as "missing"). In most cases, these persons will have low proficiency (Level 1 or below) in numeracy when assessed in the test language(s) of the country concerned.

DISTRIBUTION OF PROFICIENCY SCORES ACROSS COUNTRIES/ECONOMIES

Mean proficiency scores in numeracy

Mean numeracy scores among adults in the countries/economies participating in the Survey of Adult Skills are presented in Figure 2.13. Countries/economies with mean scores that are not statistically different from those of other countries/economies are identified. For example, the mean score among adults in France (254 points) is similar to that of adults in Ireland (256 points) and the United States (253 points), but is significantly different from that of adults in other countries/economies at the 95% confidence level (Box 2.3).

Figure 2.13 ■ **Comparison of average numeracy proficiency**

Mean numeracy proficiency scores of 16-65 year-olds

Significantly **above** the average
Not significantly different from the average
Significantly **below** the average

Mean	Comparison country/economy	Countries/economies whose mean score is NOT significantly different from the comparison country/economy
288	Japan	
282	Finland	Flanders (Belgium), Netherlands
280	Flanders (Belgium)	Denmark, Finland, Netherlands, Norway, Sweden
280	Netherlands	Finland, Flanders (Belgium), Norway, Sweden
279	Sweden	Denmark, Flanders (Belgium), Netherlands, Norway
278	Norway	Denmark, Flanders (Belgium), Netherlands, Sweden
278	Denmark	Flanders (Belgium), Norway, Sweden
276	Slovak Republic	Austria, Czech Republic
276	Czech Republic	Austria, Slovak Republic
275	Austria	Czech Republic, Estonia, Slovak Republic, Russian Federation[1]
273	Estonia	Austria, Germany, New Zealand, Russian Federation[1]
272	Germany	Estonia, New Zealand, Russian Federation[1]
271	New Zealand	Estonia, Germany, Russian Federation[1]
270	Russian Federation[1]	Australia, Austria, Canada, Estonia, Germany, New Zealand, Cyprus,[2] Lithuania
268	Australia	Canada, Lithuania, Russian Federation[1]
267	Lithuania	Australia, Canada, Cyprus,[2] Russian Federation[1]
265	Canada	Australia, Cyprus,[2] Lithuania, Russian Federation[1]
265	Cyprus[2]	Canada, Korea, Lithuania, Russian Federation[1]
263	Korea	England (UK), Cyprus[2]
263	**OECD average**	**England (UK), Korea, Cyprus[2]**
262	England (UK)	Korea, Northern Ireland (UK), Poland
260	Poland	England (UK), Northern Ireland (UK), Slovenia
259	Northern Ireland (UK)	England (UK), Ireland, Poland, Slovenia, Singapore
258	Slovenia	Ireland, Northern Ireland (UK), Poland, Singapore
257	Singapore	Ireland, Northern Ireland (UK), Slovenia
256	Ireland	France, Northern Ireland (UK), Slovenia, United States, Singapore
254	France	Ireland, United States
253	United States	France, Greece, Ireland, Israel
252	Greece	Israel, United States
251	Israel	Greece, United States
247	Italy	Spain
246	Spain	Italy
219	Turkey	
210	Jakarta (Indonesia)	Chile
206	Chile	Jakarta (Indonesia)

Note: Statistical significance is at the 5% level. Literacy-related non-response (missing) is excluded from the calculation of mean scores.
1. See note at the end of this chapter.
2. See note 1 under Figure 2.1.
Countries and economies are ranked in descending order of the mean score.
Source: Survey of Adult Skills (PIAAC) (2012, 2015), Table A2.5.
StatLink ᴍᴤ http://dx.doi.org/10.1787/888933365873

The average numeracy score across the OECD countries/economies that participated in the assessment is 263 points. Japan had the highest average level of proficiency in numeracy (288 points), followed by Finland (282 points). Chile (206 points), Jakarta (Indonesia) (210 points) and Turkey (219 points) recorded the lowest average scores. An adult with a score equal to the national average in Israel (251 points) or Greece (252 points) could successfully complete around two-thirds of items at Level 2. By contrast, the average adult in Austria, the Czech Republic and the Slovak Republic scored at the upper limit of Level 2 and lower limit of Level 3, and as such could complete around 80% of items at Level 2 difficulty and around half of the items at Level 3 difficulty. The average adult in Chile, Jakarta (Indonesia) and Turkey could successfully complete most items at Level 1 difficulty, but only a few items at Level 2 difficulty and very few, if any, items at Level 3.

Overall, the variation in mean scores among countries/economies is relatively substantial. Some 82 points separate the mean scores of the highest- and lowest-performing countries/economies. However, the majority of countries/economies (26 out of 33) differ by 29 score points or less (mean scores within the range of 251 to 280 points). By way of comparison, the average score-point gap in numeracy between the highest- and lowest-performing 25% of adults (interquartile range) across all countries/economies is 68 score points (see Table A2.5 in Annex A).

Figure 2.14 ■ **Distribution of numeracy proficiency scores**

Mean numeracy proficiency and distribution of numeracy scores, by percentile

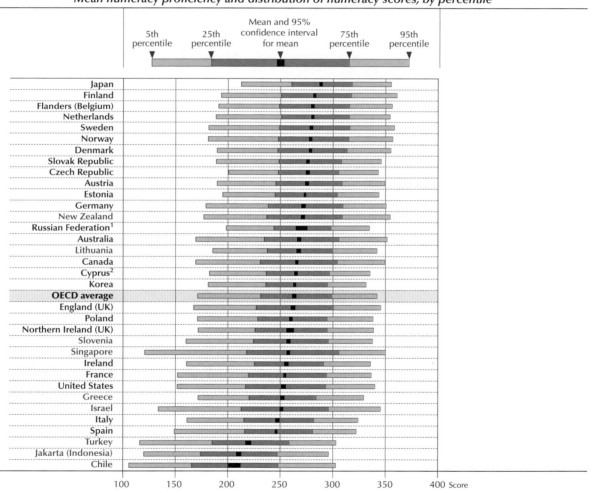

Notes: Mean scores are shown with a 95% confidence interval. Literacy-related non-response (missing) is excluded from the calculation of mean scores.
1. See note at the end of this chapter.
2. See note 1 under Figure 2.1.
Countries and economies are ranked in descending order of the mean score .
Source: Survey of Adult Skills (PIAAC) (2012, 2015), Table A2.5.
StatLink ⟐ http://dx.doi.org/10.1787/888933365881

While adults' mean scores in literacy and numeracy are similar in most countries/economies, there are some notable exceptions. Adults in Korea and England (United Kingdom), for example, scored around the international average in numeracy, but above average in literacy. Adults in Ireland, Northern Ireland (United Kingdom) and Poland performed around the international average in literacy, but below average in numeracy. Adults in the United States performed better than the international average in literacy, but much worse in numeracy (see Figure 2.22 below).

Variation of proficiency scores within countries and economies

As with literacy proficiency, the variation in performance within a country is examined by identifying the score points below which 5%, 25%, 75%, and 95% of adults perform. Figure 2.14 presents the distribution of scores within countries/economies in addition to the mean score. A longer bar indicates greater variations in numeracy proficiency within a country/economy; a shorter bar indicates smaller variations.

On average, 68 score points separate the highest and lowest 25% of performers in numeracy. The narrowest distribution of scores on the numeracy scale is observed among adults in the Russian Federation (54 score-point difference), the Czech Republic (57-point difference) and Japan (57-point difference). The widest gaps between the lowest- and the highest-performing adults are observed in Singapore (88 points), Israel (83 points) and Chile (82 points).

As observed with literacy proficiency, a moderately strong inverse relationship (r= -0.52) is found between the overall level of proficiency in numeracy and the degree of score variation (expressed in terms of interquartile range) (Figure 2.15). In general, countries/economies with higher average numeracy scores (e.g. the Czech Republic, Estonia, Japan and the Slovak Republic) have the smallest variations in proficiency, while countries/economies with the lowest average scores in numeracy (Chile, Jakarta [Indonesia], Turkey and Israel) show the largest variations in numeracy scores. Singapore is the only exception to this general trend: its mean score in numeracy is close to the OECD average, but it has the greatest variation in numeracy scores among adults. The wide gap in numeracy performance – as in literacy performance – among adults in Singapore could be partly due to older cohorts having lower educational attainment and more often having been educated in a language other than the test language than younger cohorts.

Figure 2.15 ▪ **Average and distribution of numeracy scores**
Relationship between mean numeracy proficiency score and variability

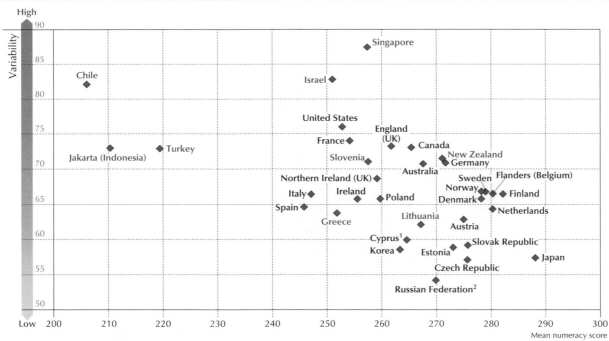

Note: The measure of variability used is the interquartile range (difference between the third quartile and the first quartile).

1. See note 1 under Figure 2.1.

2. See note at the end of this chapter.

Source: Survey of Adult Skills (PIAAC) (2012, 2015), Table A2.5.

StatLink ⟲ http://dx.doi.org/10.1787/888933365890

PROFICIENCY IN PROBLEM SOLVING IN TECHNOLOGY-RICH ENVIRONMENTS

The Survey of Adult Skills defines problem solving in technology-rich environments as "using digital technology, communication tools and networks to acquire and evaluate information, communicate with others and perform practical tasks". It focuses on "the abilities to solve problems for personal, work and civic purposes by setting up appropriate goals and plans, and accessing and making use of information through computers and computer networks" (OECD, 2012a).

Table 2.3 **Description of proficiency levels in problem solving in technology-rich environments**

Level	Score range	Percentage of adults able to perform tasks at each level (average)	The types of tasks completed successfully at each level of proficiency
No computer experience	Not applicable	10.0%	Adults in this category reported having no prior computer experience; therefore, they did not take part in the computer-based assessment but took the paper-based version of the assessment, which did not include the problem solving in technology-rich environment domain.
Failed ICT core	Not applicable	4.7%	Adults in this category had prior computer experience but failed the ICT core test, which assesses the basic ICT skills, such as the capacity to use a mouse or scroll through a web page, needed to take the computer-based assessment. Therefore, they did not take part in the computer-based assessment, but took the paper-based version of the assessment, which did not include the problem solving in technology-rich environment domain.
"Opted out" of taking computer-based assessment	Not applicable	9.6%	Adults in this category opted to take the paper-based assessment without first taking the ICT core assessment, even if they reported some prior experience with computers. They also did not take part in the computer-based assessment, but took the paper-based version of the assessment, which did not include the problem solving in technology-rich environment domain.
Below Level 1	Below 241 points	14.2%	Tasks are based on well-defined problems involving the use of only one function within a generic interface to meet one explicit criterion without any categorical or inferential reasoning, or transforming of information. Few steps are required and no sub-goal has to be generated.
1	241 to less than 291 points	28.7%	At this level, tasks typically require the use of widely available and familiar technology applications, such as e-mail software or a web browser. There is little or no navigation required to access the information or commands required to solve the problem. The problem may be solved regardless of the respondent's awareness and use of specific tools and functions (e.g. a sort function). The tasks involve few steps and a minimal number of operators. At the cognitive level, the respondent can readily infer the goal from the task statement; problem resolution requires the respondent to apply explicit criteria; and there are few monitoring demands (e.g. the respondent does not have to check whether he or she has used the appropriate procedure or made progress towards the solution). Identifying content and operators can be done through simple match. Only simple forms of reasoning, such as assigning items to categories, are required; there is no need to contrast or integrate information.
2	291 to less than 341 points	25.7%	At this level, tasks typically require the use of both generic and more specific technology applications. For instance, the respondent may have to make use of a novel online form. Some navigation across pages and applications is required to solve the problem. The use of tools (e.g. a sort function) can facilitate the resolution of the problem. The task may involve multiple steps and operators. The goal of the problem may have to be defined by the respondent, though the criteria to be met are explicit. There are higher monitoring demands. Some unexpected outcomes or impasses may appear. The task may require evaluating the relevance of a set of items to discard distractors. Some integration and inferential reasoning may be needed.
3	Equal to or higher than 341 points	5.4%	At this level, tasks typically require the use of both generic and more specific technology applications. Some navigation across pages and applications is required to solve the problem. The use of tools (e.g. a sort function) is required to make progress towards the solution. The task may involve multiple steps and operators. The goal of the problem may have to be defined by the respondent, and the criteria to be met may or may not be explicit. There are typically high monitoring demands. Unexpected outcomes and impasses are likely to occur. The task may require evaluating the relevance and reliability of information in order to discard distractors. Integration and inferential reasoning may be needed to a large extent.

Note: The proportion of adults scoring at different levels of proficiency adds up to 100% when 1.9% of literacy-related non-respondents across countries/economies are taken into account. Adults in the missing category were not able to provide enough background information to impute proficiency scores because of language difficulties, or learning or mental disabilities (see section on literacy-related non-response above).

Problem solving in technology-rich environments does not measure the cognitive skill required to solve problems in isolation. It measures both problem-solving and basic computer literacy skills (i.e. the capacity to use ICT tools and applications). This is done by assessing how well adults can use ICT tools and applications to assess, process, evaluate and analyse information in a goal-oriented way. For more details about the characteristics and some examples of problem solving tasks, see OECD, 2013c.

A prerequisite for displaying proficiency in problem solving in technology-rich environments is having some rudimentary skills in using computer tools and applications. Given the very different levels of familiarity with computer applications in the countries/economies participating in the Survey of Adult Skills, the proportions of the population to which the estimates of proficiency in this domain refer vary widely among countries/economies. For this reason, the presentation of results focuses on defining the proportions of the population by proficiency level rather than on comparing mean proficiency scores.[5]

The survey provides two different, albeit related, pieces of information regarding the capacity of adults to manage information in technology-rich environments. The first is the proportion of adults who have sufficient familiarity with computers to use them to perform information-processing tasks. The second is the proficiency of adults with at least some ICT skills in solving the types of problems commonly encountered in their roles as workers, citizens and consumers in a technology-rich world.

Levels of proficiency in problem solving in technology-rich environments across countries and economies

The scale of problem solving in technology-rich environments is divided into four levels of proficiency (Levels 1 through 3 plus below Level 1). The features of the tasks at these levels are described in detail in Table 2.3 (some examples of problem-solving items are available in OECD, 2013a and OECD, 2013c).

Figure 2.16 presents the proportion of adults across all participating countries/economies at the four proficiency levels of the problem solving in technology-rich environments scale.

Only 5.4% of adults in participating OECD countries/economies scored at Level 3, the highest proficiency level, while around one in four adults (25.7%) scored at Level 2. Taken together, on average, around one in three adults (31.1%) is proficient at the two highest levels of problem-solving proficiency (Level 2 or 3). The proportion varies from more than four in ten adults in New Zealand (44.2%), Sweden (44.0%), Finland (41.6%), the Netherlands (41.5%) and Norway (41.0%), to fewer than one in ten (7.8%) in Turkey and around one in seven in Greece (14.0%) and Chile (14.6%).

Across all countries/economies, the largest proportion of adults (28.7%) scored at Level 1 and around one in seven adults (14.2%) scored below Level 1. More than one in four adults in Chile (26.8%) and Lithuania (25.5%) scored below Level 1 on the problem-solving scale. By contrast, fewer than one in ten adults in Japan (7.6%), the Slovak Republic (8.9%), Australia (9.2%), Korea (9.8%) and Austria (9.9%) scored at this level.

The proportion of adults without basic ICT skills

In each participating country/economy, a substantial proportion of adults was unable to display any proficiency in problem solving in technology-rich environments since they took the assessment in the paper-based format.[6] Three separate groups of adults fall in this category: adults with no computer experience, those who failed the "ICT core" test and thus did not have basic computer skills needed for the computer-based assessment, and adults who opted to take the paper-based version of the assessment even though they reported having previous computer experience.

Overall, around one in ten adults (10.0%) reported having no prior computer experience. This ranged from less than 2% in Sweden (1.6%) and Norway (1.6%) to more than one in three adults in Turkey (35.6%) and more than one in five adults in Italy (24.4%) and the Slovak Republic (22.0%).

A further 4.7% of adults did not have the basic ICT skills that were assessed by the ICT core test, such as the capacity to use a mouse or scroll through a web page (see Figure 2.5 in Box 2.2). This was true of around 2% of adults in Cyprus[4] (1.9%), the Czech Republic (2.2%) and the Slovak Republic (2.2%). Large proportions of adults in Japan (10.7%),[7] Korea (9.1%), Chile (7.8%) and Singapore (7.1%) did not pass the ICT core test (see Table A2.6 in Annex A).

Figure 2.16 ▪ **Proficiency in problem solving in technology-rich environments among adults**

Percentage of 16-65 year-olds scoring at each proficiency level

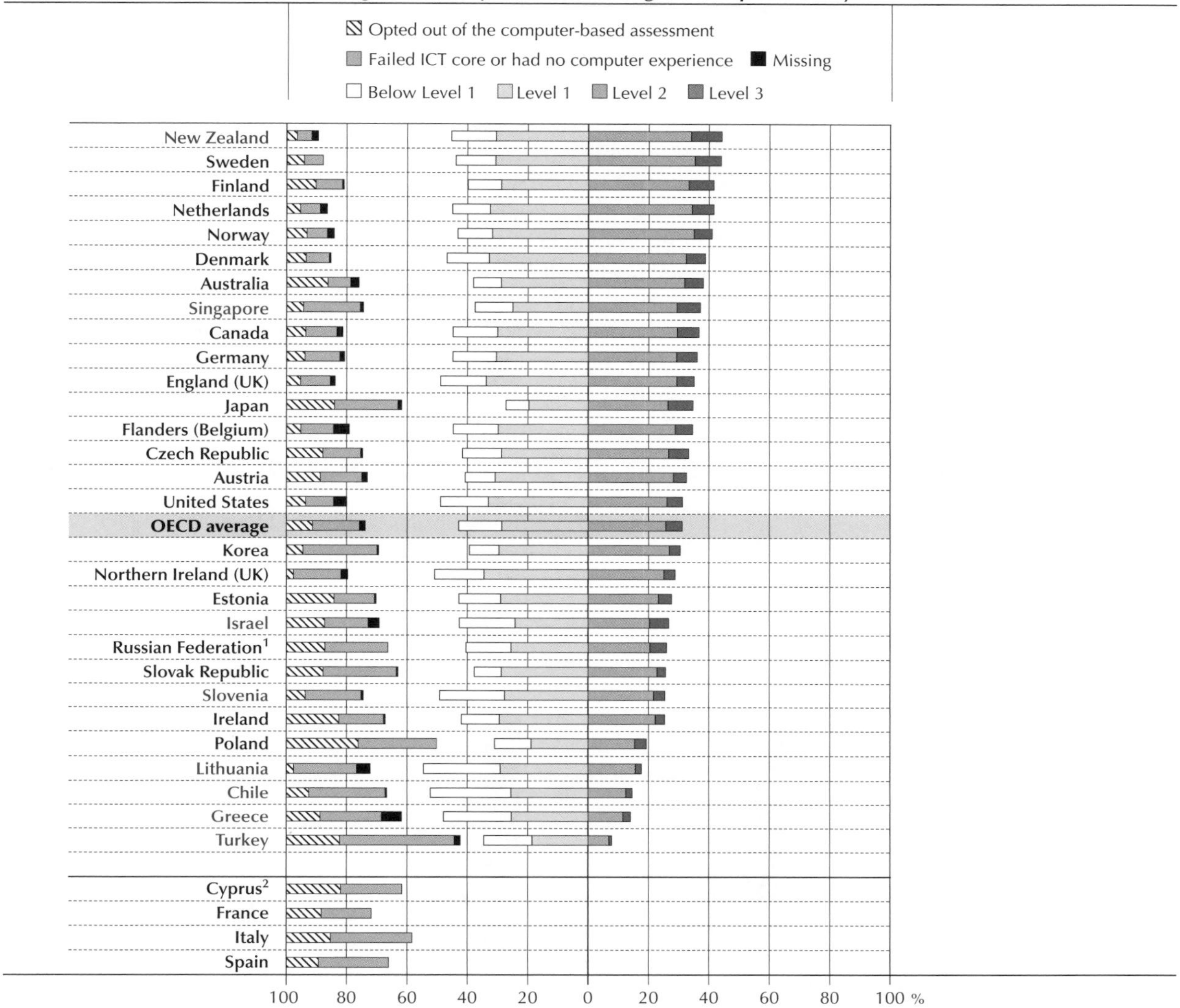

Legend:
- ▨ Opted out of the computer-based assessment
- ▦ Failed ICT core or had no computer experience   ■ Missing
- ☐ Below Level 1   ☐ Level 1   ☐ Level 2   ☐ Level 3

Countries (top to bottom): New Zealand, Sweden, Finland, Netherlands, Norway, Denmark, Australia, Singapore, Canada, Germany, England (UK), Japan, Flanders (Belgium), Czech Republic, Austria, United States, OECD average, Korea, Northern Ireland (UK), Estonia, Israel, Russian Federation[1], Slovak Republic, Slovenia, Ireland, Poland, Lithuania, Chile, Greece, Turkey, Cyprus[2], France, Italy, Spain

Notes: Adults included in the missing category were not able to provide enough background information to impute proficiency scores because of language difficulties, or learning or mental disabilities (referred to as literacy-related non-response). The missing category also includes adults who could not complete the assessment of problem solving in technology-rich environments because of technical problems with the computer used for the survey. Cyprus,[2] France, Italy, Jakarta (Indonesia) and Spain did not participate in the problem solving in technology-rich environments assessment. Results for Jakarta (Indonesia) are not shown since the assessment was administered exclusively in paper and pencil format.

1. See note at the end of this chapter.
2. See note 1 under Figure 2.1.
Countries and economies are ranked in descending order of the combined percentages of adults scoring at Level 2 and at Level 3.
Source: Survey of Adult Skills (PIAAC) (2012, 2015), Table A2.6.
StatLink ⟐▤ http://dx.doi.org/10.1787/888933365903

Some adults preferred not to use a computer in an assessment situation, even if they reported some prior experience with computers. On average, around one in ten adults (9.6%) opted to take the paper-based version of the assessment without first taking the ICT core test (Box 2.2). Large proportions of adults in Poland (23.8%), Cyprus[4] (18.0%), Turkey (17.7%) and Ireland (17.4%) "opted out" of the computer-based assessment, while relatively small proportions of adults in Northern Ireland (United Kingdom) (2.3%), Lithuania (2.3%) and New Zealand (3.4%) did so.

It is not known why these people chose to take the paper-based assessment.[8] However, information regarding the characteristics of these people and their patterns of ICT use is available and can be used to make inferences about their likely level of ICT skills and/or comfort with using a computer in a test situation. In short, the evidence suggests that many in the "opt out" group are likely to have relatively poor computer skills (Box 2.4).

Box 2.4 **Adults who "opted out" of taking the computer-based assessment**

Respondents who opted out of the computer-based assessment were much more similar in age, level of educational attainment and occupation to the respondents who failed the ICT core test than to those who passed and took the assessment in its computer-based format (Figure 2.17). Overall, respondents who opted out of taking the computer-based assessment were younger than those with no computer experience but older than those who failed and those who passed the ICT core test and took the computer-based assessment. For example, around 55% of adults who reported no computer experience were 55-65 year-olds, compared to 35% of those who "opted out", 24% of those who failed the ICT core test, and only 13% of those who took the computer-based assessment. Adults who "opted out" of the computer-based assessment had similar levels of education and occupational status as the respondents who failed the ICT core test, and lower levels of education and less likelihood of being employed in skilled occupations than those who passed the core test. The opt-out group reported less frequent use of ICTs in everyday life and at work compared to those who failed and those who passed the ICT core test. Adults who opted out had somewhat higher mean literacy and numeracy scores than those who failed the ICT core test, but they had lower scores than adults who passed the ICT core test (Figures 2.18 and 2.19).

Figure 2.17 ▪ **Socio-demographic characteristics of adults with varying levels of ICT experience**

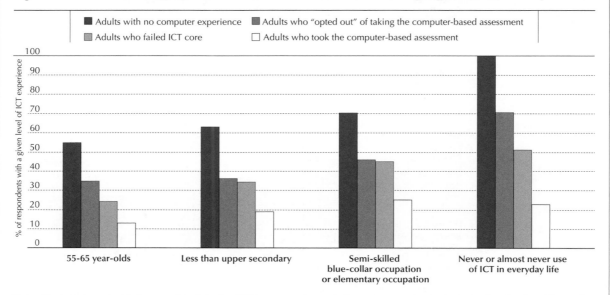

Notes: The bars shown in this figure are based on the OECD averages; the results for each country/economy can be found in the tables cited in the source. International average is computed for OECD participating countries/economies.
Source: Survey of Adult Skills (PIAAC) (2012, 2015), Tables B2.4, B2.5, B2.6, B2.7, B2.8.
StatLink ▪ http://dx.doi.org/10.1787/888933365918

THE RELATIONSHIP AMONG THE THREE PROFICIENCIES

Proficiency in literacy is closely related to proficiency in numeracy, with a correlation of 0.86. The correlation varies between 0.93 in Singapore to 0.79 in the Russian Federation (for the full list of correlation coefficients across countries/economies, see Table A2.7 in Annex A). This level of correlation is in line with expectations. Similar levels of correlation (r=0.85) are found in PISA between 15-year-olds' reading literacy and mathematical literacy (OECD, 2012b, p. 194), and in the Adult Literacy and Lifeskills Survey between prose and document literacy and numeracy (r=0.83 and r=0.86 respectively). Even higher levels of correlation (r=0.93) between prose literacy and numeracy were found in the International Adult Literacy Survey.

Given that adults use similar cognitive strategies in comparable work and life situations, those with a high level of proficiency in one skills domain will be more likely to have a higher level of skills in the other domain and vice versa. Nevertheless, literacy and numeracy represent distinct domains, each defined by its respective conceptual framework.

In particular, each is characterised by a different type of content (textual vs. mathematical) to which adults must respond, and also by different cognitive strategies required to engage with this content. As such, the strength of the relationship between proficiency and other outcomes, such as employment and wages, differs between literacy and numeracy. Proficiency in numeracy, for example, has a stronger relationship with wages than does literacy proficiency (Hanushek, et al., 2013). Likewise, countries' mean scores can vary substantially between the two domains, both in relation to those of other countries and to the OECD average (Figure 2.22).

In order to take a closer look at the relationship between proficiency in the two core domains and proficiency in problem solving in technology-rich environments, the mean literacy (Figure 2.18) and numeracy (Figure 2.19) scores are presented across the four proficiency levels of the problem solving in technology-rich environments scale. In addition, average literacy and numeracy scores are also shown for those adults with no or only basic ICT skills and for those who opted not to take the computer-based assessment.

Figure 2.18 ▪ **Relationship between literacy and problem solving in technology-rich environments**
Mean literacy proficiency, by proficiency level in problem solving in technology-rich environments

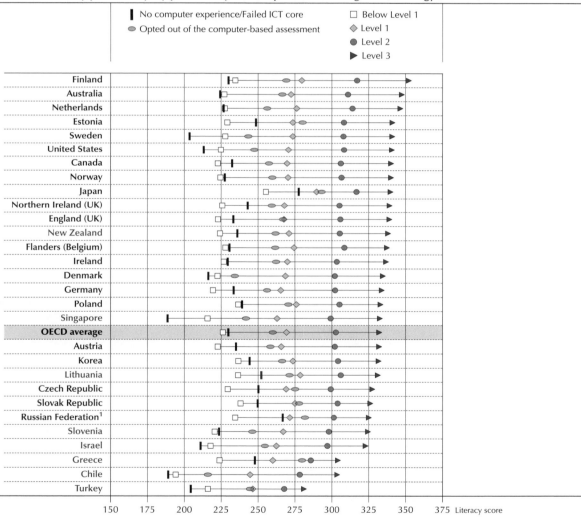

Note: Cyprus,[2] France, Italy, Jakarta (Indonesia) and Spain did not participate in the problem solving in technology-rich environments assessment.
1. See note at the end of this chapter.
2. See note 1 under Figure 2.1.
Countries and economies are ranked in descending order of the mean literacy score of adults scoring at Level 3 on the problem solving in technology-rich environments scale.
Source: Survey of Adult Skills (PIAAC) (2012, 2015), Table A2.8.
StatLink ⟐ http://dx.doi.org/10.1787/888933365924

Figure 2.19 ■ **Relationship between numeracy and problem solving in technology-rich environments**

Mean numeracy proficiency, by proficiency level in problem solving in technology-rich environments

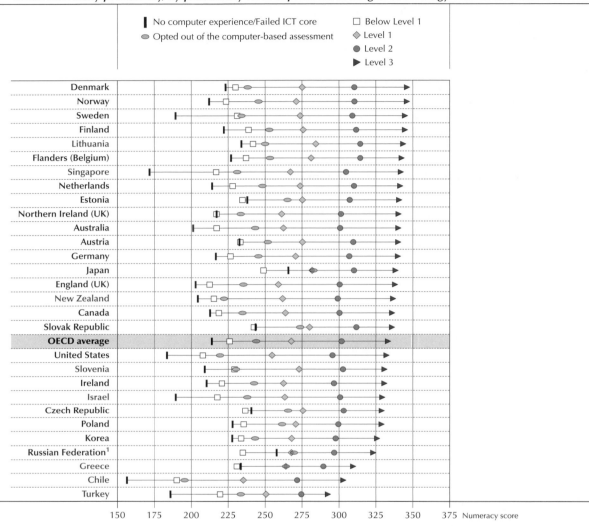

Note: Cyprus,[2] France, Italy, Jakarta (Indonesia) and Spain did not participate in the problem solving in technology-rich environments assessment.

1. See note at the end of this chapter.

2. See note 1 under Figure 2.1.

Countries and economies are ranked in descending order of the mean numeracy score of adults scoring at Level 3 on the problem solving in technology-rich environments scale.

Source: Survey of Adult Skills (PIAAC) (2012, 2015), Table A2.9.

StatLink ⟐⟐ http://dx.doi.org/10.1787/888933365938

As expected, there is a strong positive relationship between problem-solving proficiency on the one hand and literacy and numeracy proficiency on the other. The higher the average literacy and numeracy scores, the higher the proficiency in problem solving. On average, individuals who scored at Level 3 on the problem solving in technology-rich environments scale scored at the lower range of Level 4 on the literacy and numeracy scales (average scores are 332 score points in literacy and 333 points in numeracy). Those who scored at Level 2 on the problem solving in technology-rich environments scale scored, on average, at the middle range of Level 3 on the literacy and numeracy scales (303 and 302 points, respectively). Those who scored at Level 1 on the problem solving in technology-rich environments scale, on average, scored at the top of Level 2 or at the lower end of Level 3 on the literacy and numeracy scales (269 and 268 points, respectively). Those who scored below Level 1 in problem solving scored, on average, at the bottom of Level 2 or the top of Level 1 on the literacy and numeracy scales (226 points in both cases).

There is relatively little variation across countries in this regard. One exception is Japan, where those who scored at or below Level 1 on the problem solving in technology-rich environments scale scored considerably higher in literacy and numeracy than adults in other participating countries with a similar level of proficiency in problem solving. Adults in Chile, Greece and Turkey who scored at the two highest levels on the problem-solving scale scored substantially lower in literacy and numeracy, on average, than adults in other countries who scored similarly in problem solving.

The literacy and numeracy proficiency of those who opted out of the computer-based assessment is slightly higher than that among people with no or only basic computer skills, both on average across participating countries and in each individual country. Adults who opted out of the computer-based assessment scored, on average, at the middle range of Level 2 in literacy and numeracy (260 and 244 points, respectively), while those with no or only basic ICT skills scored at the bottom of Level 2 or at the top of Level 1 on the literacy and numeracy scales.

High proficiency in literacy and numeracy goes hand-in-hand with high proficiency in problem solving in technology-rich environments and vice versa. Low proficiency in literacy and numeracy may, therefore, present significant barriers to using ICT applications to manage information and solve more complex problems.

As has been noted, another potential barrier to developing problem-solving skills in computer-rich environments is a lack of basic ICT skills. These skills, in themselves, require a minimum level of proficiency in literacy and numeracy. However, even if adults have some computer skills, it is difficult for those with low proficiency in literacy and numeracy to handle many of the information-management and information-processing tasks that they are likely to encounter in everyday life. In modern societies, it has become increasingly common – and, in some places, it has become the norm – to use information found via computers for such everyday tasks as informing oneself, communicating, shopping, managing services and interacting with authorities. Given that text-based and numeric information occupies a considerable portion of the digital world, access to that world depends not only on ICT skills but also on basic proficiency in literacy and numeracy. In other words, the digital divide may also reflect a literacy and numeracy divide.

COMPARISON OF THE RESULTS FROM THE SURVEY OF ADULT SKILLS WITH THOSE OF PREVIOUS SURVEYS

The Survey of Adult Skills was designed to provide valid comparisons with the results of the International Adult Literacy Survey (IALS), which was conducted in 21 countries between 1994 and 1998, and the Adult Literacy and Life Skills Survey (ALL), which was conducted in 13 countries between 2003 and 2007. In total, 19 countries/economies participating in the Survey of Adult Skills participated in IALS and seven participated in both IALS and ALL.

An overview of the relationship between the Survey of Adult Skills and IALS and ALL is provided in Chapter 5 of the Reader's Companion to this report (OECD, 2016a). A detailed comparative analysis of the IALS, ALL and PIAAC results and related issues can be found in a separate working paper on the topic (Paccagnella, forthcoming). As noted in the Reader's Companion, given the large gap in time between IALS and PIAAC (between 13 and 18 years), differences in the mode of delivery and in operational procedures, and low response rates in some countries/economies, a degree of caution is advised in interpreting the variations in proficiency observed between PIAAC and the previous surveys.

For example, the domains covered in the surveys are somewhat different (OECD and Statistics Canada, 2000 and 2011, Statistics Canada and OECD, 2005). The Survey of Adult Skills reports results for a single domain of literacy, which covers the reading of both prose and document texts as well as digital texts; IALS and ALL report literacy as two separate domains: prose literacy and document literacy. Similarly, even though the concept of numeracy has remained largely unchanged between ALL (in which the concept was introduced) and the Survey of Adult Skills, there is significantly more information available from the Survey of Adult Skills for constructing the numeracy scale.

To allow for comparisons of change over time, the results for prose and document literacy in IALS and ALL have been combined and re-estimated so that that they can be presented on a common scale with those from the Survey of Adult Skills. The results for numeracy in ALL have also been re-estimated for the countries that participated in both surveys. Comparisons between the results of the Survey of Adult Skills and those of previous surveys should, therefore, be made only on the basis of the revised data from IALS and ALL. These comparisons are presented in Figures 2.20 and 2.21 below.

In considering trends in literacy proficiency, three distinct groups of countries/economies can be identified. First, in most countries/economies (13 of 19), results have not changed substantially over the past two decades. For example, in Chile, the Czech Republic, Finland, Flanders (Belgium) and Ireland, average scores in literacy in IALS and the Survey of Adult Skills are almost identical. In the second group of countries, which includes Denmark, Germany, Norway and Sweden, mean scores substantially decreased between IALS and the Survey of Adult Skills, with an especially large decrease in Sweden. Finally, a sizeable increase in the national average is observed in Italy, Poland and Slovenia. Poland has seen by far the largest change in average scores in literacy: an increase of 35 score points.

Figure 2.20 ■ **Changes in literacy scores in IALS, ALL and PIAAC surveys**

*Mean literacy proficiency in the International Adult Literacy Survey (IALS),
the Adult Literacy and Lifeskills Survey (ALL) and the Survey of Adult Skills (PIAAC)*

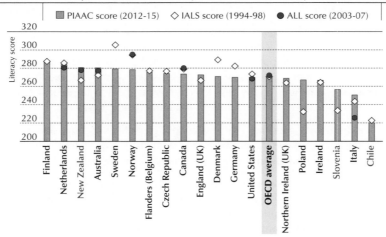

Countries and economies are ranked in descending order of the mean score on the Survey of Adult Skills (PIAAC).
Sources: Survey of Adult Skills (PIAAC) (2012, 2015), International Adult Literacy Survey (IALS) and Adult Literacy and Lifeskills Survey (ALL), see Table A2.10.
StatLink http://dx.doi.org/10.1787/888933365943

Figure 2.21 ■ **Changes in numeracy scores in PIAAC and ALL surveys**

*Mean numeracy proficiency in the Adult Literacy and Lifeskills Survey (ALL)
and the Survey of Adult Skills (PIAAC)*

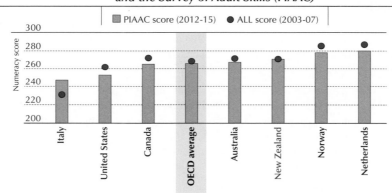

Countries are ranked in descending order of the mean score on the Survey of Adult Skills (PIAAC).
Sources: Survey of Adult Skills (PIAAC) (2012, 2015), and Adult Literacy and Lifeskills Survey (ALL), see Table A2.11.
StatLink http://dx.doi.org/10.1787/888933365958

Changes in numeracy scores between ALL and the Survey of Adult Skills are not as pronounced, except in Italy, where scores improved substantially over the period. A moderate decrease in numeracy scores was observed in Canada, the Netherlands, Norway and the United States.

The major trend observed is a considerable reduction in the gap between the lowest- and highest-performing countries, resulting in a more equal distribution of mean scores across countries/economies. Part of the reason for this trend may be differences in educational attainment across age groups. Younger adults have more similar levels of educational attainment across countries than older adults do (Figures 2.2, 2.3 and 2.4 Box 2.1). For example, the proportion of tertiary-educated adults doubled in Italy, Poland and Slovenia during the past three decades, while countries where national averages decreased saw no change (Germany) or only a slight rise in educational attainment among younger generations (in this latter group of countries, however, initial levels of educational attainment were substantially higher than in the former group). Interestingly, national wealth is not directly correlated with an increase in proficiency scores. In Poland, for example, both GDP and proficiency scores have increased substantially over the past two and a half decades, while in Chile and Ireland, sharp rises in GDP over the past 25 years were not matched by improvements in literacy and numeracy proficiency.

The decrease in literacy scores observed in Denmark, Norway and Sweden between IALS (and ALL in the case of Norway) and the Survey of Adult Skills may partly be the result of a number of demographic factors, such as population ageing and an increase in the proportion of immigrants in the population. However, it may also indicate somewhat lower academic standards among younger adults who are consequently not attaining as high levels of literacy and proficiency as their older compatriots did. For example, even though the number of students with tertiary degrees has increased over the years, younger adults may have poorer skills than older adults who have attained the same level of education (Paccagnella, 2016).

SUMMARISING PERFORMANCE ACROSS COUNTRIES AND ECONOMIES

Figure 2.22 summarises the proficiency of adults in participating countries/economies in each of the three domains assessed. It provides an overview of the average proficiency in each participating country/economy relative to the average in each domain.

Figure 2.22 ▪ **Summary of proficiency in key information-processing skills**

Mean proficiency scores of 16-65 year-olds in literacy and numeracy, and the percentage of 16-65 year-olds scoring at Level 2 or 3 in problem solving in technology-rich environments

Significantly **above** the average
Not significantly different from the average
Significantly **below** the average

	Literacy	Numeracy	Problem solving in technology-rich environments
	Mean score	Mean score	% at Level 2 or 3
OECD countries and economies			
Australia	280	268	38
Austria	269	275	32
Canada	273	265	37
Chile	220	206	15
Czech Republic	274	276	33
Denmark	271	278	39
England (UK)	273	262	35
Estonia	276	273	28
Finland	288	282	42
Flanders (Belgium)	275	280	35
France	262	254	m
Germany	270	272	36
Greece	254	252	14
Ireland	267	256	25
Israel	255	251	27
Italy	250	247	m
Japan	296	288	35
Korea	273	263	30
Netherlands	284	280	42
New Zealand	281	271	44
Northern Ireland (UK)	269	259	29
Norway	278	278	41
Poland	267	260	19
Slovak Republic	274	276	26
Slovenia	256	258	25
Spain	252	246	m
Sweden	279	279	44
Turkey	227	219	8
United States	270	253	31
OECD average	**268**	**263**	**31**
Partners			
Cyprus[1]	269	265	m
Jakarta (Indonesia)	200	210	m
Lithuania	267	267	18
Russian Federation[2]	275	270	26
Singapore	258	257	37

Note: Cyprus,[1] France, Italy, Jakarta (Indonesia) and Spain did not participate in the problem solving in technology-rich environments assessment.

1. See note 1 under Figure 2.1.

2. See note at the end of this chapter.

Countries and economies are listed in alphabetical order.

Source: Survey of Adult Skills (PIAAC) (2012, 2015), Tables A2.3, A2.5 and A2.6.

StatLink ⧉ http://dx.doi.org/10.1787/888933365964

It also indicates whether the country's/economy's mean score is statistically greater than, equal to, or less than the average across participating OECD countries/economies. In the case of problem solving in technology-rich environments, the average proficiency is not presented because of variations across countries/economies in the proportions of respondents who did not take the computer-based version and were not assessed in the problem-solving domain. Instead, the figure shows the proportion of the total population performing at Level 2 or 3 on this scale.

Adults in 11 of 33 countries/economies show above-average levels of proficiency in all three domains. Among these, adults in Japan had the highest average scores in literacy and numeracy, while New Zealand and Sweden had the largest proportion of adults scoring at Level 2 or 3 in problem solving in technology-rich environments.

In five countries – Chile, Greece, Israel, Slovenia and Turkey – adults' mean scores were statistically significantly below average in all three domains; and in four of the five countries/economies that did not participate in the assessment of problem solving – France, Italy, Jakarta (Indonesia) and Spain – mean scores in both literacy and numeracy were below average. Adults in Jakarta (Indonesia) and Chile had the lowest average score in literacy and numeracy, respectively, while Turkey had the smallest proportion of adults at Level 2 or 3 in problem solving in technology-rich environments. Adults in the remaining 14 countries/economies had mixed results. A closer look at the results of the countries/economies that participated in Round 2 is provided in Box 2.5.

Box 2.5 Skills proficiency among adults in the countries/economies that participated in Round 2 of the Survey of Adult Skills (PIAAC)

The proficiency of adults in the nine countries/economies that participated in Round 2 of the Survey of Adult Skills varies substantially, reflecting the diversity of the countries'/economies' current economic situation and their social, educational and economic development over the past five decades.

Among the adults in the nine Round-2 countries/economies, those in New Zealand averaged the highest scores, by far, in the three domains assessed. In fact, along with Sweden, New Zealand had the largest proportion of adults who scored at the two highest levels of proficiency in problem solving in technology-rich environments (Levels 2 and 3) of all countries/economies that participated in both rounds of the study, and had the fourth highest score in literacy. Adults in New Zealand did not score as high in numeracy as in literacy, but their mean numeracy score was still significantly above the international average.

Adults in Lithuania performed close to the international mean in literacy but showed better-than-average performance in numeracy. Somewhat surprisingly, their proficiency in problem solving in technology-rich environments was substantially lower than the international average, with only 18% of adults reaching one of the two highest levels. The relatively large proportion of adults who reported having no computer experience (16%) suggests that these results may reflect the low level of ICT skills in the country.

By contrast, the mean literacy and numeracy scores among adults in Singapore were somewhat below the international average, but scores in problem solving in technology-rich environments were much higher than average. There are large differences in levels of educational attainment among age cohorts in Singapore: younger adults have attained much higher levels of education than older adults. In fact, compared to their peers in other countries/economies, young adults in Singapore were among the most proficient in the three domains assessed. In addition, a sizable proportion of those in the older cohorts who were relatively better-educated were educated in a language other than the test language. These could be some of the reasons why Singapore shows the largest variations in literacy and numeracy scores.

Adults in Slovenia scored somewhat lower than average in all three domains. A comparison between Slovenia's performance in IALS and in the Survey of Adult Skills suggests that there has been substantial improvement in literacy proficiency among adults over the past 15 years. These results may reflect the outcome of some of the intense political and economic transformations that Slovenia underwent over the past few decades.

The mean scores of adults in Israel were also consistently somewhat below the international average in all three domains. After Singapore, Israel shows the second highest dispersion of individual scores, indicating a heterogeneous distribution of skills across the adult population.

...

Adults in Greece achieved mean scores in literacy and numeracy similar to those of adults in Slovenia and Israel, scoring around 12 points lower than the international average. However, they scored much lower in problem solving in technology-rich environments, with only 14% reaching one of the two highest levels of proficiency in this domain – the second smallest proportion among countries/economies that participated in the two rounds of the survey.

The mean literacy and numeracy scores among adults in Turkey were more than 40 points lower than the international average (around one standard deviation). This means that the average literacy and numeracy proficiency of adults in Turkey (which is between the upper end of Level 1 and the lower end of Level 2) was almost one proficiency level lower than the international average (the upper end of Level 2). In addition, a majority of adults in Turkey showed no or very low levels of proficiency in problem solving in technology-rich environments. Only 8% of adults attained one of the two highest proficiency levels in this domain. Given that almost 40% of adults reported no computer experience or failed the ICT core test, the lack of the basic ICT skills among a large proportion of adults may be chiefly responsible for the poor performance of Turkish adults in this domain.

Adults in Chile had the lowest mean scores in numeracy and the second lowest in literacy among all countries in both rounds of the survey. The mean literacy score of adults in Chile was 48 score points lower than the international average. In numeracy, the mean score was 57 score points lower than the international average. In relative terms, adults in Chile performed better in problem solving in technology-rich environments, where a slightly larger proportion of adults scored at one of the two highest proficiency levels compared to the proportion of adults in Turkey and Greece who scored at that level. Together with Singapore and Israel, Chile is also one of the countries with the greatest variations in both literacy and numeracy proficiency. The average literacy proficiency among Chilean adults seems to have changed little in the 15 years that separate the IALS from the Survey of Adult Skills.

The average scores of adults in Jakarta (Indonesia) are the lowest among participating countries/economies in literacy and the second lowest in numeracy. Furthermore, there is a relatively high level of individual variation in scores, in spite of the fact that few adults scored at the two highest proficiency levels. Since only the paper-based assessment module was used in Jakarta (Indonesia), there is no information in the domain of problem-solving in technology rich environments.

SUMMARY

The Survey of Adult Skills measures proficiency in literacy, numeracy and problem solving in technology-rich environments among 16 to 65 year-olds. It finds that the variation in average scores in the three domains, across countries, is substantial, although many countries score within relatively close range of each other. However, even relatively small differences in national averages (e.g. 10 score points) are significant since average scores at the national level represent the proficiency of a country's entire working-age population. Thus substantial effort and cost is associated with improving the proficiency scores of each person.

Variations in scores among adults in individual countries are even larger than those across countries. Countries/economies with higher mean scores tend to have less variation in scores among their adults. On the one hand, this relationship could be seen as an encouraging sign for all countries/economies, given that it implies that higher levels of literacy proficiency go hand-in-hand with – or at least do not hinder – a more equal and homogeneous distribution of skills proficiency across the adult population. On the other hand, it could also be seen as an indication of the urgency for the countries with low proficiency and large variations in scores, such as Chile, to act, both to improve general levels of proficiency and to reduce inequalities.

Among the Round-2 countries/economies, New Zealand performed the best, scoring significantly above average in all three domains. Adults in Lithuania and Singapore performed better than average in some domains (numeracy and problem solving, respectively) and at or slightly below average in others. Adults in Greece, Israel and Slovenia performed below average in all three domains but, with the exception of problem solving in technology-rich environments in Greece, scored relatively close to the OECD average. Mean scores in all three domains in Chile and Turkey were substantially below the OECD average, presenting significant policy challenges. In addition, Chile, Israel and Singapore showed the widest dispersion of scores among adults, indicating the need for policies to focus specifically on adults with low proficiency.

As expected, literacy and numeracy proficiency are closely related: adults who are highly proficient in one domain are likely to be highly proficient in the other. Nevertheless, literacy and numeracy require different cognitive strategies and constitute distinct abilities. There is also a strong positive relationship between literacy and numeracy, on the one hand, and problem solving in technology-rich environments on the other.

Low-skilled adults are numerous in all countries/economies, with the proportion ranging from one in ten to one in two adults who are proficient at or below Level 1 in the domain of literacy or numeracy. At these levels, adults can usually complete simple reading and numeracy tasks, such as locating information in a short text or performing simple one-step arithmetic operations; but they have trouble extracting information from longer and more complex texts or performing numerical tasks involving several steps and mathematical information represented in different ways.

In all countries/economies that participated in the Survey of Adult Skills, a considerable proportion of adults has no or very limited ICT skills. In addition, nearly half of adults have low proficiency in problem solving in technology-rich environments. This means that they are able to use only familiar applications to solve problems that involve few steps and explicit criteria, such as sorting e-mails into pre-existing folders. Given these findings, governments may need to rethink the way they conceive and implement policies relating to the digital economy, particularly concerning e-government and online access to public services.

Notes

1. The lower number of proficiency levels for the domain of problem solving in technology rich-environments indicates a less precise scale due to the far smaller number of items that are used in the assessment of problem solving (16 items) compared to literacy (58 items) and numeracy (56 items).

2. The common denomination of the levels (e.g. Level 1, 2 or 3) does not imply any underlying similarity of the factors affecting the difficulty of tasks at any given level in each of the domains. The descriptors for each of the levels in each of the domains reflect the features of the relevant framework and the specific factors determining difficulty in each domain.

3. English was the only test language in Singapore.

4. See notes regarding Cyprus under Figure 2.1.

5. For this reason, the presentation of results focuses on the proportions of the population by proficiency level rather than the comparison of mean proficiency scores.

6. Proficiency in problem solving in technology-rich environments was assessed only in computer-based formats; numeracy and literacy were assessed in both paper- and computer-based formats.

7. This may represent an overestimate of the proportion of Japanese adults with poor ICT skills. In particular, literacy and numeracy proficiency among these adults was far higher compared to that of adults in other countries who reported no prior computer use. At the same time, the majority of those in Japan who failed the core test reported limited use of ICTs in everyday life.

8. Presumably they regarded themselves as having poor ICT skills, or felt more comfortable with or believed that they would perform better on the paper-based version of the assessment than on the computer-based assessment.

A note regarding the Russian Federation

The sample for the Russian Federation does not include the population of the Moscow municipal area. The data published, therefore, do not represent the entire resident population aged 16-65 in the Russian Federation but rather the population of the Russian Federation *excluding* the population residing in the Moscow municipal area.

More detailed information regarding the data from the Russian Federation as well as that of other countries can be found in the *Technical Report of the Survey of Adult Skills, Second Edition* (OECD, forthcoming).

References and further reading

Autor, D., F. Levy and **R.J. Murnane** (2003), "The skill content of recent technological change: An empirical exploration", *Quarterly Journal of Economics*, No. 118/4, pp. 1279-1334.

Grotlüschen, A. et al. (2016), "Adults with low proficiency in literacy or numeracy", *OECD Education Working Papers*, No. 131, OECD Publishing, Paris, http://dx.doi.org/10.1787/5jm0v44bnmnx-en.

Hanushek, E.A. et al. (2013), "Returns to skills around the world: Evidence from PIAAC", *OECD Education Working Papers*, No. 101, OECD Publishing, Paris, http://dx.doi.org/10.1787/5k3tsjqmvtq2-en.

Levy, F. and **R.J. Murnane** (2006), "Why the changing American economy calls for twenty-first century learning: Answers to educators' questions", *New Directions for Youth Development*, No. 110, pp. 53-62.

OECD (forthcoming), *Technical Report of the Survey of Adult Skills, Second Edition*.

OECD (2016a), *The Survey of Adult Skills: Reader's Companion, Second Edition,* OECD Skills Studies, OECD Publishing, Paris, http://dx.doi.org/10.1787/9789264258075-en.

OECD (2016b), *Survey of Adult Skills (PIAAC)* (Database 2012, 2015), www.oecd.org/site/piaac/publicdataandanalysis.htm.

OECD (2015), *Country Statistical Profiles* (database), http://stats.oecd.org (accessed on 2 May 2016).

OECD (2013a), *The Survey of Adult Skills: Reader's Companion,* OECD Publishing, Paris, http://dx.doi.org/10.1787/9789264204027-en.

OECD (2013b), *Technical Report of the Survey of Adult Skills,* www.oecd.org/site/piaac/_Technical%20Report_17OCT13.pdf.

OECD (2013c), *OECD Skills Outlook 2013: First Results from the Survey of Adult Skills,* OECD Publishing, Paris, http://dx.doi.org/10.1787/9789264204256-en.

OECD (2012a), *Literacy, Numeracy and Problem Solving in Technology-Rich Environments: Framework for the OECD Survey of Adult Skills,* OECD Publishing, Paris, http://dx.doi.org/10.1787/9789264128859-en.

OECD (2012b), *PISA 2009 Technical Report, PISA*, OECD Publishing, Paris, http://dx.doi.org/10.1787/9789264167872-en.

OECD and **Statistics Canada** (2011), *Literacy for Life: Further Results from the Adult Literacy and Life Skills Survey*, OECD Publishing, Paris, http://dx.doi.org/10.1787/9789264091269-en.

OECD and **Statistics Canada** (2005), *Learning a Living: First Results of the Adult Literacy and Life Skills Survey*, OECD Publishing, Paris, http://dx.doi.org/10.1787/9789264010390-en.

OECD and **Statistics Canada** (2000), *Literacy in the Information Age: Final Report of the International Adult Literacy Survey*, OECD Publishing, Paris, http://dx.doi.org/10.1787/9789264181762-en.

Paccagnella, M. (forthcoming), "Literacy and numeracy proficiency in IALS, ALL, and PIAAC", *OECD Education Working Papers*, OECD Publishing, Paris.

Paccagnella, M. (2016), "Age, ageing and skills: Results from the Survey of Adult Skills", *OECD Education Working Papers*, No. 132, OECD Publishing, Paris, http://dx.doi.org/10.1787/5jm0q1n38lvc-en.

World Bank (2015), "GDP per capita (constant 2005 US$)", http://data.worldbank.org/indicator/NY.GDP.PCAP.KD (accessed 2 May, 2016).

3

The socio-demographic distribution of key information-processing skills

This chapter examines differences in skills proficiency between different groups of individuals, defined by age, gender, socio-economic status, educational attainment, and immigrant and language background. The main focus of the analysis is on literacy proficiency; results for numeracy are generally similar, and are discussed in detail when this is not the case. Results for problem solving in technology-rich environments are discussed separately.

A note regarding Israel

The statistical data for Israel are supplied by and under the responsibility of the relevant Israeli authorities. The use of such data by the OECD is without prejudice to the status of the Golan Heights, East Jerusalem and Israeli settlements in the West Bank under the terms of international law.

Knowing the proficiency levels of different subgroups of the population makes it easier for policy makers to target policy interventions, and to identify strengths and weaknesses of particular policies. To this end, this chapter tries to identify the groups that may be at particular risk of suffering from low proficiency in literacy, numeracy and/or problem-solving skills. A lack of information-processing skills could be a major obstacle to full participation in modern societies and could lead to social and economic exclusion and marginalisation.

OVERVIEW OF SOCIO-DEMOGRAPHIC DIFFERENCES IN PROFICIENCY

Figure 3.1 presents an overview of proficiency differences associated with various socio-demographic characteristics, as revealed in the Survey of Adult Skills, a product of the OECD Programme for the International Assessment of Adult Competencies (PIAAC). The bars show raw (unadjusted) differences, while the dots represent adjusted differences, estimated after accounting for the impact of other background characteristics.[1] While the analysis focuses on literacy proficiency, results for numeracy are generally similar.

Of all the socio-demographic characteristics examined in this chapter, educational attainment has the strongest relationship with proficiency, both before and after accounting for the influence of other socio-demographic characteristics. When considering educational attainment, the adjusted differences are generally close to the unadjusted differences, meaning that background characteristics like age, gender or family background have little impact on the strength of the relationship between educational attainment and proficiency. In fact, accounting for differences in educational attainment generally results in a much weaker association between proficiency and other background characteristics. In other words, while education explains a substantial part of the difference in proficiency between older and younger adults, the opposite is not true: differences in proficiency among adults with different levels of education remain substantial, even after taking account of age.

Among the main findings discussed in this chapter:

- The largest gaps in literacy proficiency are usually related to differences in educational attainment, with tertiary-educated 25-65 year-olds scoring some 60 points higher, on average, than adults in this age group who have not attained an upper secondary qualification. The magnitude of the gap varies from more than 100 score points in Singapore, to about 30 to 40 score points in the Russian Federation[2] and Greece.

- Proficiency is strongly related to age. Cognitive abilities are generally found to peak between the mid-20s and the early 30s and then gradually decline (see Desjardins and Wanke, 2012; Paccagnella, 2016, and references therein); proficiency in information-processing skills follows a similar trajectory. In the Survey of Adult Skills, older adults (55-65 year-olds) scored almost 30 points below 25-34 year-olds, on average. However, there is substantial variation in the strength of the relationship between proficiency and age across countries. This suggests that the evolution of proficiency over a lifetime is not determined solely by biological factors. Accounting for other background characteristics – notably, education – strongly reduces observed age-related differences in proficiency, especially in countries/economies that expanded access to higher education over the past three decades.

- The difference in literacy proficiency between men and women is negligible. In numeracy, men have a more substantial advantage, scoring about 10 points higher than women, on average. Gender gaps in proficiency are more pronounced among older cohorts. This could reflect either the fact that gender gaps in educational attainment are wider, or that women's skills depreciate more over time, possibly because they participate less in the labour market.

- Native-born adults scored 24 points higher than foreign-born adults, on average. However, migrants whose native language is the same as that of the host country tended to score significantly higher than other migrants, and are often nearly as proficient as native-born adults. The magnitude of the differences, and the extent to which other background characteristics might account for them, varies enormously across countries/economies, reflecting countries'/economies' vastly different migration histories and policies.

- Socio-economic background exerts a significant influence on adults' proficiency in literacy. Having at least one parent with tertiary qualifications is associated with a 40 score-point advantage over adults with neither parent having attained an upper secondary degree. A significant portion of this difference (about half) is explained by other socio-demographic characteristics, most notably the fact that children of high-educated parents are themselves more likely to attain higher levels of education.

Figure 3.1 ▪ **Socio-demographic differences in literacy proficiency**

Adjusted and unadjusted differences in literacy scores between contrast categories within various socio-demographic groups

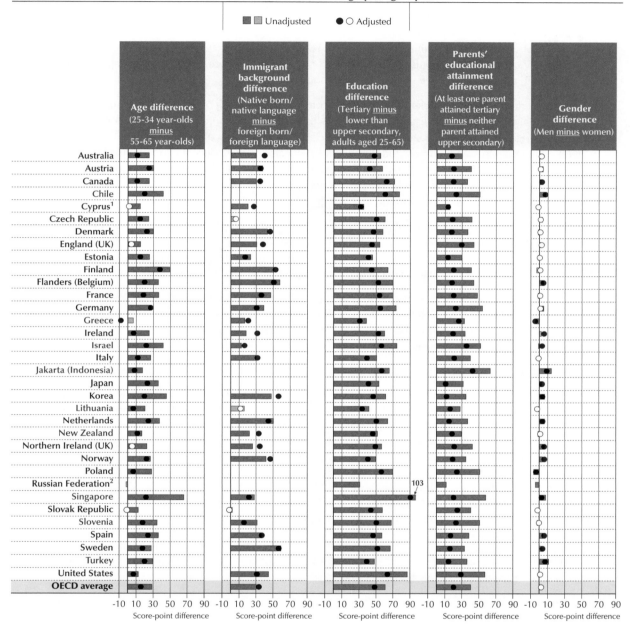

Notes: Statistically significant differences are marked in a darker tone. Estimates based on a sample size less than 30 are not shown (i.e. immigrant background differences in Chile, Jakarta [Indonesia], Japan, Poland and Turkey). Unadjusted differences are the differences between the two means for each contrast category. Adjusted differences are based on a regression model and take account of differences associated with the following variables: age, gender, education, immigrant and language background and parents' educational attainment. Only the score-point differences between two contrast categories are shown, which is useful for showing the relative significance of each socio-demographic variable vis-a-vis observed score-point differences. All adjusted differences and immigrant background estimates for the Russian Federation are missing due to the lack of language variables.

1. *Note by Turkey:* The information in this document with reference to "Cyprus" relates to the southern part of the Island. There is no single authority representing both Turkish and Greek Cypriot people on the Island. Turkey recognises the Turkish Republic of Northern Cyprus (TRNC). Until a lasting and equitable solution is found within the context of the United Nations, Turkey shall preserve its position concerning the "Cyprus issue".

Note by all the European Union Member States of the OECD and the European Union: The Republic of Cyprus is recognised by all members of the United Nations with the exception of Turkey. The information in this document relates to the area under the effective control of the Government of the Republic of Cyprus.

2. See note at the end of this chapter.

Countries and economies are listed in alphabetical order.

Source: Survey of Adult Skills (PIAAC) (2012, 2015), Tables A3.1 (L), A3.2 (L), A3.5 (L), A3.9 (L), A3.12 (L) and A3.14 (L).

StatLink ⟨⟩ http://dx.doi.org/10.1787/888933365979

DIFFERENCES IN SKILLS PROFICIENCY RELATED TO EDUCATIONAL ATTAINMENT

Learning and skills development can take place in many different contexts and in many different forms. However, most knowledge and skills are acquired through education and training programmes delivered by educational institutions such as schools, colleges and universities. While children learn in their families, and adults continue to learn, develop and maintain skills in the workplace, schools and some adult training providers are the only institutions whose primary, explicit goal is to equip individuals with the proficiency in reading and numeracy they need in order to participate fully in society. The very existence of compulsory education indicates the importance attached to formal schooling, and the shared belief that it is the most effective vehicle for educating young people.

The link between education and proficiency is complex. Instruction is only one of the possible channels through which the two are related. People with higher innate ability are likely to be both more proficient in information-processing skills and to earn higher educational qualifications, in which case the direction of causality would run from proficiency to education, rather than the other way around. More highly educated individuals are also more likely to be employed, which gives them more opportunities to practice their skills and prevent (or slow) the decline in cognitive functions normally associated with ageing. This implies that people with different educational qualifications also differ in terms of other relevant characteristics associated with proficiency.

Moreover, educational qualifications are not perfectly comparable across countries, or over time. Countries differ in the selectivity of their education systems and in the content of curricula, especially at higher levels of education. Even within the same country, the changing nature of education systems and policies implies that an individual who earned a tertiary degree some 30 years ago probably had a very different experience in tertiary education than a more recent graduate.

The analysis of proficiency differences according to educational attainment is further complicated by the fact that, among the youngest age groups that participated in the Survey of Adult Skills, a sizeable share of respondents are still in education. For this reason, this section will analyse the proficiency of 16-24 year-olds separately. The core analysis of proficiency differences related to educational qualifications applies to the subsample of 25-65 year-olds.

Proficiency in literacy and numeracy among low- and high-educated adults

As expected, in all countries, high-educated 25-65 year-olds (those who have attained at least a tertiary degree) scored higher in both literacy and numeracy than adults with an upper secondary education as their highest level of attainment; and they, in turn, scored higher than adults who have not completed upper secondary education (hereafter "low-educated adults"). Across OECD countries and economies participating in the survey, tertiary-educated adults scored 292 points on the literacy scale, on average, while adults with upper secondary education scored 264 points, and low-educated adults scored 231 points. On average, 42% of low-educated adults scored at or below Level 1, more than double the proportion of upper secondary graduates at that level (slightly below 20%). Less than 10% of tertiary-educated adults scored below Level 2, and 21% scored at Level 4 or 5. The score differences by educational attainment are generally even larger in the case of numeracy proficiency (see Tables A3.3 [L] and A3.3 [N]).

Figure 3.2 shows both average literacy proficiency by level of educational attainment (in the left panel) and proficiency differences between tertiary-educated adults and adults without an upper secondary education (on the right). Countries/economies differ to a great extent along both dimensions.

Low-educated adults in Chile, Israel, Jakarta (Indonesia), Singapore and Turkey scored particularly poorly (see Table A3.3 [L]). In Chile, 87% of adults without upper secondary education scored at or below Level 1; in Jakarta (Indonesia), 90% of such adults scored at that level. This is particularly significant, given that in Chile low-educated adults make up 32% of the total population, compared to 21% in Singapore and 13% in Israel (see Table B3.1). In Jakarta (Indonesia), low-educated adults represent almost 40% of the total population. In Lithuania and New Zealand, low-educated adults scored above the average: fewer than one in three scored at or below Level 1, and about a quarter scored at or above Level 3.

In Chile and Turkey, the vast majority of tertiary graduates scored below Level 3 in literacy; less than 5% scored at Level 4 or 5. Similar results were obtained by tertiary graduates in Jakarta (Indonesia). The literacy proficiency of tertiary graduates is only slightly better in Greece and Israel, where about 50% of tertiary graduates scored below Level 3 and less than 15% scored at Level 4 or 5. In contrast, the proficiency of tertiary graduates in Lithuania, Singapore and Slovenia is close to the international average,[3] while it is almost 10 points above average in New Zealand, where 26% of tertiary graduates scored at Level 4 or 5 (compared to an average of 21% among OECD countries/economies participating in the survey).

Singapore stands out as the country in which the difference in proficiency between high- and low-educated 25-65 year-olds is greatest – around 100 score points. This is mainly due to the comparatively low performance among low-educated adults. The same explanation applies to the large differences found in Chile, Israel and the United States. By contrast, higher educational attainment is much less closely associated with high proficiency in Greece, Lithuania and Turkey. However, in Lithuania, only 6% of adults reported that they had low educational attainment, a share much smaller than in most other countries and economies that participated in the Survey of Adult Skills. In Lithuania, the difference in proficiency between tertiary-educated adults and those with upper secondary as their highest level of attainment is close to the international average. In Greece and Turkey, the relatively small differences in proficiency between high- and low-educated adults are mainly due to low proficiency among tertiary graduates. In Jakarta (Indonesia), the difference between high- and low-educated adults is similar to the international average: across all levels of educational attainment, literacy proficiency is below the international average by roughly the same amount (approximately 60 score points).

Figure 3.2 ▪ **Differences in literacy proficiency, by educational attainment**
Adults aged 25-65

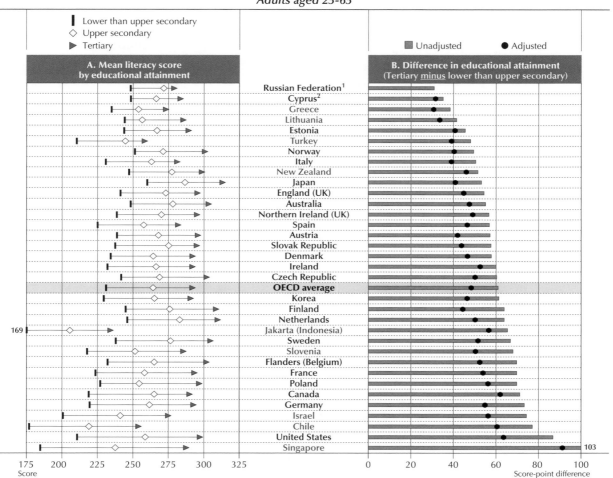

Notes: All differences in Panel B are statistically significant. Unadjusted differences are the differences between the two means for each contrast category. Adjusted differences are based on a regression model and take account of differences associated with other factors: age, gender, immigrant and language background and parents' educational attainment. Only the score-point differences between two contrast categories are shown in Panel B, which is useful for showing the relative significance of educational attainment vis-a-vis observed score-point differences. Lower than upper secondary includes ISCED 1, 2 and 3C short. Upper secondary includes ISCED 3A, 3B, 3C long and 4. Tertiary includes ISCED 5A, 5B and 6. Where possible, foreign qualifications are included as the closest corresponding level in the respective national education systems. Adjusted difference for the Russian Federation is missing due to the lack of language variables.

1. See note at the end of this chapter.

2. See note 1 under Figure 3.1.

Countries and economies are ranked in ascending order of the unadjusted differences in literacy scores (tertiary minus lower than upper secondary).

Source: Survey of Adult Skills (PIAAC) (2012, 2015), Tables A3.1 (L) and A3.2 (L).

StatLink ᵃⁱˢᵖ http://dx.doi.org/10.1787/888933365986

Accounting for other socio-demographic characteristics tends to reduce the gap in proficiency associated with educational attainment. In all countries/economies, adults with high educational attainment tend to come from advantaged backgrounds, or have other characteristics that tend to be positively associated with literacy proficiency. The effect of such other background characteristics, however, is weak, and does not vary greatly from one country to another. This is further evidence of the strong link between formal education and proficiency in information-processing skills.

Proficiency in problem solving in technology-rich environments among low- and high-educated adults

The proficiency advantage among high-educated adults is even more striking when looking at proficiency in problem solving in technology-rich environments (Figure 3.3). Only about 7% of low-educated adults scored at Level 2 or 3 on the problem-solving assessment, compared to 48% of adults who had attained tertiary education.

In this respect, between-country/economy differences are small. The share of low-educated adults showing high proficiency in problem solving in technology-rich environments is below 3% in a large and diverse group of countries that includes Chile, Greece, Ireland, Korea, Poland, Singapore, the Slovak Republic, Turkey and the United States, and exceeds 10% in only five countries (Australia, Denmark, the Netherlands, New Zealand and Norway).

Figure 3.3 ■ Problem-solving proficiency, by educational attainment

Percentage of low- and high-educated adults scoring at Level 2 or 3 in problem solving in technology-rich environments or having no computer experience (adults aged 25-65)

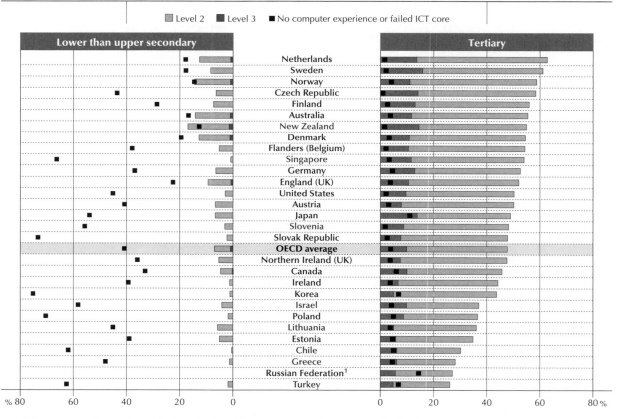

Notes: Percentages on the problem solving in technology-rich environments scale are computed so that the sum of percentages for the following mutually exhaustive categories equals 100%: opted out of the computer-based assessment; no computer experience; failed ICT core test; below Level 1, Level 1, Level 2 and Level 3. For more detailed results for each category, see corresponding table mentioned in the source below. Lower than upper secondary includes ISCED 1, 2 and 3C short. Upper secondary includes ISCED 3A, 3B, 3C long and 4. Tertiary includes ISCED 5A, 5B and 6. Where possible, foreign qualifications are included as the closest corresponding level in the respective national education systems. Cyprus,[2] France, Italy, Jakarta (Indonesia) and Spain did not participate in the problem solving in technology-rich environments assessment.

1. See note at the end of this chapter.

2. See note 1 under Figure 3.1.

Countries and economies are ranked in descending order of the combined percentages of adults with tertiary attainment scoring at Level 2 or 3.

Source: Survey of Adult Skills (PIAAC) (2012, 2015), Table A3.3 (P).

StatLink ⟨⟩ http://dx.doi.org/10.1787/888933365994

There is much more variation at the bottom of the proficiency distribution, however. An average of 41% of low-educated adults reported having no experience at all with ICTs, or failed the ICT core test. This share ranges from more than 70% in Korea, Poland and the Slovak Republic, to around 60% in Chile, Israel, Singapore, Slovenia and Turkey, to 48% in Greece, to below 20% in a large number of countries, including New Zealand, Norway and Sweden.

When looking at high-educated adults, the opposite pattern emerges: between-country/economy differences are much more pronounced at the top than at the bottom of the proficiency distribution. The share of tertiary-educated adults who failed the ICT core test, or who reported having no ICT experience, ranges from 2% in New Zealand and Slovenia to 7% in Turkey (and 12% in Japan). By contrast, less than 30% of high-educated adults in Greece and Turkey scored at Level 2 or higher, compared to between 54% and 63% in ten other countries/economies, including Australia, the Netherlands, New Zealand, Singapore and Sweden.

Skills and education among younger adults

In most countries, young adults (16-24 year-olds) are at a stage of their life when they make choices with significant long-term implications for their educational careers. While the situation in each country is different, it is usually between the ages of 16 and 24 that participation in education ceases to be compulsory, and young people have to decide whether or not to stay in school, whether or not to complete upper secondary education, and whether or not to enrol in higher education.

Figure 3.4 ▪ **Differences in literacy proficiency by educational attainment, young adults aged 16-24**

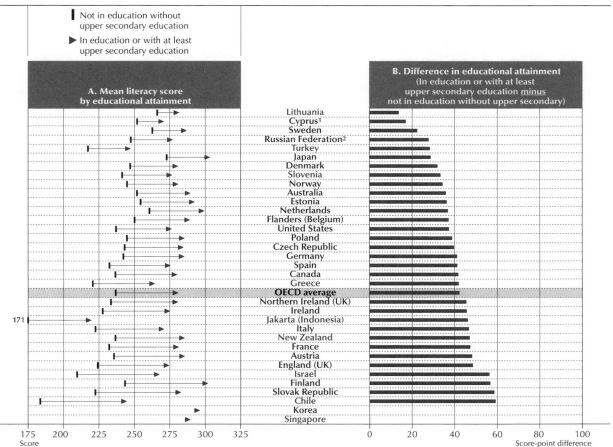

Notes: All differences in Panel B are statistically significant. Estimates based on a sample size of less than 30 are not shown in Panels A and B (Korea and Singapore). Upper secondary includes ISCED 3A, 3B, 3C long and 4. Where possible, foreign qualifications are included as the closest corresponding level in the respective national education systems.

1. See note 1 under Figure 3.1.

2. See note at the end of this chapter.

Countries and economies are ranked in ascending order of the differences in literacy scores (In education or with at least upper secondary education minus not in education without upper secondary).

Source: Survey of Adult Skills (PIAAC) (2012, 2015), Table A3.4 (L).

StatLink ᐃᔅᐠ http://dx.doi.org/10.1787/888933366007

In many countries, students also have to choose whether they want to enrol in an academically-oriented or in a vocational programme. Although it is theoretically possible to go back to school at any time, from a practical point of view many of the choices made in young adulthood tend to be irreversible.

Given the dynamic nature of this phase of life, particularly the transitions from one level of education to another and from education into the labour market, this subsection takes a closer look at the proficiency of 16-24 year-olds. In this analysis, the population is divided in three broad groups, reflecting three key transition points in young people's educational careers. The first group is composed of early school leavers, i.e. those who left formal education without an upper secondary degree. The second group is composed of those who completed upper secondary education, but decided not to enrol in tertiary education. The third group comprises young adults who are either enrolled in tertiary education or who have already earned a tertiary qualification. When looking at this latter group, the analysis will be restricted to 20-24 year-olds, because country differences in the typical age at which students graduate from upper secondary school would generate large (and somewhat artificial) differences in the share of 16-19 year-olds who are enrolled in tertiary education.

Figure 3.5 ▪ **Differences in literacy proficiency by educational attainment, young adults aged 20-24**

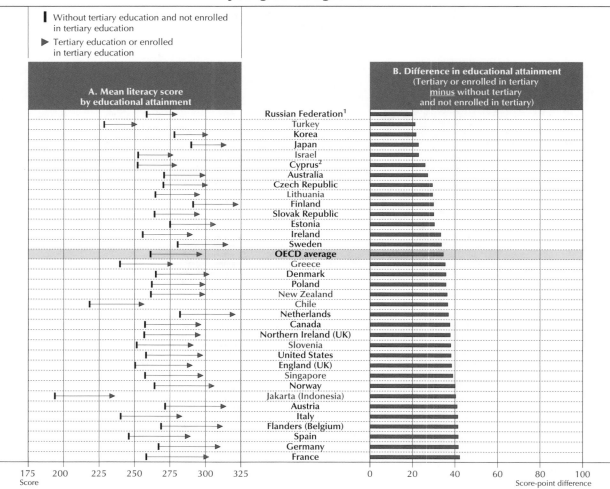

Notes: All differences in Panel B are statistically significant. Tertiary includes ISCED 5A, 5B and 6. Where possible, foreign qualifications are included as the closest corresponding level in the respective national education systems.

1. See note at the end of this chapter.

2. See note 1 under Figure 3.1.

Countries and economies are ranked in ascending order of the differences in literacy scores (Tertiary or enrolled in tertiary minus without tertiary and not enrolled in tertiary).

Source: Survey of Adult Skills (PIAAC) (2012, 2015), Table A3.4 (L).

StatLink ⌗ http://dx.doi.org/10.1787/888933366017

In many countries, leaving education before earning an upper secondary qualification is a significant and worrying phenomenon. In 2013, enrolment rates among 15-19 year-olds averaged 84% across OECD countries/economies, but ranged from well above 90% in Ireland and Slovenia, to 69% in Turkey and 65% in Israel (OECD, 2015a). In the Survey of Adult Skills, early school leavers are identified as 16-24 year-olds who have not attained an upper secondary qualification and who are not currently enrolled in formal education. Using this definition, an average of 10% of 16-24 year-olds are early school leavers, ranging from 1% in Singapore, to about 5% in Israel and Slovenia, 23% in Spain and 31% in Turkey. The share of early school leavers (18%) is also relatively high in Jakarta (Indonesia) (Table B3.2).

Figure 3.4 shows that leaving the education system without earning an upper secondary qualification is strongly associated with large deficits in literacy proficiency compared with young people who had attained an upper secondary education. The average gap is about 40 score points, which is larger than the score-point difference separating tertiary-educated from upper secondary-educated 25-65 year-olds. On average, early school leavers scored 237 points on the literacy scale, meaning that they barely attained Level 2; in Chile, Greece, Israel, Turkey and Jakarta (Indonesia), the average scores were below 225 points. In no country was the average score of early school leavers high enough to place them at proficiency Level 3. The largest differences in literacy proficiency (around 60 score points) between early school leavers and other 16-24 year-olds are found in Chile, Finland, Israel and the Slovak Republic; in Lithuania, the gap is less than 15 score points.

Young adults (20-24 year-olds) enrolled in tertiary education, or who have already earned a tertiary degree, are more proficient than their peers of the same age who didn't enter higher education (Figure 3.5). The average difference is about 34 score points, which is slightly less than the 39 score-point difference that separates 25-65 year-olds with and without a tertiary degree (see Table A3.4 [L]). But this may be an underestimation of the proficiency gap between the two groups, since many 20-24 years-old are still working to complete their tertiary degree, and one could expect the gap to grow with each year spent in tertiary education.

DIFFERENCES IN SKILLS PROFICIENCY RELATED TO AGE

The evolution of proficiency in information-processing skills over a lifetime can be thought of as the result of distinct and conceptually separate processes. First, there is a "natural", or biological, process by which cognitive abilities are developed as people grow and mature, and then inevitably decline because of ageing. However, this process can be influenced considerably by individual choices, such as pursuing higher education and/or a particular career and practicing information-processing skills both in and outside the workplace. Moreover, the extent to which such individual choices affect the age-proficiency profile varies across countries, because of differences in the quality of education, the quality of and access to lifelong learning, industry structure and labour market institutions, to name just a few factors.

The Survey of Adult Skills offers a snapshot of the proficiency level of adults of different ages at a particular point in time, and therefore does not allow for tracking how the proficiency of the same age cohorts evolves over time. As a result, it is not possible to disentangle age effects (i.e. the consequences of growing older), cohort effects (the consequences of being born at different times) and period effects (the consequences of influences that vary through time, such as economic recessions).

In spite of these limitations, observed age differences as measured in the Survey of Adult Skills still provide useful information to policy makers. Between-country comparisons, coupled with detailed knowledge of how policies and institutions evolved in individual countries/economies, can help identify where strengths and weaknesses lie. On an even more basic level, understanding how information-processing skills are distributed among different age groups can help to target policies more accurately to particularly vulnerable individuals. Foreign-born adults are excluded from the analysis below because the demographic structure of the immigrant population tends to be different from that of native-born adults.

Figure 3.6 plots the average age-proficiency profile in literacy and numeracy in the OECD countries/economies that participated in the Survey of Adult Skills. It also plots the country-specific profiles in literacy proficiency for the nine Round-2 countries/economies.[4] The age-proficiency profiles vary considerably across countries although, on average and in the majority of countries, proficiency tends to peak at around age 30, and then gradually declines with age (Desjardins and Warnke, 2012; Paccagnella, 2016).

Unlike the profile found in most countries, in Lithuania, Slovenia and Turkey, there seems to be very little improvement in proficiency between the ages 16 and 30. This is also the case in Jakarta (Indonesia). Various factors could explain this pattern, from entry rates into tertiary education, to quality of education, to the extent to which earlier years in the labour market are conducive to the development of proficiency in information-processing skills. In Greece, a small decline in proficiency between the ages of 16 and 25 is observed, after which the age-proficiency profile is unusually flat before a small and gradual decline in proficiency begins at around age 55.

Figure 3.6 ▪ **Relationship between skills proficiency and age**

Trend scores by age, foreign-born adults excluded

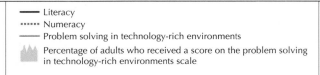

——— Literacy
▪▪▪▪▪▪ Numeracy
——— Problem solving in technology-rich environments
Percentage of adults who received a score on the problem solving in technology-rich environments scale

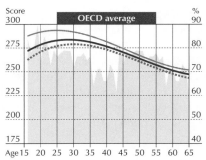

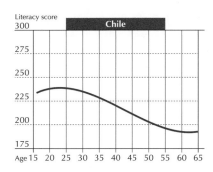

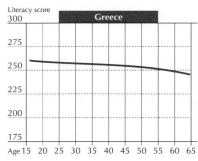

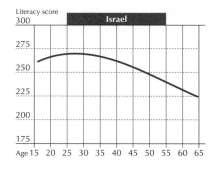

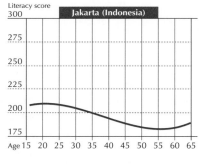

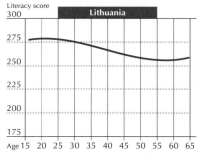

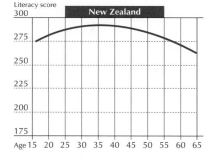

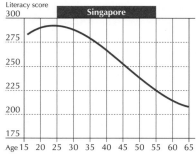

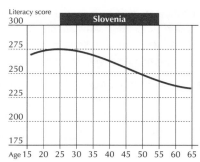

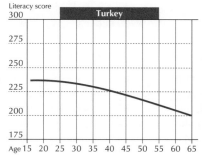

Notes: A cubic specification of the trend curves is found to be most accurate in reflecting the distribution of scores by age in most countries/economies. Results account for cross-country differences in OECD average scores by age cohort. Foreign-born adults are excluded from the analysis. See corresponding tables mentioned in the source below for regression parameters and significance estimates. Only countries and economies participating in the second round of the survey are shown. Similar results for the countries and economies participating in the first round are available in OECD (2013), Figure 5.2b (L).
Countries and economies are listed in alphabetical order.
Source: Survey of Adult Skills (PIAAC) (2012, 2015), Tables A3.6 (L), A3.6 (N) and A3.6 (P).
StatLink ⌨ http://dx.doi.org/10.1787/888933366025

Proficiency in literacy and numeracy among older and younger adults

Figure 3.7 presents average proficiency among different age groups (left panel) and differences in literacy proficiency among 55-65 year-olds and 25-34 year-olds, i.e. the two age groups that, in most countries, show the lowest and the highest literacy proficiency, respectively (right panel). While there are some countries/economies where 16-24 year-olds scored higher than 25-34 year-olds, the differences in proficiency between these two age groups are generally small, at less than five score points in Chile, Greece, Jakarta (Indonesia), Lithuania, Singapore and Turkey. In most countries/economies, however, 25-34 year-olds have higher average proficiency than 16-24 year-olds, with a difference of about seven points in Israel and New Zealand, and well above 10 points in England (United Kingdom), Finland and Norway.

Figure 3.7 ▪ **Age differences in literacy proficiency**

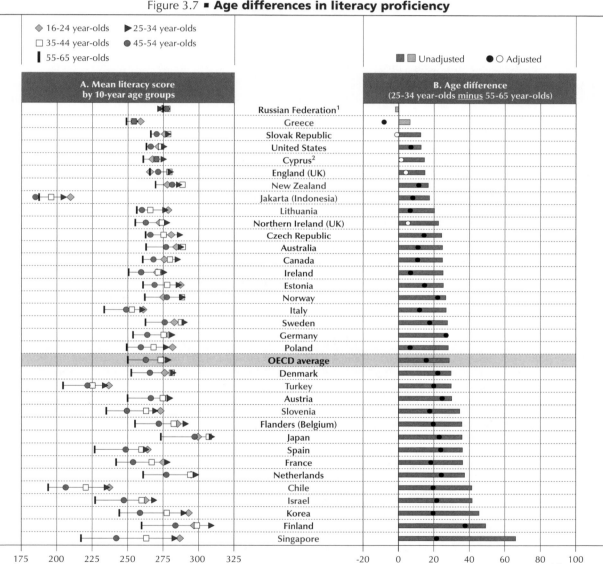

Notes: Statistically significant differences in Panel B are marked in a darker tone. Unadjusted differences are the differences between the two means for each contrast category. Adjusted differences are based on a regression model and take account of differences associated with other factors: gender, education, immigrant and language background and parents' educational attainment. Only the score-point differences between two contrast categories are shown in Panel B, which is useful for showing the relative significance of age vis-a-vis observed score-point differences. Adjusted difference for the Russian Federation is missing due to the lack of language variables.

1. See note at the end of this chapter.

2. See note 1 under Figure 3.1.

Countries and economies are ranked in ascending order of the unadjusted difference in literacy scores (25-34 year-olds minus 55-65 year-olds).

Source: Survey of Adult Skills (PIAAC) (2012, 2015), Tables A3.1 (L) and A3.5 (L).

StatLink ▦🔜 http://dx.doi.org/10.1787/888933366032

The literacy proficiency of 55-65 year-olds is particularly low in Chile, Israel, Singapore and Turkey. In these countries, the share of older adults who scored at or below Level 1 on the literacy scale ranges from 44% in Israel to 73% in Chile (Table A3.7 [L]). Similar results were recorded in Jakarta (Indonesia), where 76% of adults aged 55-65 scored at or below Level 1. In New Zealand the share is 16%, well below the international average of 28%, and one of the smallest shares among all the countries that participated in the survey. New Zealand had the largest share (slightly above 10%) of older adults who scored at Level 4 or 5.

In Chile and Turkey, adults aged 25-34 have particularly low levels of literacy proficiency: some 40% of them scored at or below Level 1 (the OECD average is less than 15%). The share is even higher in Jakarta (Indonesia), at 66%. In Greece, around 25% of 25-34 year old adults scored at or below Level 1. In New Zealand and Singapore, adults in the same age group scored above the average, although well below the best-performing adults of the same age in Finland, Japan and the Netherlands. This difference in proficiency is due to both a larger share of individuals scoring at the bottom of the proficiency distribution, and a smaller share attaining the highest levels of proficiency.

Interpreting age differences in literacy proficiency is complicated by the fact that, inevitably, age differences include both age and cohort effects. The relative strength of cohort effects is likely to vary widely across countries because the expansion of education opportunities (an important determinant of cohort effects, although not the only one) occurred in different countries at different points in time. This is clearly seen in the right panel of Figure 3.7, where adjusting for other characteristics (including educational attainment) has different effects on the magnitude of differences related to age.[5]

Adjusted and unadjusted age differences in literacy proficiency are, in fact, similar in Germany, New Zealand and Norway, where differences in educational attainment between 55-65 year-old and 25-34 year-old adults are not very large. In Germany, the share of tertiary-educated adults is very similar in the two age groups; in New Zealand and Norway, this share is larger among 25-34 year-olds by 8 and 10 percentage points, respectively (Table B3.4).

By contrast, in Chile, Korea, Lithuania, Poland and Singapore, adjusted differences are much smaller than unadjusted differences. These are all countries in which tertiary graduation rates increased by more than 20 percentage points over the recent past. In Chile and Lithuania, the share of tertiary-educated adults aged 25-34 is around 20 percentage points larger than the share of tertiary-educated adults aged 55-65; in Korea, the share is 46 percentage points larger, and in Singapore it is 53 percentage points larger.

In Israel, there is no large difference in educational attainment between the two age groups. Rather, adjusted differences in literacy proficiency are much smaller than unadjusted differences because of the difference in the share of foreign-born adults in the two age groups. Only 47% of 55-65 year-olds in Israel are native speakers born in the country (compared to 86%, on average across OECD countries/economies participating in the survey), while 73% of 25-34 year-olds are (Table B3.6). The picture is even more striking in Singapore, where only 15% of older adults are native speakers born in the country, while 67%, although born in the country, are not native speakers in the language of the assessment (which was English). Among 25-34 year-olds, the former share increases to 27%, and the latter decreases to 45%.

The two most extreme cases (Germany and Singapore) illustrate how the expansion of education generates cohort effects that deeply influence the observed age differences in cross-sectional data. In Germany, the levels of educational attainment among 25-34 year-olds are virtually identical to those among older adults. In both age groups, some 35% have a tertiary degree, about 55% are upper secondary graduates, and 10% did not complete upper secondary education (Table B3.1). In Singapore, the share of tertiary-educated adults is 21% among 55-65 year-olds, but increases to 74% among 25-34 year-olds (Table B3.4). Meanwhile, the share of adults who have not attained upper secondary education has shrunk from 40% to just below 5%.

Nevertheless, educational attainment does not explain everything. Cognitive decline related to ageing, as well as cohort effects related to unobservable factors, such as quality of schooling, still play a significant role, although to different extents in different countries. As a result, adjusted differences in age-proficiency profiles average about 16 score points, ranging from -8 points in Greece to 38 points in Finland. The negative estimate in Greece is due to the fact that the large expansion in education (only 15% of 25-34 year-olds have not completed upper secondary education, compared to 50% of older adults) has not translated into an improvement in literacy proficiency. In Greece, 25-34 year-olds scored only six points higher than 55-65 year-olds did.

Proficiency in problem solving in technology-rich environments among older and younger adults

Age-related differences are even more pronounced when it comes to proficiency in problem solving in technology-rich environments. This assessment relied on familiarity with ICTs to a greater extent than the assessments of literacy and numeracy. Given that the widespread use of ICTs is a relatively recent phenomenon, older adults were clearly in a position of relative disadvantage compared to younger adults, as indicated by the large share of 55-65 year-olds who skipped the problem-solving assessment because of lack of computer experience, or because they failed the ICT core test. Moreover, the rate of penetration of ICTs varies widely across countries. Although levels of use are converging, between-country differences remain.

This is well illustrated in Figure 3.8. On average, some 45% of 25-34 year-olds scored at Level 2 or 3 in the problem-solving assessment, compared to only 11% of older adults. Proficiency in problem solving in technology-rich environments among younger adults varies widely across countries. In Chile, Greece and Turkey, between 12% and 24% of respondents scored at Level 2 or 3, compared to 55% or more in Denmark, the Netherlands, New Zealand, Norway, Singapore and Sweden, and to 67% in Finland. In New Zealand, 24% of older adults scored at Level 2 or 3, but in most other countries this share was smaller than 10%.

Figure 3.8 ■ **Problem-solving proficiency among younger and older adults**

Percentage of adults aged 25-34 and 55-65 scoring at Level 2 or 3 in problem solving in technology-rich environments or having no computer experience

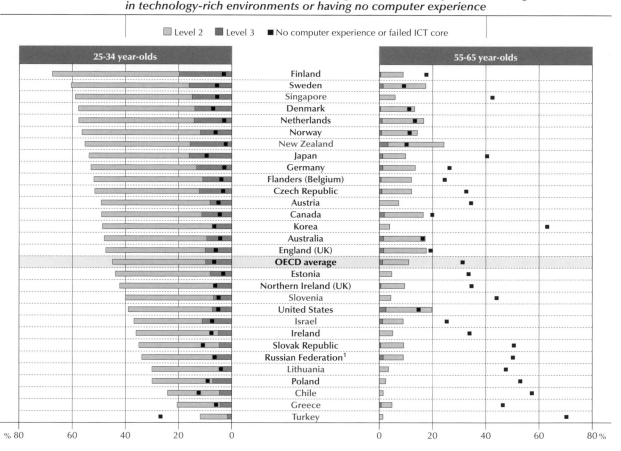

Notes: Percentages on the problem solving in technology-rich environments scale are computed so that the sum of percentages for the following mutually exhaustive categories equals 100%: opted out of the computer-based assessment; no computer experience; failed ICT core test; below Level 1, Level 1, Level 2 and Level 3. For more detailed results for each category, see corresponding table mentioned in the source below. Cyprus,[2] France, Italy, Jakarta (Indonesia) and Spain did not participate in the problem solving in technology-rich environments assessment.

1. See note at the end of this chapter.

2. See note 1 under Figure 3.1.

Countries and economies are ranked in descending order of the combined percentages of adults aged 25-34 scoring at Level 2 or 3.

Source: Survey of Adult Skills (PIAAC) (2012, 2015), Table A3.7 (P).

StatLink ᵃᵐˢ᠍ᵖ http://dx.doi.org/10.1787/888933366049

At the same time, few 25-34 year-olds skipped the problem-solving assessment because of a lack of computer experience, or because they failed the ICT core test (well below 10% in most countries, although 27% in Turkey). Lack of familiarity with ICTs, however, constituted a major obstacle for older adults. On average, 32% of 55-65 year-olds were not able to take the assessment; but this share ranges from about 10% in New Zealand and Sweden to almost 50% in Greece and Lithuania, almost 60% in Chile, and 71% in Turkey.

Age differences in familiarity with ICTs are also likely to influence the relationship between proficiencies across domains. Figure 3.9 shows the share of 25-34 year-olds and 55-65 year-olds who scored at Level 2 or 3 in problem solving in technology-rich environments, by level of literacy proficiency (the scope of the analysis is limited by small samples in a number of countries). As expected, at every level of proficiency, 25-34 year-olds are much more likely than older adults to score at Level 2 or 3 in the problem-solving assessment. On average, 90% of 25-34 year-olds who scored at Level 4 or 5 in literacy, and more than 60% of those who scored at Level 3, also scored at Level 2 or 3 in the problem-solving assessment. Even among those who only scored at Level 2, almost one in five reached high levels of proficiency in problem-solving (actual probabilities varying from 7% in Lithuania to almost 30% in Singapore). Given that older adults are much less likely to attain high levels of proficiency in problem solving, the relationship between literacy and problem-solving proficiency turns out to be stronger among older adults. In fact, moving from Level 2 to Level 3 on the literacy scale is associated with a more than seven-fold increase (from 3% to 23%) in the probability of a 55-65 year-old scoring at Level 2 or 3 in problem solving; among 25-34 year-olds, the corresponding increase in probability is less than four-fold (from 18% to 63%, on average).

Figure 3.9 ▪ **Relationship between literacy and problem solving in technology-rich environments, by age**

Percentage of adults scoring at Level 2 or 3 in problem solving in technology-rich environments, by literacy level among younger and older adults

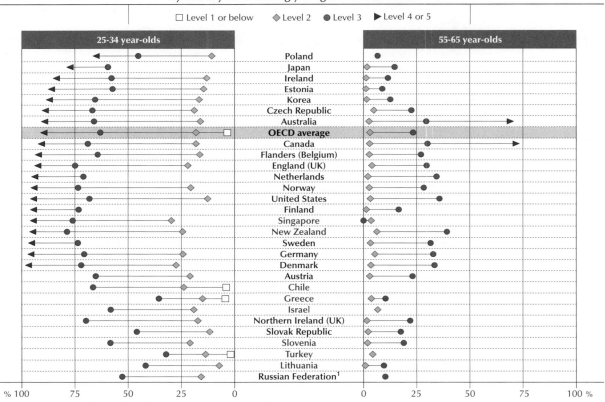

Notes: Cyprus,[2] France, Italy, Jakarta (Indonesia) and Spain did not participate in the problem solving in technology-rich environments assessment. Estimates based on low sample size are not shown.

1. See note at the end of this chapter.

2. See note 1 under Figure 3.1.

Countries and economies are ranked in descending order of the percentage of adults aged 25-34 scoring at Level 2 or 3 on the problem solving in technology-rich environments scale among adults of the same age scoring at Level 4 or 5 on the literacy scale.

Source: Survey of Adult Skills (PIAAC) (2012, 2015), Table A3.8 (L).

StatLink ᗏᗌ http://dx.doi.org/10.1787/888933366059

DIFFERENCES IN SKILLS PROFICIENCY RELATED TO GENDER

The expansion of education in many countries over the past decades not only raised the populations' average level of schooling, but also resulted in a substantial narrowing of the gender gap in educational achievement. Girls outperform boys in reading at age 15, and are more likely to enrol in tertiary education (OECD, 2015b).

The Survey of Adult Skills shows small gender differences in literacy proficiency, and larger differences in numeracy, where men have a clear advantage. Given that gender gaps in educational attainment have shrunk considerably over the past few decades, differences in skills proficiency are much more pronounced among older adults, and are almost non-existent among younger adults.

Proficiency in literacy and numeracy among men and women

Figure 3.10 clearly shows that in most countries there is no significant difference in literacy proficiency between men and women. Even in countries/economies where a statistically significant difference can be detected, the gap is small: men have an advantage of 11 score points in Turkey and of 8 score points in Chile, while women score about 5 points higher than men in Greece and 6 points higher than men in Poland. The largest difference is recorded in Jakarta (Indonesia), where men have a 14-point advantage over women.

Figure 3.10 ▪ **Gender differences in literacy and numeracy proficiency**

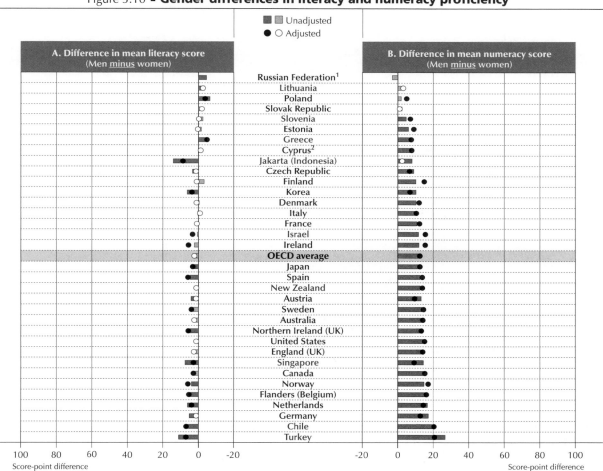

Notes: Statistically significant differences are marked in a darker tone. Unadjusted differences are the differences between the two means for each contrast category. Adjusted differences are based on a regression model and take account of differences associated with other factors: age, education, immigrant and language background and parents' educational attainment. Adjusted difference for the Russian Federation is missing due to the lack of language variables.

1. See note at the end of this chapter.
2. See note 1 under Figure 3.1.

Countries and economies are ranked in ascending order of the unadjusted difference in numeracy scores (men minus women).

Source: Survey of Adult Skills (PIAAC) (2012, 2015), Tables A3.1 (L), A3.9 (L) and A3.9 (N).

StatLink ᵐˢᵖ http://dx.doi.org/10.1787/888933366065

When it comes to numeracy, though, the picture is different. In the vast majority of countries, men scored 12 points higher than women in the numeracy assessment, on average. Wider gender gaps (about 20 score points) are observed in Chile and Turkey, while in the Central and Eastern European countries of Estonia, Lithuania, Poland, Slovenia and the Slovak Republic, gender differences in numeracy proficiency are small. Only in Jakarta (Indonesia) are gaps smaller in numeracy (8 score points) than in literacy (14 score points).

The magnitude of the gender gaps in literacy and numeracy proficiency appears to be related to respondents' age. Especially in numeracy, gender gaps appear to be narrower among 16-24 year-olds and significantly wider among 25-44 and 45-65 year-olds (Figure 3.11). Age and cohort effects are both likely to play a role, but it is difficult to disentangle those effects. Accounting for differences in other observable characteristics, particularly educational attainment, generally leads to a small reduction of the gender gap among 45-65 year-olds, and to a small increase among 16-24 and 25-44 year-olds (Table A3.10 [N]).

Figure 3.11 ▪ **Gender gap in literacy and numeracy, by age**

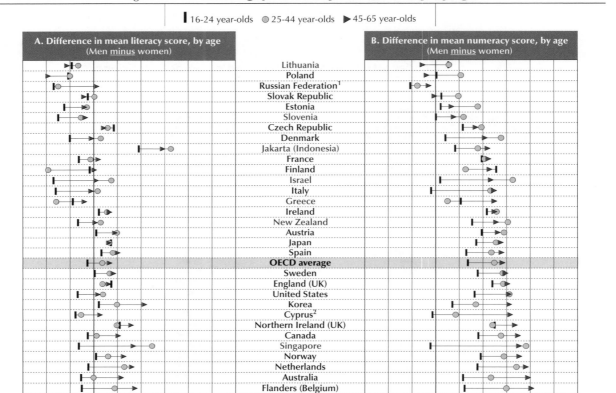

1. See note at the end of this chapter.
2. See note 1 under Figure 3.1.
Countries and economies are ranked in descending order of the gender gap in numeracy among 45-65 year-olds.
Source: Survey of Adult Skills (PIAAC) (2012, 2015), Tables A3.10 (L) and A3.10 (N).
StatLink ᵃᵍᵐᵖ http://dx.doi.org/10.1787/888933366071

The gender gaps observed among adults assessed in the survey differ from those seen among 15-year-old students assessed in the OECD Programme for International Student Assessment (PISA), where girls tend to have a clear advantage in reading, and boys a clear advantage in mathematics. The assessment of reading literacy and numeracy/mathematical literacy in PIAAC and PISA are based on slightly different conceptual frameworks, given the difference in the reference population. While this prevents a direct comparison of PISA and PIAAC scores, the frameworks are sufficiently similar to allow a qualitative comparison of gender gaps across the two surveys.

Figure 3.12 ▪ **Problem-solving proficiency among women and men**

Percentage of women and men scoring at Level 2 or 3 in problem solving in technology-rich environments or having no computer experience

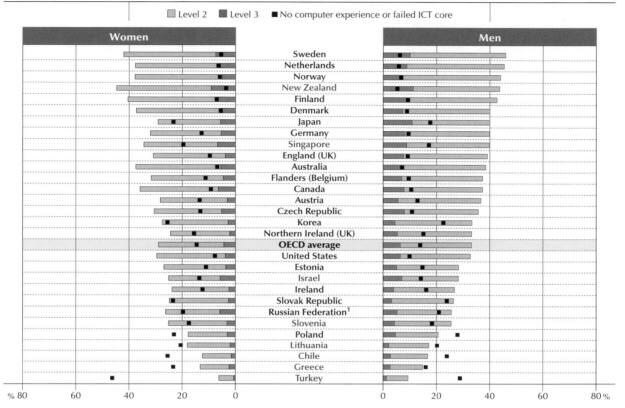

Notes: Percentages on the problem solving in technology-rich environments scale are computed so that the sum of percentages for the following mutually exhaustive categories equals 100%: opted out of the computer-based assessment; no computer experience; failed ICT core test; below Level 1, Level 1, Level 2 and Level 3. For more detailed results for each category, see corresponding table mentioned in the source below. Cyprus,[2] France, Italy, Jakarta (Indonesia) and Spain did not participate in the problem solving in technology-rich environments assessment.

1. See note at the end of this chapter.

2. See note 1 under Figure 3.1.

Countries and economies are ranked in descending order of the combined percentages of men scoring at Level 2 or 3.

Source: Survey of Adult Skills (PIAAC) (2012, 2015), Table A3.11 (P).

StatLink ⏷ http://dx.doi.org/10.1787/888933366088

Comparing the two assessments gives a more complete picture of the evolution of gender differences in proficiency over a lifetime (acknowledging that cohort effects are also at work). It appears that gender gaps in literacy narrow (and are often reversed) as people age; in numeracy, men either retain or increase their advantage. These processes seem to stop once people complete their transition into adulthood: the gender gaps are of similar magnitude among 25-44 year-olds and 45-65 year-olds. Explaining these patterns is a subject for future research, and is outside the scope of this report. One possible explanation for the observed evolution of gender gaps is the higher employment rates among men than women (possibly for reasons unrelated to skills proficiency). Arguably, reading is a transversal skill that is practiced across a wide range of occupations, so that men may have more opportunities to practice their reading skills than women do. Men are also much more likely than women to pursue careers in fields that require more intensive use of numeracy skills – which may explain why they tend to retain or increase their advantage in numeracy.

Proficiency in problem solving in technology-rich environments among men and women

Gender differences in proficiency in problem solving in technology-rich environments are small, although men tend to have a slight advantage over women. On average, 33% of men scored at Level 2 or 3, compared to 29% of women. However, the proportions of men and women who have no computer experience, or who failed the ICT core test, is much more balanced, and is even slightly larger among men in a number of countries/economies. Only in Turkey, and to a lesser extent in Greece, are women significantly more likely to lack computer experience or to have failed the ICT core test.

DIFFERENCES IN SKILLS PROFICIENCY RELATED TO COUNTRY OF ORIGIN AND LANGUAGE

OECD countries have long aimed to better integrate immigrants into their societies. The global economic crisis and the recent influx of refugees have underscored the urgency of the need to improve integration, not only for the well-being of the immigrants population, but for the functioning and progress of society as a whole.

About 12% of the adults who participated in the Survey of Adult Skills were born in a different country from the one in which they currently reside (see Table B3.5). While foreign-born adults represent a negligible share of the population (below 5%) in many countries/economies (including Chile, Lithuania and Turkey), about 20% of the adult population in Ireland, Israel, Singapore and Sweden are foreign-born, as are more than 25% of adults in Australia, Canada and New Zealand.

Not only the size, but also the characteristics of the immigrant population differ widely across countries, mainly because of variations in policies that influence the composition of immigrant populations (in terms of both country of origin and educational background) across OECD countries, and in the processes that aim to integrate immigrants into the labour market and society.

It is hard to think of any successful package of integration policies that does not assign a crucial role to the acquisition and development of skills, particularly in the language of the host country. In this respect, the Survey of Adult Skills provides valuable information that can help policy makers to better understand the obstacles migrants face in integrating into their host communities.

Proficiency in literacy among native- and foreign-born adults

On average, foreign-born adults scored 24 points lower in literacy than native-born adults (Figure 3.13). This is a sizeable difference, equal to about half of the international standard deviation, and similar to the difference between tertiary- and upper secondary-educated adults. However, differences in countries' immigration-related policies are reflected in large between-country differences in immigrant adults' proficiency and in the gap that separates them from native-born adults.

Foreign-born adults living in New Zealand scored 275 points, on average, in literacy. This is five score points above the international average for native-born adults, and around the level of proficiency of native-born adults in Denmark, Germany, Korea and the United States. Native-born adults in New Zealand scored only 8 points higher than foreign-born adults in the country. This difference is even smaller in Greece and Singapore, while it is about 15 points in Israel, and close to 30 points in Slovenia, where literacy proficiency among immigrants is one of the lowest across all countries/economies that participated in the Survey of Adult Skills.

In most countries, recent immigrants tend to score particularly poorly. This is likely because the more time spent in the host country, the better an immigrant's language skills, which is an important component of literacy proficiency as assessed in the Survey of Adult Skills. The only notable exception to this pattern is Singapore, where recent immigrants (those who have spent less than five years in the host country) scored almost 10 points higher than immigrants who have been in the country for more than five years, and three score points higher than native-born adults.

As noted above, knowledge of the host country's language is crucial for literacy proficiency. Language proficiency is often a key element of the points-based immigration programmes used in a number of OECD countries. Not surprisingly, Figure 3.14 shows that foreign-born adults whose native language is the same as the language of the assessment tend to perform much better than foreign-language immigrants. In fact, their proficiency level is often close to that of native-born, native-language adults. Foreign-born, native-language adults make up between 40% and 50% of the entire immigrant population in many countries, including Australia, England (United Kingdom), France, Greece, Lithuania and New Zealand. The share decreases to about 25% in Germany, Israel and the United States and to about 17% in Singapore and Slovenia (Table B3.5). On average, foreign-born native-language adults represent 4% of the entire population. This is twice the share of native-born foreign-language adults (2%), and half the share of foreign-born foreign-language adults. The share of foreign-born native-language adults over the entire population is above 10% in Australia, Estonia, Ireland and New Zealand, and about 8% in Canada and Spain. By contrast, it is below 2% in many other countries, including the Czech Republic, Denmark, Finland, Japan, Korea, Lithuania, Norway, Poland, the Slovak Republic and Turkey.

Restricting attention to native-language speakers (whether foreign- or native-born), foreign-born adults scored only seven points lower than native-born adults. They even scored slightly higher in a few countries/economies, namely Australia, Austria, Finland, Greece, Ireland, New Zealand and Northern Ireland (United Kingdom). Only in Estonia, France, Israel, Korea and the Netherlands, did foreign-born adults score much lower than native-born adults (a difference of more than 20 score points), despite the fact that they speak the language of the assessment as their mother tongue.

Figure 3.13 ▪ **Differences in literacy scores between native- and foreign-born adults**

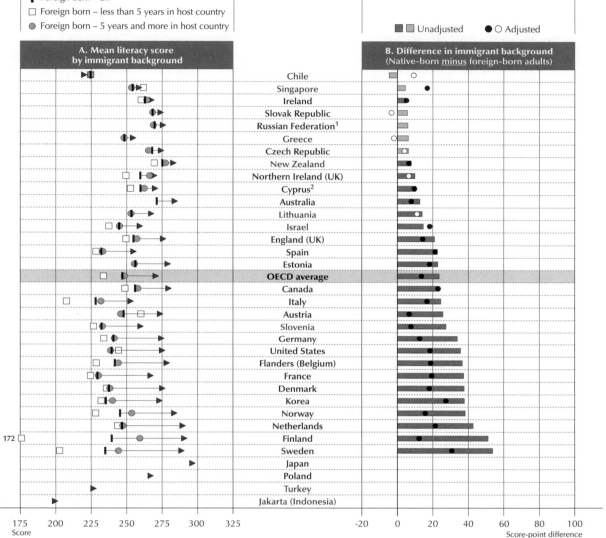

Notes: Statistically significant differences in Panel B are marked in a darker tone. Estimates based on a sample size of less than 30 are not shown in Panels A and B (Jakarta [Indonesia], Japan, Poland and Turkey). Unadjusted differences are the differences between the two means for each contrast category. Adjusted differences are based on a regression model and take account of differences associated with all of the following variables: age, gender, education, language background and parents' educational attainment. Estimates for the Russian Federation are missing due to the lack of language variables. Information about years since immigration is not available for Australia.

1. See note at the end of this chapter.

2. See note 1 under Figure 3.1.

Countries and economies are ranked in ascending order of the unadjusted difference in literacy scores (native-born minus foreign-born adults).

Source: Survey of Adult Skills (PIAAC) (2012, 2015), Table A3.12 (L).

StatLink ⸺ http://dx.doi.org/10.1787/888933366090

Singapore is a unique case. Almost one in two native-born adults in Singapore are not native speakers of the language of the assessment (English, in this case). In fact, only 27% of the respondents in Singapore were classified as native speakers. This is very small compared to the proportions of native speakers in other countries, which is always above 75% (and about 90% on average). This explains why there is just a small gap in proficiency between foreign-born and native-born adults (presented in Figure 3.13), but a sizeable difference (almost 30 score points) between native and non-native English speakers (Figure 3.14). Indeed, there is no difference in proficiency between native- and foreign-born adults, once the language of origin is taken into account. Native-language speakers scored about 277 points, regardless of their country of origin, and both native- and foreign-born, foreign-language speakers scored about 250 points.

Figure 3.14 ▪ **Differences in literacy scores, by immigrant and language background**

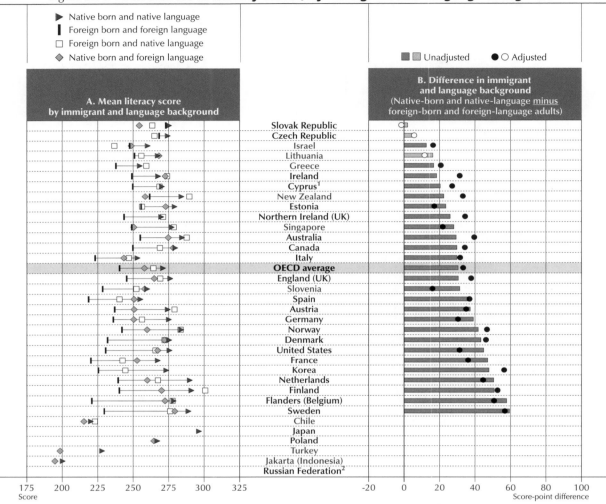

Notes: Statistically significant differences in Panel B are marked in a darker tone. Estimates based on a sample size less than 30 are not shown in Panels A and B (i.e. immigrant and language background differences in Chile, Jakarta [Indonesia], Japan, Poland and Turkey). Unadjusted differences are the differences between the two means for each contrast category. Adjusted differences are based on a regression model and take account of differences associated with all of the following variables: age, gender, education and parents' educational attainment. Only the score-point differences between two contrast categories are shown in Panel B, which is useful for showing the relative significance of an immigrant background vis-a-vis observed score-point differences. Native language refers to whether the first or second language learned as a child is the same as the language of assessment, and not whether the language has official status. Foreign language refers to whether the first or second language learned as a child is not the same as the language of assessment. Thus in some cases, foreign language might refer to minority languages in which the assessment was not administered. Estimates for the Russian Federation are missing due to the lack of language variables.

1. See note 1 under Figure 3.1.

2. See note at the end of this chapter.

Countries and economies are ranked in ascending order of the unadjusted difference in literacy scores (native-born and native-language minus foreign-born and foreign-language adults).

Source: Survey of Adult Skills (PIAAC) (2012, 2015), Tables A3.1 (L) and A3.12 (L).

StatLink ⧉ http://dx.doi.org/10.1787/888933366102

Proficiency in problem solving in technology-rich environments among native- and foreign-born adults

The share of foreign-born, foreign-language adults who scored at Level 2 or 3 on the problem solving in technology-rich environments assessment ranges from about 7% in Greece and Slovenia to about 30% in New Zealand and Singapore (Figure 3.15). When compared with native-born, native-language adults, the difference is most pronounced in Singapore (largely due to the high levels of proficiency among native-born adults) and Slovenia (mainly due to the low levels of proficiency among foreign-born adults). By contrast, the differences are small in Israel (where the proficiency of native-born adults is close to the average, but some 24% of foreign-born adults scored at Level 2 or 3) and in Greece (where the share of adults who scored at Level 2 or 3 is well below the average among both native- and foreign-born adults).

Figure 3.15 ▪ **Problem-solving proficiency among foreign-language immigrants and non-immigrants**

Percentage of foreign-born and foreign-language (immigrants) and native-born and native-language (non-immigrants) adults scoring at Level 2 or 3 in problem solving in technology-rich environments or having no computer experience

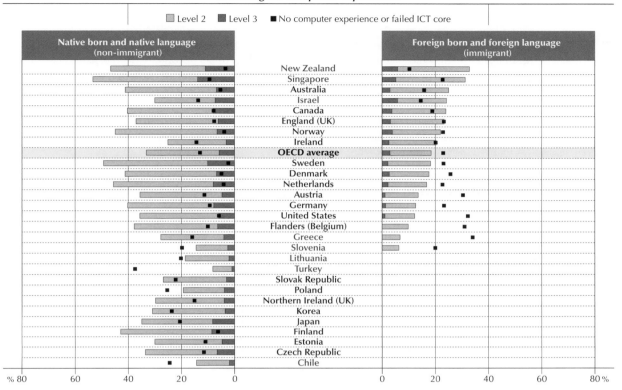

Notes: Estimates based on low sample sizes are not shown. Percentages on the problem solving in technology-rich environments scale are computed so that the sum of percentages for the following mutually exhaustive categories equals 100%: opted out of computer-based assessment; no computer experience; failed ICT core test; below Level 1, Level 1, Level 2 and Level 3. For more detailed results for each category, see corresponding table mentioned in the source below. Native language refers to whether the first or second language learned as a child is the same as the language of assessment, and not whether the language has official status. Foreign language refers to whether the first or second language learned as a child is not the same as the language of assessment. Thus in some cases, foreign language might refer to minority languages in which the assessment was not administered. Estimates for the Russian Federation are missing due to the lack of language variables. Cyprus,[1] France, Italy, Jakarta (Indonesia) and Spain did not participate in the problem solving in technology-rich environments assessment.

1. See note 1 under Figure 3.1.

Countries and economies are ranked in descending order of the combined percentages of foreign-born and foreign-language (immigrant) adults scoring at Level 2 or 3.

Source: Survey of Adult Skills (PIAAC) (2012, 2015), Table A3.13 (P).

StatLink ⌐⌐ http://dx.doi.org/10.1787/888933366113

DIFFERENCES IN SKILLS PROFICIENCY RELATED TO SOCIO-ECONOMIC BACKGROUND

There are few factors that shape individuals' lives more significantly than the family in which they grow up. This influence works not only through the characteristics of individual families, but also through the different social and cultural environments in which people are raised. This crucial factor in determining an individual's life chances is completely beyond the control of the person concerned.

Ensuring that everyone, regardless of his or her particular socio-economic background, has equal chances to develop his or her skills and make the best of his or her talents is an explicit goal of education systems in most countries. In fact, there is probably no better way to tackle growing income inequality than by providing a quality education for all.

In the Survey of Adult Skills, the educational attainment of the respondent's parents is used as a proxy for socio-economic status.[6] The results of the analysis presented below are consistent with much of the existing literature on this topic, and indicate that parents' educational attainment has a large influence on the proficiency of their offspring and, consequently, on labour market outcomes and, more broadly, individual well-being. The strength of the association between parents' educational attainment and proficiency (also called the "parental education gradient") differs across countries. It is shown in the greater likelihood that children of highly educated parents will complete higher education themselves.

The parental education gradient can also be interpreted as a measure of inequality of opportunity: the steeper the gradient, the less likely that adults whose parents attained low levels of education will attain high levels of proficiency. Given the established positive link between proficiency and a wide range of economic and non-economic outcomes, a strong link between parents' educational attainment and their children's proficiency can be a serious obstacle to broader social and intergenerational mobility.

Proficiency in literacy among adults with high- and low-educated parents

On average, almost 30% of adults with neither parent having attained an upper secondary degree scored at or below Level 1 in the literacy assessment and only 5% scored at Level 4 or 5 (Table A3.15 [L]). By contrast, among adults raised by at least one tertiary-educated parent, 20% scored at Level 4 or 5 and 8% scored at or below Level 1. The average difference in proficiency between an advantaged and a disadvantaged adult is slightly less than 60 score points in Singapore and the United States, and between 50 and 55 score points in Chile, Germany, Israel, Poland and Slovenia. A larger difference (63 score points) is recorded in Jakarta (Indonesia). In Australia, Estonia, Lithuania and New Zealand, differences are less than 30 score points (Figure 3.16).

Figure 3.16 ▪ **Differences in literacy proficiency, by parents' educational attainment**

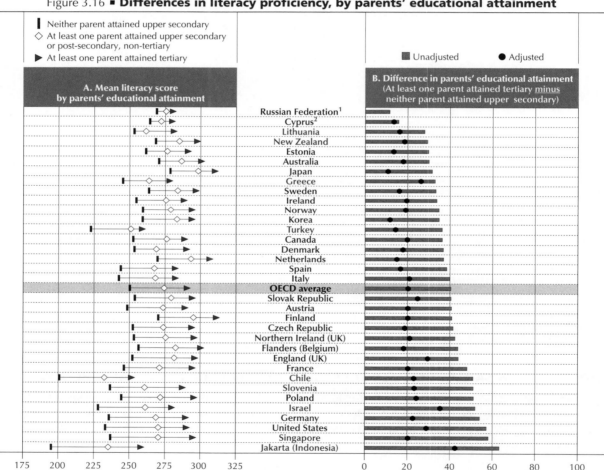

Notes: All differences in Panel B are statistically significant. Unadjusted differences are the differences between the two means for each contrast category. Adjusted differences are based on a regression model and take account of differences associated with other factors: age, gender, education, immigrant and language background. Only the score-point differences between two contrast categories are shown in Panel B, which is useful for showing the relative significance of parents' educational attainment vis-a-vis observed score-point differences. Upper secondary includes ISCED 3A, 3B, 3C long and 4. Tertiary includes ISCED 5A, 5B and 6. Adjusted difference for the Russian Federation is missing due to the lack of language variables.

1. See note at the end of this chapter.

2. See note 1 under Figure 3.1.

Countries and economies are ranked in ascending order of the unadjusted difference in literacy scores (at least one parent attained tertiary minus neither parent attained upper secondary).

Source: Survey of Adult Skills (PIAAC) (2012, 2015), Table A3.14 (L).

StatLink ⧉ http://dx.doi.org/10.1787/888933366126

Accounting for other background characteristics strongly reduces the estimated impact of parents' educational attainment, from 40 to 20 score points, on average. This suggests that a significant portion of the overall impact of parental education is explained by the intergenerational transmission of educational attainment, i.e. by the fact that children of highly educated parents are themselves more likely to attain higher levels of education. Still, even after accounting for this, proficiency differences remain substantial – similar to the gaps that are observed between native-born and foreign-born adults. In Greece and Israel (and, to a lesser extent, in Lithuania and New Zealand), accounting for other characteristics does not result in a large reduction in the impact of parents' educational attainment on proficiency.

ADULTS WITH LOW PROFICIENCY

Adults with low proficiency, defined as those who score at or below Level 1 in either literacy or numeracy, can successfully complete reading tasks that involve only short and simple texts, and mathematics tasks involving only basic operations. They are most at risk of being marginalised in modern societies and economies, where knowledge and the ability to access and process information is ever more crucial, not only in order to succeed in the labour market, but also to participate in the broader society (Grotlüschen et al., 2016).

Figure 3.17 shows how low proficiency is pervasive in most countries/economies that participated in the Survey of Adult Skills. Even in Japan, the country with highest average literacy and numeracy scores, 9% of adults are low performers in either literacy or numeracy. This share is about 20% in Lithuania and New Zealand, 31% in Singapore and Slovenia, 36% in Greece and Israel, 57% in Turkey, and 67% in Chile. In Jakarta (Indonesia), 78% of adults can be classified as low performers.

Figure 3.17 ■ **The proportion of adults who are low performers**
Percentage of adults who score at or below Level 1 in literacy and/or numeracy

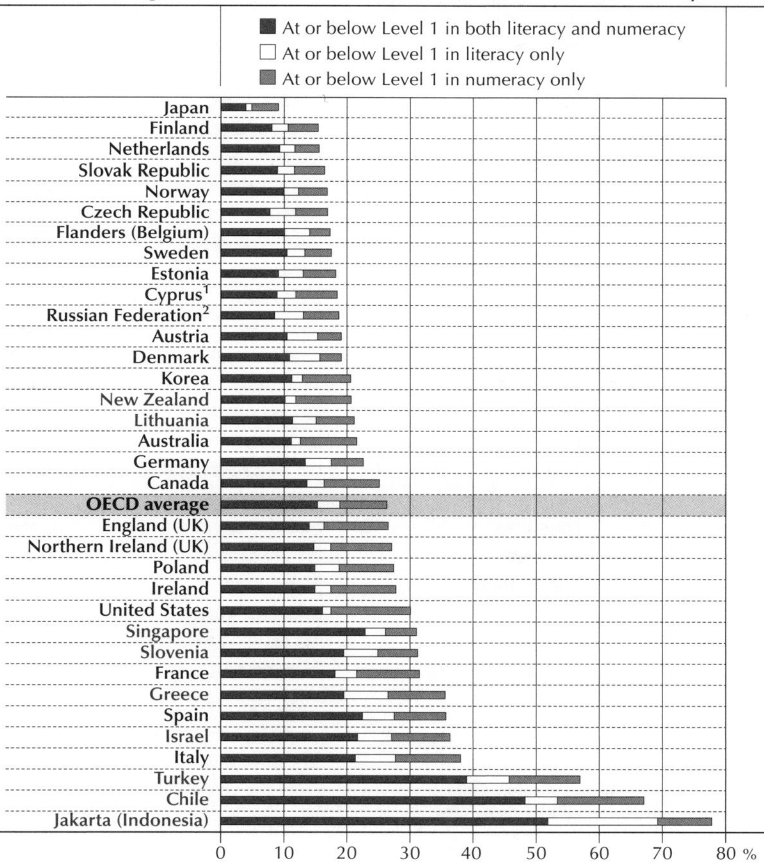

Note: Low-performing adults are defined as those who score at or below Level 1 in either literacy or numeracy.
1. See note 1 under Figure 3.1.
2. See note at the end of this chapter.
Countries and economies are ranked in ascending order of the combined percentages of adults scoring at or below Level 1 in literacy and/or numeracy.
Source: Survey of Adult Skills (PIAAC) (2012, 2015), Table A3.16.
StatLink ᶜᶜᵖᵃ http://dx.doi.org/10.1787/888933366131

Figure 3.18 ▪ **Low performers: Synthesis of socio-demographic differences**

Adjusted and unadjusted difference in the percentage of adults scoring at or below Level 1 in literacy or numeracy between contrast categories within various socio-demographic groups

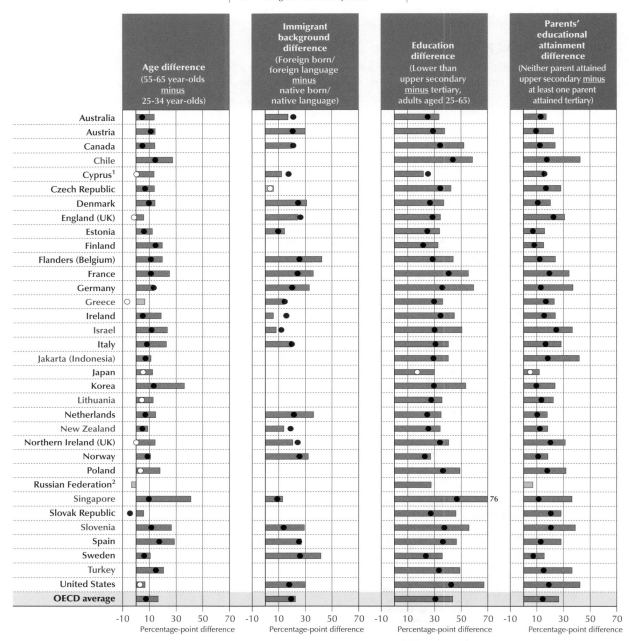

Notes: Statistically significant differences are marked in a darker tone. Estimates based on a sample size with too few observations are not shown (i.e. immigrant background differences in Chile, Finland, Jakarta [Indonesia], Japan, Korea, Lithuania, Poland, the Slovak Republic and Turkey). Unadjusted differences are those between the two means for each contrast category. Adjusted differences are based on a regression model and take account of differences associated with the following variables: age, gender, education, immigrant and language background and parents' educational attainment. Only the score-point differences between two contrast categories are shown, which is useful for showing the relative significance of each socio-demographic variable vis-a-vis observed score-point differences. Adjusted differences for the Russian Federation are missing due to the lack of language variables.

1. See note 1 under Figure 3.1.

2. See note at the end of this chapter.

Countries and economies are listed in alphabetical order.

Source: Survey of Adult Skills (PIAAC) (2012, 2015), Tables A3.17 and A3.18.

StatLink 🔗 http://dx.doi.org/10.1787/888933366144

Figure 3.18 shows how certain socio-demographic characteristics are associated with a greater likelihood of being low performers. The overall picture emerging from Figure 3.18 is similar to that in Figure 3.1. The socio-demographic factors associated with low proficiency are also associated with a higher probability of being a low performer in either literacy or numeracy.

Low educational attainment is strongly correlated with the likelihood of being a low performer. On average, the chances of being a low performer increase by more than 40 percentage points when comparing adults, 25 years or older, who have not attained upper secondary education with those who have completed tertiary education. Education is a particularly strong predictor of low performance in Singapore (where the probability that low-educated adults are also low performers is 76 percentage points higher than that for high-educated adults), Chile, Germany, Slovenia and the United States.

Accounting for other socio-demographic characteristics substantially reduces the strength of the association between educational attainment and the likelihood of being a low performer. The estimated difference in the probability of being low performer decreases, on average, from 44 to 31 percentage points. These adjusted differences remain large (above 40 percentage points) in Chile, Singapore and the United States.

Adults raised by low-educated parents are more likely to be low performers in either literacy or numeracy. The strength of the relationship is remarkably similar across countries. On average, the likelihood of being a low performer is about 25 percentage points lower for adults with at least one tertiary-educated parent, compared to adults with neither parent having attained upper secondary education. This relationship is particularly strong in Chile, Israel, Singapore, Turkey and the United States, but well below average in Finland, Japan, New Zealand and Sweden.

Accounting for other socio-demographic characteristics strongly reduces the estimated association, especially in Chile (from 43 to 18 percentage points), Germany (from 37 to 13 percentage points), Singapore (from 36 to 11 percentage points) and the United States (from 42 to 19 percentage points).

Foreign-born adults whose native language is different from that of the assessment are more likely than native-born adults to be low performers, by 22 percentage points, on average. The influence of language and immigrant background is particularly strong in Flanders (Belgium) and Sweden, where the difference is greater than 40 percentage points. However, in both countries (and in Denmark, France, Northern Ireland [United Kingdom], Norway, and Spain) a large part of the gap is explained by other socio-demographic characteristics, and adjusted differences shrink to 26 percentage points. By contrast, in the Czech Republic, Estonia, Greece, Israel and Singapore, the risk of being a low performer among foreign-born, foreign-language adults is between 4 and 15 percentage points higher than among native-born, native-language adults.

The prevalence of low performance is generally greater among older adults, but the variation across countries is substantial, reflecting different age and cohort effects, as discussed above. Older adults in Korea and Singapore are more likely than 25-34 year-olds to be low performers by more than 35 percentage points, although much of this likelihood is explained by other socio-demographic characteristics. After accounting for those characteristics, the likelihood, while still above average, shrinks to 10 percentage points in Singapore and to 13 percentage points in Korea, similar to that observed in Austria, Chile, Finland, Flanders (Belgium), France, Germany, Israel, Slovenia and Turkey. After accounting for other background characteristics, older adults in Spain are most at risk of being low performers. In England (United Kingdom) and Greece, after accounting for other socio-demographic characteristics, the differences in the probability of being low performers become negative, although statistically not different from zero.

SUMMARY

This chapter investigates differences in skills proficiency by socio-economic and demographic characteristics, in order to identify which groups of individuals are more likely to suffer from low proficiency, and in which countries more disadvantaged adults are able to perform at high levels of proficiency.

Perhaps unsurprisingly, educational attainment is found to be an accurate predictor of proficiency in information-processing skills. The relationship between education and proficiency remains strong even after taking into account differences in other socio-demographic characteristics, such as age, gender, socio-economic status or immigrant background.

Proficiency is also strongly related to age. Much of this association is explained by lower educational attainment among older adults, especially in countries that recently expanded access to education. However, there is clear evidence that biological ageing also plays a role; and the large degree of between-country/economy variation in age-proficiency profiles suggests that policies can shape the evolution of proficiency over a lifetime.

Gender differences in literacy proficiency are negligible, and are statistically indistinguishable from zero in half of the countries or economies that participated in the first or second round of the survey. In numeracy, though, men maintain a more significant advantage over women. Gender gaps are generally more pronounced among older adults, which is probably due to a combination of lower levels of education among older women and faster depreciation of proficiency among them. This latter phenomenon can be linked to the fact that women participate less in the labour market and, when they do, are more likely to pursue careers in which they have limited possibility to practice their numeracy skills.

Foreign-born adults tend to have lower levels of proficiency than native-born adults. By shaping the composition of the immigrant population, immigration policies result in large differences among countries/economies in the magnitude of the proficiency gaps between native- and foreign-born adults. Not surprisingly, being skilled in the language of the assessment is found to be a strong determinant of literacy proficiency, and immigrants whose native language is the same as that of the host country often score similarly to native-born adults in literacy.

Socio-economic background exerts a significant influence on adults' proficiency in literacy. Having at least one tertiary-educated parent is associated with a large advantage over adults with neither parent having attained an upper secondary degree – as large as the difference in proficiency between tertiary-educated adults and adults who have not attained tertiary qualifications. About half of this gap is explained by the fact that children of high-educated parents are themselves much more likely to attain high levels of education.

Notes

1. More precisely, adjusted differences are estimated through an Ordinary Least Squares regression. The dependent variable is the score in the literacy (or numeracy) assessment, which is simultaneously regressed on a set of dummy variables identifying each individuals' gender, age category, educational attainment, socio-economic status (measured by parents' highest level of educational attainment), and immigrant and language background.

2. See note regarding the Russian Federation below.

3. The international average, or average across countries, is always computed as the average across OECD countries/economies participating in the survey, whether in Round 1 or 2.

4. Similar figures for Round-1 countries can be found in Figure 5.2b (L) in OECD (2013).

5. However, controlling for observable characteristics, such as educational attainment, is not enough to separately identify age and cohort effects, because of, among other things, changes in unobservable quality of education (Green and Riddel, 2013; Paccagnella, 2016).

6. The Survey of Adult Skills does not contain enough information to compute an index of socio-economic status, as is done, for instance, in PISA. Information on the occupation of parents was collected only in some countries. No information on wealth was recorded, and, in terms of cultural possessions, the only information that was collected was the number of books in the household. While there is much socio-economic background information that is not captured in the Survey of Adult Skills (e.g. income, wealth, and occupation of parents), parents' educational attainment is one of the most important proxies of socio-economic background, given that education is an important predictor of income, wealth and occupation.

A note regarding the Russian Federation

The sample for the Russian Federation does not include the population of the Moscow municipal area. The data published, therefore, do not represent the entire resident population aged 16-65 in the Russian Federation but rather the population of the Russian Federation *excluding* the population residing in the Moscow municipal area.

More detailed information regarding the data from the Russian Federation as well as that of other countries can be found in the *Technical Report of the Survey of Adult Skills, Second Edition* (OECD, forthcoming).

References and further reading

Desjardins, R. and **A. Warnke** (2012), "Ageing and skills: A review and analysis of skill gain and skill loss over the lifespan and over time", *OECD Education Working Papers*, No. 72, OECD Publishing, Paris, http://dx.doi.org/10.1787/5k9csvw87ckh-en.

Green, D. and **W.C. Riddell** (2013), "Ageing and literacy skills: Evidence from Canada, Norway and the United States", *Labour Economics*, Vol. 22(C), pp. 16-29.

Grotlüschen, A. et al. (2016), "Adults with low proficiency in literacy or numeracy", *OECD Education Working Papers*, No. 131, OECD Publishing, Paris, http://dx.doi.org/10.1787/5jm0v44bnmnx-en.

OECD (2016), *Survey of Adult Skills (PIAAC)* (Database 2012, 2015), www.oecd.org/site/piaac/publicdataandanalysis.htm.

OECD (2015a), *Education at a Glance 2015: OECD Indicators*, OECD Publishing, Paris, http://dx.doi.org/10.1787/eag-2015-en.

OECD (2015b), *The ABC of Gender Equality in Education: Aptitude, Behaviour, Confidence*, OECD Publishing, Paris, http://dx.doi.org/10.1787/9789264229945-en.

OECD (2013), *OECD Skills Outlook 2013: First Results from the Survey of Adult Skills*, OECD Publishing, Paris, http://dx.doi.org/10.1787/9789264204256-en.

Paccagnella, M. (2016), "Age, ageing and skills. Results from the Survey of Adult Skills", *OECD Education Working Papers*, No. 132, OECD Publishing, Paris, http://dx.doi.org/10.1787/5jm0q1n38lvc-en.

4

How skills are used in the workplace

This chapter examines the use of information-processing skills at work and in everyday life, and the relationship between the use of skills and wages, job satisfaction and economy-wide productivity. It also explores the factors associated with greater or lesser use of these skills in the workplace, including proficiency, the characteristics of workers and the features of their jobs.

Having a skilled workforce is not enough to achieve growth and raise productivity. For countries to grow and individuals to thrive in the labour market, skills must be put to productive use at work. The Survey of Adult Skills, a product of the OECD Programme for the International Assessment of Adult Competencies (PIAAC), provides insights into how frequently information-processing skills are used in the workplace and how frequently they are used in daily life.

Skills use at work can be defined as the level of skills that is observed in a worker's current job within a given skills domain. This definition is rooted in sociological theory that distinguishes between "own skills" (the skills that individuals have) and "job skills" (skills as defined by jobs). In fact, skills use is affected by both the extent to which workers are motivated to use their skills in the workplace – which in turn may depend on the incentives they are offered and on their own innate motivation – and by the skills required to carry out the specific job.

The background questionnaire of the Survey of Adult Skills asks about the frequency with which individuals carry out a number of skills-related tasks in the context of their job and in their private life. This task-based approach to measuring skills use – the so-called job requirement approach (JRA) – ensures that the resulting indicators are as unbiased as possible by the actual skills held by the respondents.

The background questionnaire also elicits information from respondents on the way work is organised and jobs are designed and on the management practices adopted by the firm. This information can be used to identify the type of environments that are associated with more frequent skills use in the workplace.[1]

Among the main findings discussed in the chapter:

- Writing and problem solving are the skills most frequently used at work. Reading skills follow close behind while numeracy and ICT skills are least used.

- Among Round-2 countries/economies, New Zealand stands out as the one whose adults use almost all measured information-processing skills the most frequently at work, along with Australia and the United States from Round 1. Singapore also stands out as a country whose adults use their skills frequently at work, particularly ICT skills. In Slovenia, the use of most information-processing skills is close to the average and, unsurprisingly, close to some other Eastern European countries, such as the Czech Republic, Estonia and the Slovak Republic. In addition, workers in Slovenia are among those who use their writing skills at work the most frequently. In all other Round-2 countries/ economies once occupation and firm characteristers are taken into account, the use of information-processing skills at work is well below average and close to the bottom of the scale.

- There appears to be a strong link between skills use at work and in everyday life, suggesting that the same adults' socio-demographic characteristics and personal dispositions play a role in defining their level of engagement with literacy, numeracy and ICT in both their personal and work environments.

- Skills-use indicators do not mirror measures of skills proficiency, as countries rank differently on the two dimensions of skills proficiency and skills use. Proficiency accounts for only about 5% of the variation in adults' use of numeracy skills at work across participating OECD countries once occupation and firm characteristics are taken into account; it accounts for less of the variation in the use of reading or writing at the workplace. Put differently, the distribution of skills use among workers with different levels of proficiency overlap substantially. While the median use of both literacy and numeracy skills increases consistently as levels of proficiency increase, it is not uncommon that more proficient workers use their skills at work less intensively than less proficient workers do. Skills use is a strong predictor of productivity.

- In all the countries and economies covered in the Survey of Adult Skills, differences in skills use between socio-demographic groups are strongly associated with the type of jobs held by workers.

- High-Performance Work Practices – including work organisation and management practices – are positively related to the use of information-processing skills at work. They account for between 14% and 27% of the variation in skills use across individuals. The way work is organised – the extent of team work, autonomy, task discretion, mentoring, job rotation and applying new learning – influences the degree of internal flexibility to adapt job tasks to the skills of new hires. Some management practices – bonus pay, training provision and flexibility in working hours – provide incentives for workers to use their skills at work more fully.

This chapter begins with a picture of how frequently information-processing skills are used in the workplace. It then compares skills use at work with skills use in everyday life and goes on to examine key factors related to skills use at work, such as workers' socio-demographic traits and the characteristics of jobs and firms.

MEASURING SKILLS USE IN THE WORKPLACE AND IN EVERYDAY LIFE

The Survey of Adult Skills (PIAAC) includes detailed questions about the frequency with which respondents perform specific tasks in their jobs and in everyday life. Based on this information, the survey measures the use of information-processing skills – reading, writing, numeracy, ICT and problem solving – which can be related to those measured in the direct assessment.

However, although there are some parallels between the skills included in the direct assessment – literacy, numeracy and problem solving in technology-rich environments – and the use of reading, numeracy, problem-solving and ICT skills at work and in everyday life, there are important differences. For instance, while information about the frequency of writing tasks is available in the background questionnaire, writing skills are not tested in the survey's direct assessment. Similarly, questions about the use of problem-solving and ICT skills at work are not to be confused with the assessment of proficiency in problem solving in technology-rich environments. Even when there is a parallel between skills use and skills proficiency – notably between the use of reading skills and literacy proficiency, and between the use of numeracy skills and proficiency – there is no direct correspondence between the questions about the tasks performed at work (or in everyday life) and those asked in the survey's direct assessment of skills. In light of these differences, the term "skills use" should not be interpreted as necessarily referring to the use of skills that are measured in the survey's direct assessment, but rather as the use of information-processing skills more generally.

Given the large amount of information collected in the background questionnaire, it is helpful to construct indices that group together tasks associated with the use of similar information-processing skills. Five indicators were created (see Table 4.1) referring to the use of reading, writing, numeracy, ICT skills and problem solving at work. Following the same procedure, indicators of the use of reading, writing, numeracy and ICT in everyday life were also constructed.[2]

Box 4.1 lists the individual items associated with each of the skills-use indicators. For example, the reading and writing indices are derived from a large set of questions concerning the frequency with which several types of documents (directions, instructions, memos, e-mails, articles, manuals, books, invoices, bills and forms) are read or written during one's regular work activity. Higher values on the indices correspond to more frequent use of literacy skills.

Box 4.1 **Measuring the use of information-processing skills in the Survey of Adult Skills**

The Survey of Adult Skills elicits information on the use of a number of information-processing skills at work and in everyday life. These include reading, writing, numeracy, ICT and problem solving. Rather than asking workers directly about how frequently and in what context they use their skills, the survey enquires about the frequency with which tasks relevant to each skill are carried out (a complete list is provided in Table 4.1).

Table 4.1 **Indicators of skills use at work and in everyday life**

		Skills put to use at work	Group of tasks measured in the survey
Skills use at work	Skills use in everyday life	Reading	Reading documents (directions, instructions, letters, memos, e-mails, articles, books, manuals, bills, invoices, diagrams, maps)
		Writing	Writing documents (letters, memos, e-mails, articles, reports, forms)
		Numeracy	Calculating prices, costs or budgets; using fractions, decimals or percentages; using calculators; preparing graphs or tables; using algebra or formulas; using advanced mathematics or statistics (calculus, trigonometry, regressions)
		ICT skills	Using e-mail, Internet, spreadsheets, word processors, programming languages; conducting transactions on line; participating in online discussions (conferences, chats)
	n.a.	Problem solving	Facing hard problems (at least 30 minutes of thinking to find a solution)

Frequency is measured as follows: a value of 1 indicates that the task is never carried out; a value of 2 indicates that it is carried out less than once a month; a value of 3 indicates that it is carried less than once a week but at least once a month; a value of 4 indicates that it is carried out at least once a week but not every day; and a value of 5 indicates that it is carried out every day.

...

For most skills-use domains, information is collected for a large number of tasks, improving the reliability of the derived variable. The only exception is problem-solving skills, the use of which is measured through a single question that asks: "How often are you usually confronted with more complex problems that take at least 30 minutes to find a good solution?" Thus, indices are constructed for reading, writing, numeracy and ICT skills use and used as such in the analyses. Respondents' answer to the question on problem-solving skills use is included directly the analyses.

The composite variables – those derived from multiple task-related questions – are constructed using sum scales. Cronbach's Alpha, a statistical technique, is used to ensure that the items used to derive each skills-use composite variable are grouped appropriately. The resulting scale for these variables is semi-continuous and ranges from 1 to 5 as is the case for the underlying items: a value close to 1 indicates that the person does not use that particular skill at work while a value close to 5 suggests that the person uses the skill every day.

Questions concerning ICT-related tasks at work are only asked of adults who reported using a computer at work; thus few adults reported "never" using their ICT skills at work. In order to ensure comparability with the other skills-use scales, adults who reported that they do not use a computer at work are assigned to "never" carrying out ICT-related tasks at work.

Because all indices are expressed on the same scale ranging from 1 to 5, numerical comparisons between countries/economies and indicators are possible. Nevertheless, some comparisons may not be conceptually meaningful. For instance, the appropriate frequency of use of reading skills may not be the same as the frequency with which workers are required to solve complex problems. One additional concern is that the semi-continuous indices of skills use created for this chapter and used in related publications (OECD, 2016a; Quintini, 2014) implicitly assume that the distance between values is linear and equivalent. For instance, the distance between "never carried out" (value of 1) and "less than once a month" (value of 2) is the same as the distance between "at least once a week" (value of 4) and "every day" (value of 5). This is a strong assumption, and it could have implications when using skills use in regression analysis. The *First Results from the Survey of Adult Skills* (OECD, 2013) shows that results are similar when focusing on the share of workers who use each skill – i.e. carry out each set of tasks – frequently.

Sources:

OECD (2016a), *OECD Employment Outlook 2016*, OECD Publishing, Paris, http://dx.doi.org/10.1787/empl_outlook-2016-en.

OECD (2013), *OECD Skills Outlook 2013: First Results from the Survey of Adult Skills*, OECD Publishing, Paris, http://dx.doi.org/10.1787/9789264204256-en.

Quintini, G. (2014), "Skills at work: How skills and their use matter in the labour market", *OECD Social, Employment and Migration Working Papers*, No. 158, OECD Publishing, Paris, http://dx.doi.org/10.1787/5jz44fdfjm7j-en.

LEVELS OF SKILLS USE IN THE WORKPLACE AND IN EVERYDAY LIFE

On average across countries, the skills most frequently used at work are writing and problem solving. In both cases, the average-use indicator has a value close to three. Reading skills at work follows close behind, while numeracy and ICT are the least frequently used, with an index value closer to two (Figure 4.1).

New Zealand stands out as the country where adults use almost all information-processing skills the most frequently, along with Australia and the United States.[3] Among Round-2 countries/economies, Singapore also stands out with relatively high skills use in all five domains; and it has the most frequent use of ICT skills at work among all participating countries and economies. In Slovenia, the use of most information-processing skills is close to the OECD average and, unsurprisingly, close to some other Eastern European countries, such as the Czech Republic, Estonia and the Slovak Republic. In addition, Slovenian workers are among those who use their writing skills at work the most frequently. In all other Round-2 countries/economies, the use of information-processing skills at work is well below average and close to the bottom of the scale.

Across countries and economies, writing and numeracy skills are used less frequently in everyday life than in the workplace (Figure 4.2). In most cases, country/economy rankings of skills use in everyday life are similar to those presented for skills use at work. New Zealand ranks highest in using information-processing skills most frequently in everyday life, Slovenia ranks close to the average and most other Round-2 countries/economies are close to the bottom, well below the average. An exception is Singapore, which ranks just below the average for skills use in everyday life, compared to a fairly frequent use of information-processing skills in the workplace.

Figure 4.1 ■ **Information-processing skills used at work**

Average skills use, working population aged 16 to 65

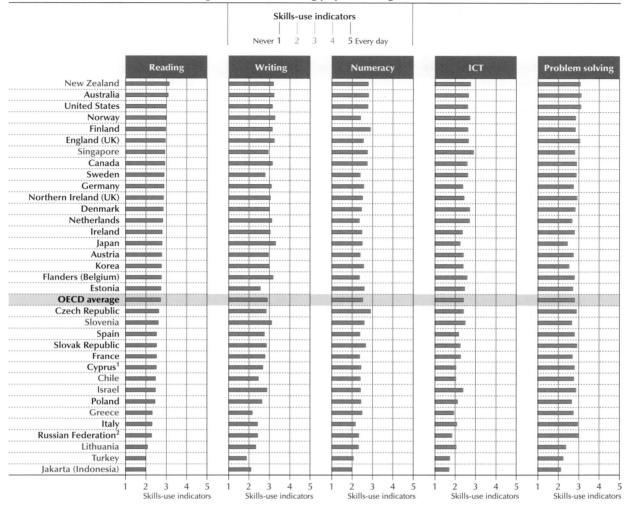

Note: For reading, writing, numeracy and ICT skills, skills-use indicators are scaled between 1 "Never" and 5 "Every day". Problem-solving skills use refers to respondents' answers to "How often are you usually confronted with more complex problems that take at least 30 minutes to find a good solution?". The set of possible answers also ranges between 1 "Never" and 5 "Every day".

1. *Note by Turkey:* The information in this document with reference to "Cyprus" relates to the southern part of the Island. There is no single authority representing both Turkish and Greek Cypriot people on the Island. Turkey recognises the Turkish Republic of Northern Cyprus (TRNC). Until a lasting and equitable solution is found within the context of the United Nations, Turkey shall preserve its position concerning the "Cyprus issue".

Note by all the European Union Member States of the OECD and the European Union: The Republic of Cyprus is recognised by all members of the United Nations with the exception of Turkey. The information in this document relates to the area under the effective control of the Government of the Republic of Cyprus.

2. See note at the end of this chapter.

Countries and economies are ranked in descending order of the average use of reading skills at work.

Source: Survey of Adult Skills (PIAAC) (2012, 2015), Table A4.1.

StatLink 🔗 http://dx.doi.org/10.1787/888933366159

As Figures 4.1 and 4.2 suggest, the use of skills in everyday life and at work are highly correlated at the country/economy level. The correlation coefficient between the average use of skills at work and in everyday life ranges between 0.81 for numeracy skills to 0.94 for reading skills. This strong link is confirmed at the individual level, when the responses about the use of skills in everyday life are compared to those about the use of skills at work. However, in this case, the correlation is lower than at the country /economy level, and varies between 0.40 for numeracy skills and 0.56 for reading skills (not shown). Since the time available outside of work may affect the relationship between skills use in the two contexts – e.g. those working longer hours may have less time to read, write, use ICT or perform numeracy-related tasks in their free time – the figures are adjusted to account for working hours. When this is done, the correlation at the individual level is stronger and closer to the country /economy-level correlation, ranging from 0.66 for numeracy skills to 0.80 for writing skills (not shown).

Figure 4.2 ▪ **Information-processing skills used in everyday life**

Average skills use, working population aged 16 to 65

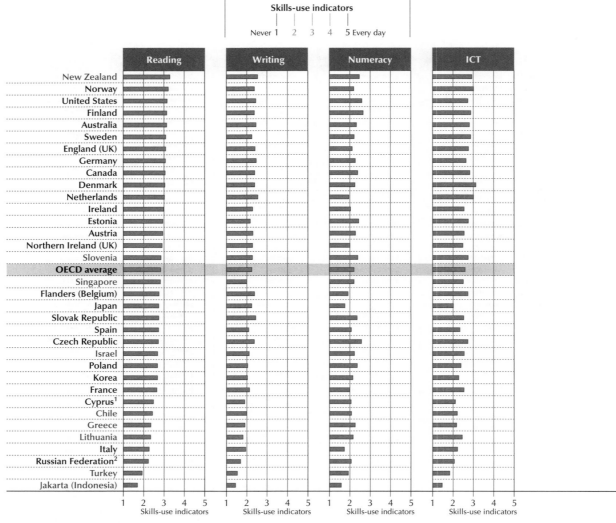

Note: Skills use in everyday life indicators are scaled between 1 "Never" and 5 "Every day".
1. See note 1 under Figure 4.1.
2. See note at the end of this chapter.
Countries and economies are ranked in descending order of the average use of reading skills in everyday life.
Source: Survey of Adult Skills (PIAAC) (2012, 2015), Table A4.2.
StatLink ⬛ http://dx.doi.org/10.1787/888933366163

The strong link between skills use at work and in everyday life suggests that adults' socio-demographic characteristics and attitudes towards learning play a role in defining a similar level of engagement with literacy, numeracy and ICT in their personal life, in and outside of the workplace.[4] At the same time, the use of skills at work is also influenced by job-related characteristics, such as the occupation and industry in which an adult works, which are unlikely to affect skills use in everyday life beyond the time constraints they may impose.

WHY SKILLS USE AT WORK MATTERS
Skills use, wages and job satisfaction

As shown in Chapter 5, workers who use their skills more frequently also tend to have higher wages, even after accounting for differences in educational attainment, skills proficiency and occupation. The use of ICT and reading skills are the most closely related to hourly wages. By contrast, while using numeracy and problem-solving skills at work matters as much as proficiency, their correlation with wages is much weaker than that of ICT and reading skills (OECD, 2016a).

More effective skills use has also been linked to greater job satisfaction and employee well-being. For this reason, the concept of skills use has sometimes been closely associated with that of job quality (e.g. Green et al., 2013), with possible spill-over effects into life satisfaction, more generally, and better health. A study conducted by the OECD in parallel to this report (OECD, 2016a) shows how, on average across countries, skills use is related to the likelihood of being extremely satisfied at work. It emerges that the use of information-processing skills has a stronger association with job satisfaction than a workers' actual skills or years of education. Although magnitudes vary, patterns across countries are similar, on average. The relationships between the use of reading, writing and ICT skills at work and job satisfaction are statistically significant in nearly all countries, while this is not always the case for the use of numeracy and problem-solving skills.

Skills use and productivity

Many skills are not actually used at work – for example, among workers who are mismatched in their job – making skills use a potentially stronger determinant of wages and productivity than skills proficiency. This is also argued in the relevant literature that finds, for instance, that at the level of the firm, better skills use results in higher productivity and lower staff turnover (UKCES, 2014). Some have also argued that better skills use stimulates investment, employees' engagement, and innovation (Wright and Sissons, 2012).

Figure 4.3 shows that the use of reading skills at work correlates strongly with output per hour worked. This is also the case for writing skills. One possible explanation for this is that using skills simply reflects workers' proficiency in those skills. In other words, they both represent the human capital available to the firm. If so, the link between the use of reading skills at work and productivity could actually reflect a relationship between literacy proficiency and productivity.

Figure 4.3 ▪ **Labour productivity and the use of reading skills at work**

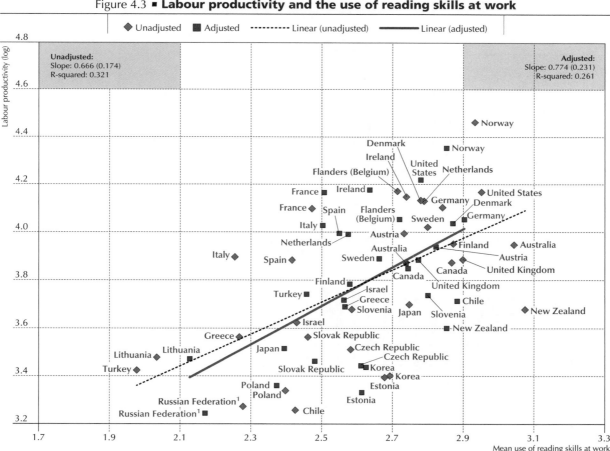

Notes: Lines are best linear predictions. Labour productivity is equal to the GDP per hour worked, in USD current prices 2012 for Round-1 and 2014 for Round-2 countries/economies. Adjusted estimates are based on OLS regressions including controls for literacy and numeracy proficiency scores. Standard errors in parentheses.

1. See note at the end of this chapter.

Source: Survey of Adult Skills (PIAAC) (2012, 2015), Table A4.3.

StatLink ⇲ http://dx.doi.org/10.1787/888933366179

But this is not what the data show. The positive link between labour productivity and reading at work remains strong even after accounting for average proficiency scores in literacy and numeracy.[5] Once these adjustments are made, the average use of reading skills accounts for less of the variation in labour productivity across countries (26% compared to 32% before the adjustment) but remains statistically significant. Put simply, the frequency with which skills are used at work is important, in itself, in explaining differences in labour productivity over and above the effect of proficiency.

The strength of the link across countries/economies varies, depending on a number of factors, such as the capital stock, the quality of production technologies, and the efficiency of the match between workers and jobs.[6] Similarly, these additional factors may influence output per hour along with human capital as captured by skills use and proficiency. The *OECD Employment Outlook* (OECD, 2016a) tests the link between skills use and productivity further by looking at individual industries. Not only does this analysis confirm the relationship, found at the country/economy level, between productivity and the use of reading and writing skills, but it also confirms an association between productivity and the use of problem-solving and ICT skills.

THE LINK BETWEEN PROFICIENCY AND USE OF INFORMATION-PROCESSING SKILLS

One key question concerning skills use is whether it simply reflects proficiency. Figure 4.4 sheds some light on the relationship between skills use and proficiency at the country/economy level. Though countries/economies that have higher skills proficiency tend to show more frequent skills use, it is also apparent that countries/economies rank differently on the two dimensions of skills proficiency and skills use, which suggests that proficiency and use are two different, albeit to some extent related, concepts.

Figure 4.4 ■ **Skills use at work and skills proficiency of the working population**

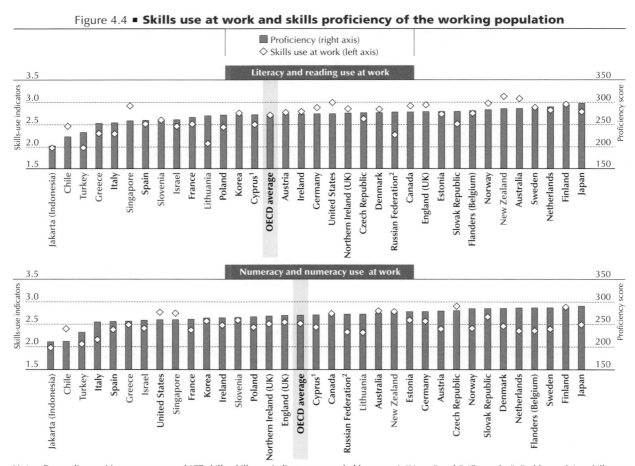

Notes: For reading, writing, numeracy and ICT skills, skills-use indicators are scaled between 1 "Never" and 5 "Every day". Problem-solving skills use refers to respondents' answers to "How often are you usually confronted with more complex problems that take at least 30 minutes to find a good solution?". The set of possible answers also ranges between 1 "Never" and 5 "Every day". Proficiency scores range from 0 to 500.
1. See note 1 under Figure 4.1.
2. See note at the end of this chapter.
Countries and economies are ranked in ascending order of the proficiency score.
Source: Survey of Adult Skills (PIAAC) (2012, 2015), Tables A4.1 and A4.4.
StatLink ᴹˢᴸ http://dx.doi.org/10.1787/888933366180

This could be the result of the way skills are measured in the direct assessment and in the questionnaire; but it could also point to a more fundamental discrepancy between the skills held by workers and the extent to which they are used on the job or to the way other factors (e.g. the way work is organised) allows for skills to be used more frequently.[7]

A similar picture emerges when looking at how skills use varies across proficiency levels. Figure 4.5 shows that, across countries and economies, the distributions of skills use among workers with different levels of proficiency overlap substantially. While the median use of literacy skills increases consistently as levels of proficiency increase, it is not uncommon that more proficient workers use their skills at work less frequently than less proficient workers do. This may reflect the limited comparability between skills proficiency as measured in the survey's direct assessment and tasks included in the skills-use indicators. However, it also suggests that the use of skills may depend on factors other than workers' actual skills.

Figure 4.5 ▪ **Skills use at work, by proficiency level**
Median, 25th and 75th percentiles of the distribution of skills use, by level of proficiency

○ 25th percentile ◆ Median ▶ 75th percentile

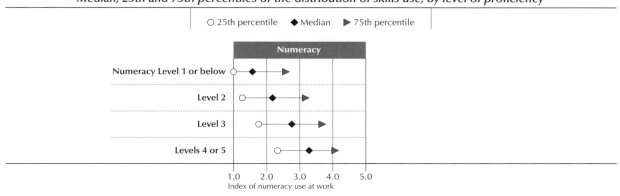

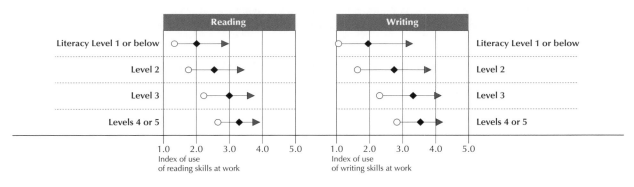

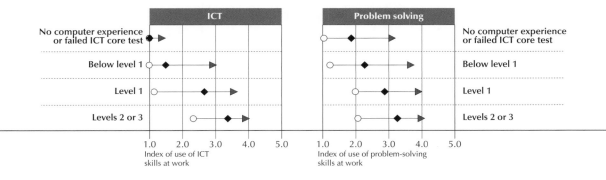

Notes: The data correspond to the average of OECD countries/economies participating in the Survey of Adult Skills (PIAAC). For reading, writing, numeracy and ICT skills, skills-use indicators are scaled between 1 "Never" and 5 "Every day". Problem-solving skills use refers to respondents' answers to "How often are you usually confronted with more complex problems that take at least 30 minutes to find a good solution?". The set of possible answers also ranges between 1 "Never" and 5 "Every day".
Source: Survey of Adult Skills (PIAAC) (2012, 2015), Tables A4.5 (L), A4.5 (N) and A4.5 (P).
StatLink http://dx.doi.org/10.1787/888933366193

THE VARIATION OF SKILLS USE AT WORK

Figure 4.6 shows the extent to which various factors – including individual proficiency, job/firm characteristics and human-resource practices – explain the variation of skills use at work. As the figure shows, after considering workers' occupation and the way their work is organised, proficiency accounts for a small part of the variation in skills use at work among adults (from around 1% in problem solving and reading to just under 6% in ICT), with the main role played by occupation and human-resource practices.[8] This is not to say that skills proficiency is unrelated to skills use. Skills proficiency and use are related as selection to occupations and firms that make more frequent use of skills depends on skills proficiency. Human-resource practices account for up to 27% of the variation in the use of reading skills at work while occupation accounts for up to 25% of the variation in ICT use at work. The relationship between skills proficiency and skills use at work is thus not direct but mediated by variables like workers' occupation and work organisation.

Occupations are important predictors of skills use at work. They account for 25% of the variance in ICT skills use at work, around 14% of the variance in reading, writing and numeracy skills, and 6% of the variance in problem-solving skills use at work. Skills use varies by occupation: skills use is lowest among workers in elementary occupations and highest among managers and professionals. ICT and writing skills use varies across occupations. While managers, professionals, technicians and clerical-support workers use these skills relatively often, workers in service and sales, agriculture, forestry and fishery, craft and trades, plant and machine operators, and elementary occupations use these skills more frequently (OECD, 2013, 2016a).

The *OECD Employment Outlook* (OECD, 2016a) also confirms that human-resource practices are highly correlated with skills use at work. This finding is in line with a growing body of literature showing that participatory practices at work – such as those allowing workers more flexibility in determining the way and rhythm at which they carry out their tasks – encourage better use of skills in the workplace. Management practices also help, with bonuses, training and working time flexibility all providing incentives for workers to use their skills at work more fully.

Overall, these results suggest that the job-requirement approach (JRA) to measuring skills use at work has succeeded in reflecting job-specific demands and skills use in the workplace. It clarifies the complex relationship between workers' proficiency and actual skills use. High skills proficiency may set the foundation for high skills use, but this is not necessary. The JRA's success in measuring skills use is important, as this methodology was applied to improve the quality of data over that collected from self-reports, in which workers' views would be more influenced by their level of proficiency.

Figure 4.6 ■ **Explaining information-processing skills used at work**
Percentage of the variance in skills use explained by each factor

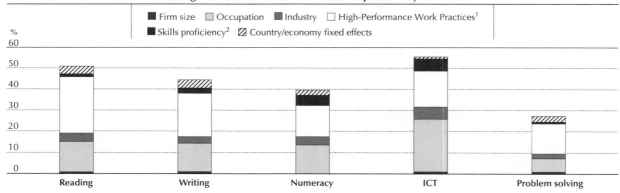

Notes: The figures presented in this table are based on a pooled regression of all OECD countries/economies in the Survey of Adult Skills, including country/economy fixed effects. Individual country results can be found in the tables cited in the source. For reading, writing, numeracy and ICT skills, skills-use indicators are scaled between 1 "Never" and 5 "Every day". Problem-solving skills use refers to respondents' answers to "How often are you usually confronted with more complex problems that take at least 30 minutes to find a good solution?". The set of possible answers also ranges between 1 "Never" and 5 "Every day".

1. High-Performance Work Practices include the following variables: choosing and changing the sequence of your tasks, the speed of work and how to do your work, organising your own time and planning your own activities; co-operating with others; instructing, teaching or training people; sharing information with co-workers; bonus; participating in training; flexible working hours.

2. For reading and writing, skills proficiency refers to proficiency in literacy; for numeracy, skills proficiency refers to proficiency in numeracy; for ICT and problem solving, skills proficiency refers to proficiency in problem solving in technology-rich environments (hence, the analysis excludes countries for which this proficiency domain is not tested). Using literacy proficiency to include all countries when decomposing the variance of ICT and problem solving use does not change the main thrust of the results presented here.

Source: Survey of Adult Skills (PIAAC) (2012, 2015), Table A4.6.

StatLink 🔗 http://dx.doi.org/10.1787/888933366204

THE DISTRIBUTION OF SKILLS USE, BY WORKERS' GENDER, AGE AND EDUCATIONAL ATTAINMENT

Gender

With only a few country/economy exceptions, differences in reading, writing and ICT use at work related to gender are small (Figure 4.7). Larger differences, generally showing more frequent use by men than women, are observed in the use of numeracy and problem-solving skills in the workplace. Differences between men and women in the use of skills may be the result of gender discrimination, but may also be explained by differences in skills proficiency (in numeracy) and/or in the nature of the job (part-time versus full-time, and occupation).

Figure 4.7 ■ **Information-processing skills used at work, by gender**

Adjusted and unadjusted gender differences in the mean use of skills, in percentage of the average use of skills by women

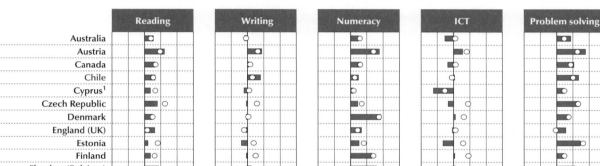

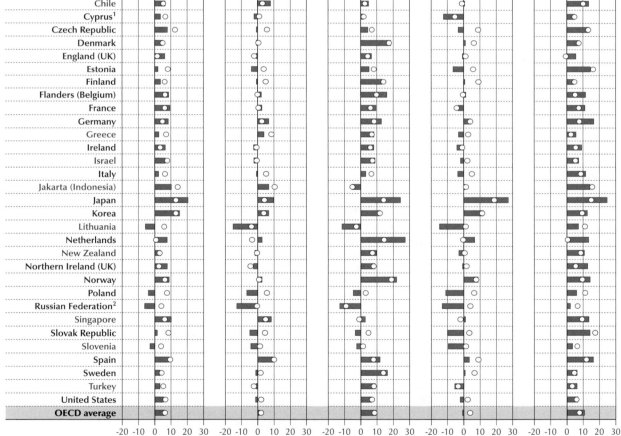

Note: Adjusted estimates are based on OLS regressions including controls for literacy and numeracy proficiency scores, hours worked, and occupation dummies (ISCO 1-digit).

1. See note 1 under Figure 4.1.

2. See note at the end of this chapter.

Countries and economies are listed in alphabetical order.

Source: Survey of Adult Skills (PIAAC) (2012, 2015), Tables A4.7a and A4.7b.

StatLink ⟡ http://dx.doi.org/10.1787/888933366214

For instance, if numeracy skills were used less frequently in part-time jobs than in full-time jobs, this may explain part of the difference in skills use between the genders, as women are more likely than men to work part time.[9] This reasoning could apply to occupations as well, with women more likely to be found in jobs that presumably require less intensive use of certain skills, such as problem solving. For instance, women may sort themselves into jobs that require less investment in human capital during the period of childrearing.

However, as Figure 4.7 suggests, adjusting for hours worked, occupation and proficiency levels does not change the sign or order of magnitude of the differences. Looking closer at the results, this appears to be because some of the adjustments cancel each other out. Hours worked and proficiency tend to reduce gender differences as expected; but occupation increases them. In other words, when the type of job held is taken into account, the differences in how men and women use their skills at work are larger. This is particularly striking for the use of ICT skills at work, where the gender gap in skills use increases markedly in most countries/economies after accounting for occupation. This is somewhat surprising, given that the concentration of women in low-paying occupations is often considered one of the key determinants of gender discrimination and the gender gap in wages (Blau and Kahn, 2000, 2003; Goldin, 1986; OECD, 2012). One possible explanation is that, while women tend to be concentrated in certain occupations, they use their skills more intensively than do the relatively few men who are employed in similar jobs.

Looking at countries and economies individually, large gender differences across most skills-use domains are observed in Japan and Korea, where men use their skills up to 20-30% more than their female counterparts, and also in Austria and Spain, where differences are smaller but still reach 15% in some domains. The type of jobs women do and their working hours reduce the differences markedly only in Japan. Interestingly, Lithuania and the Russian Federation stand out as countries where women use their skills in the workplace more than men, although this is mostly due to differences in the jobs they hold. Focusing on Round-2 countries/economies, New Zealand and Turkey both show small differences between the genders, although they stand at the two opposite ends of the distribution of skills use at work: the average use of skills in Turkey is among the least frequent in most domains, while in New Zealand it is among the most frequent.

Age

In all countries/economies except the Russian Federation, 16-24 year-old workers and 55-65 year-old workers use information-processing skills at work less than do workers of prime age (25-54 year-olds) (Figure 4.8). Differences tend to be more pronounced between younger and prime-age adults, but the size of those differences varies across countries/economies.

Contrary to the conventional wisdom that young people are more intense users of ICTs, it is precisely in ICT use that young people lag behind prime-age workers the most. In Canada, Denmark, Finland, Israel, the Netherlands, New Zealand, Norway and Sweden, 16-24 year-olds use ICT at work about 30% less than 25-54 year-olds do. The opposite picture emerges for the use of ICT in everyday life (not shown): 16-24 year-old workers use ICT consistently more at home than prime-age and older workers do. Of course, some of the computer activities in which young adults engage at home (playing videogames, browsing the Internet, chatting) may not be the same as those required on the job. Nevertheless, it would be useful to explore differences in skills use between younger and older cohorts in more depth, including by shedding light on whether young people's ICT skills might be underused in the labour market.

Focusing on other Round-2 countries/economies, in Singapore, Turkey and, to a lesser extent, Chile and Slovenia, raw differences in skills use at work between older (55-65 year-old) and prime-age workers are the most pronounced. This is also the case in Korea among Round-1 countries and economies.

The fact that skills use appears to peak between the ages of 25 and 54 can be interpreted in several ways. For instance, it is possible that older workers move into less demanding positions prior to retirement while young people follow the opposite path as they move out of entry-level jobs into more stable career positions. Alternatively, skills use may decline as skills proficiency does. Skills accumulate in the initial stages of one's career, reach a maximum in the early 30s, and then depreciate over time due to a lack of investment in training and lifelong learning activities (see Chapter 3).[10] Finally, some of the countries with a pronounced difference in skills use at work between older and prime-age workers have seen a marked increase in educational attainment – and presumably skills – over time. In these cases, the decline in proficiency may be due to a cohort effect, possibly in addition to age-related skills depreciation.

The role of proficiency in explaining differences in skills use over a lifetime is supported by differences between raw and adjusted figures in skills use at work, particularly for older workers relative to prime-age workers. Large differences in proficiency seem to be substantially more important in explaining differences in skills use between prime-age and older workers than between prime-age and younger workers.[11]

Figure 4.8 ▪ **Information-processing skills used at work, by age group**

*Adjusted and unadjusted age differences in the mean use of skills,
in percentage of the average use of skills by prime-age workers*

▪ Difference between younger and prime-age workers (unadjusted)
● Difference between younger and prime-age workers (adjusted)
□ Difference between older and prime-age workers (unadjusted)
● Difference between older and prime-age workers (adjusted)

	Reading	Writing	Numeracy	ICT	Problem solving
Australia					
Austria					
Canada					
Chile					
Cyprus[1]					
Czech Republic					
Denmark					
England (UK)					
Estonia					
Finland					
Flanders (Belgium)					
France					
Germany					
Greece					
Ireland					
Israel					
Italy					
Jakarta (Indonesia)					
Japan					
Korea					
Lithuania					
Netherlands					
New Zealand					
Northern Ireland (UK)					
Norway					
Poland					
Russian Federation[2]					
Singapore					
Slovak Republic					
Slovenia					
Spain					
Sweden					
Turkey					
United States					
OECD average					

-60 -40 -20 0 20   -60 -40 -20 0 20   -60 -40 -20 0 20   -60 -40 -20 0 20   -60 -40 -20 0 20
Percentage difference   Percentage difference   Percentage difference   Percentage difference   Percentage difference

Notes: Adjusted estimates are based on OLS regressions including controls for literacy and numeracy proficiency scores and contract type. Younger workers are 16 to 25 years old, prime-age workers are 26 to 54, and older workers are 55 to 65.
1. See note 1 under Figure 4.1.
2. See note at the end of this chapter.
Countries and economies are listed in alphabetical order.
Source: Survey of Adult Skills (PIAAC) (2012, 2015), Tables A4.8a and A4.8b.
StatLink ⌦ http://dx.doi.org/10.1787/888933366224

Educational attainment

Although skills are developed in a variety of settings and evolve with age, formal education remains the primary source of learning, and it seems natural to expect greater use of skills among better-educated individuals.

For this analysis, only three groups of workers are considered: those who have less than upper secondary education, those who have completed upper secondary education, and those who have completed tertiary education.[12] With very few exceptions, the results show that workers with higher educational qualifications use their information-processing skills more intensively in their jobs than upper secondary graduates (Figure 4.9). The opposite is true for workers without an upper secondary qualification.

Figure 4.9 ▪ **Information-processing skills used at work, by educational attainment**

Adjusted and unadjusted differences in the mean use of skills, by educational attainment,
in percentage of the average use of skills by workers with upper secondary education

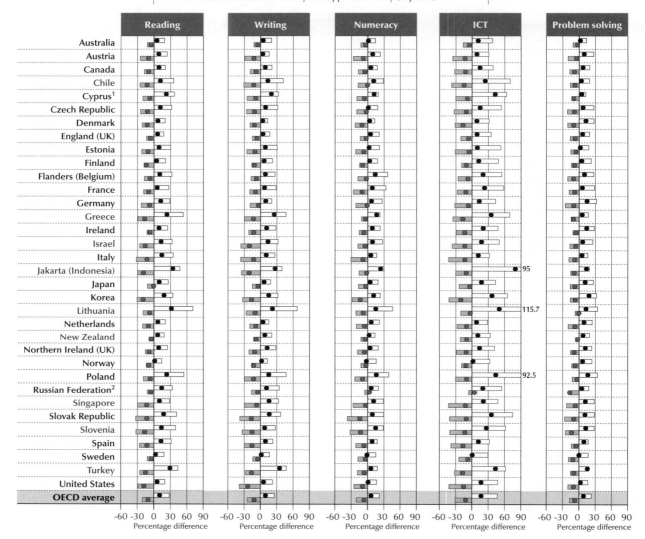

Note: Adjusted estimates are based on OLS regressions including controls for literacy and numeracy proficiency scores and occupation dummies (ISCO 1-digit).
1. See note 1 under Figure 4.1.
2. See note at the end of this chapter.
Countries and economies are listed in alphabetical order.
Source: Survey of Adult Skills (PIAAC) (2012, 2015), Tables A4.9a and A4.9b.
StatLink ⊞≡ http://dx.doi.org/10.1787/888933366239

Differences are large – comparable to those observed between age groups and larger than those found between men and women. The gap in skills use between tertiary and upper secondary graduates is largest in ICT, with raw differences of 50-60% in several countries. As for other socio-demographic characteristics, differences in skills proficiency and in the distribution of workers across occupations explain most of the variation in skills use between people with different educational qualifications. However, it is the jobs that people hold – as reflected by their occupations – rather than their competency in literacy and numeracy that have the greatest impact on skills use by educational attainment.

Despite the adjustment for skills proficiency and occupation, differences in ICT use at work between tertiary and upper secondary graduates remain sizeable, particularly in some Eastern European countries, including Lithuania, Poland, the Slovak Republic and Slovenia, and in Greece, Jakarta (Indonesia), Korea and Turkey.

While unsurprising, it is something of a wasted opportunity that the best-educated workers are also those who use their skills the most frequently at work. The use of skills at work can, and should, complement initial education in helping workers to acquire new skills and master those they already have. This calls for identifying incentive mechanisms for employers to encourage further skills use and development.

THE DEMAND SIDE: HOW FIRM AND JOB CHARACTERISTICS INFLUENCE SKILLS USE

Analysis of data from Survey of Adult Skills shows that how workers are distributed across occupations has a strong impact on skills use. In fact, accounting for occupation (along with skills proficiency) significantly reduces the differences in skills use between key socio-demographic groups. But these differences persist after occupation has been accounted for, suggesting that other factors may be at play. For instance, occupation categories – particularly when defined by broad groups of jobs[13] – can mask differences between jobs that are identified by the same occupation code. In addition, how firms are organised and managed could also influence the extent of skills use.

This section examines additional job and firm characteristics likely to be related to skills use. In most cases, only the average use of skills across countries is shown in the figures, as the high number of categories would make a presentation of results by country too cumbersome.

Table 4.2 **Industries with highest and lowest skills use at work**

Skills use at work	Top 5 industries (ISIC 2-digit code)	Bottom 5 industries (ISIC 2-digit code)
Reading	69 – Legal and accounting activities 71 – Architectural and engineering activities; technical testing and analysis 72 – Scientific research and development 62 – Computer programming, consultancy and related activities 70 – Activities of head offices; management consultancy activities	81 – Services to buildings and landscape activities 56 – Food and beverage service activities 15 – Manufacture of leather and related products 10 – Manufacture of food products 38 – Waste collection, treatment and disposal activities; materials recovery
Writing	70 – Activities of head offices; management consultancy activities 65 – Insurance, reinsurance and pension funding, except compulsory social security 69 – Legal and accounting activities 61 – Telecommunications 64 – Financial service activities, except insurance and pension funding	81 – Services to buildings and landscape activities 56 – Food and beverage service activities 96 – Other personal service activities 14 – Manufacture of wearing apparel 15 – Manufacture of leather and related products
Numeracy	65 – Insurance, reinsurance and pension funding, except compulsory social security 70 – Activities of head offices; management consultancy activities 64 – Financial service activities, except insurance and pension funding 71 – Architectural and engineering activities; technical testing and analysis 66 – Activities auxiliary to financial service and insurance activities	87 – Residential care activities 80 – Security and investigation activities 81 – Services to buildings and landscape activities 88 – Social work activities without accommodation 53 – Postal and courier activities
ICT	63 – Information service activities 66 – Activities auxiliary to financial service and insurance activities 64 – Financial service activities, except insurance and pension funding 70 – Activities of head offices; management consultancy activities 62 – Computer programming, consultancy and related activities	81 – Services to buildings and landscape activities 56 – Food and beverage service activities 16 – Manufacture of wood and of products of wood and cork, except furniture; manufacture of articles of straw and plaiting materials 49 – Land transport and transport via pipelines 96 – Other personal service activities
Problem solving	64 – Financial service activities, except insurance and pension funding 63 – Information service activities 61 – Telecommunications 70 – Activities of head offices; management consultancy activities 62 – Computer programming, consultancy and related activities	81 – Services to buildings and landscape activities 56 – Food and beverage service activities 15 – Manufacture of leather and related products 53 – Postal and courier activities 96 – Other personal service activities

Notes: Industries with two-digit codes on the ISIC classification are ranked on the basis of their average skills use. The top five and bottom five in the ranking are reported in the table.

Industry, firm size and sector

Only limited information is available in the Survey of Adult Skills concerning the characteristics of the respondents' employer: the number of employees, the industry in which the firm operates, and whether the firm operates in the public or private sector. To be more precise, survey questions refer to the geographical location where the job is mainly carried out or based – i.e. not the firm but the establishment where the worker is based – a relevant distinction in the case of large firms operating in several branches or regions.

Starting with skills use by industry, it emerges that information-processing skills are most frequently used in the "activities of head offices and consultancy", "financial services" and, to a lesser extent, "computer programming" (Table 4.2). At the other end of the scale, skills are least frequently used in "services to buildings", "food and beverage services" and also in "personal services" and the "manufacturing of leather products". Overall, the results are not surprising; but it is interesting to note that both the top and bottom rankings are consistent across most of the information-processing skills analysed in this chapter.

Figure 4.10 ▪ **Information-processing skills used at work, by sector**

Adjusted and unadjusted sector differences in the mean use of skills, in percentage of the average use of skills in private sector

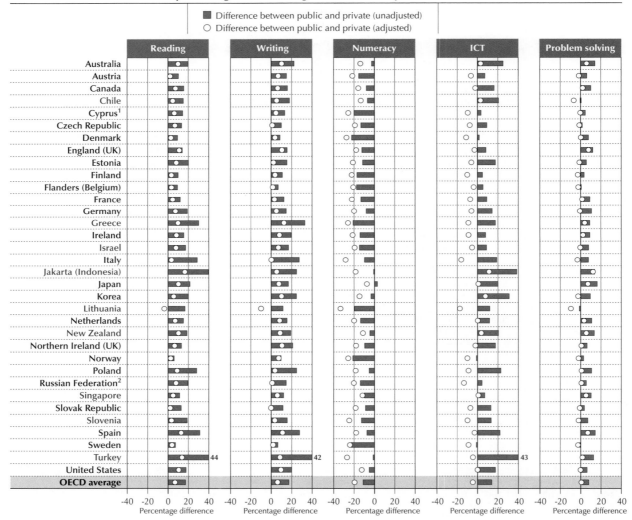

Note: Adjusted estimates are based on OLS regressions including controls for literacy and numeracy proficiency scores, hours worked and occupation dummies (ISCO 1-digit).

1. See note 1 under Figure 4.1.

2. See note at the end of this chapter.

Countries and economies are listed in alphabetical order.

Source: Survey of Adult Skills (PIAAC) (2012, 2015), Tables A4.10a and A4.10b.

StatLink ᴍ𝘴ᵖ http://dx.doi.org/10.1787/888933366247

Comparing public and private sector firms delivers a mixed picture (Figure 4.10). Reading and writing at work are more frequently used among adults working in public sector firms. The difference in the use of these skills between adults working in the public and private sectors is largest in Turkey, followed by Jakarta (Indonesia), Spain and Greece. The situation is inverted for numeracy skills: adults working in the private sector reported using their numeracy skills at work more frequently, although in some countries, the differences are small. The picture is mixed for ICT and, to a lesser extent, problem-solving skills, which tend to be used more frequently by workers in the public sector, although the differences are smaller than for reading and writing skills.

The nature of the jobs and the proficiency of workers in the two sectors explain the differences somewhat, particularly for reading, writing and problem-solving skills use at work. But adults working in the private sector appear to make more frequent use of numeracy and ICT skills once the difference between sectors is adjusted to take account of differences in the composition of workers across occupations and in workers' proficiency levels.

Another factor that determines how workers use their skills is the size of the firm in which they work. It could be expected that workers employed in small firms use their skills differently than do those employed in large firms, even within the same occupational group and the same industrial sector. One possibility is that large firms employ more skilled workers and adopt more sophisticated production technologies (Brown and Medoff, 1989; Gibson and Stillman, 2009), resulting in better use of information-processing skills relative to smaller firms. But small start-up firms may also distinguish themselves by giving their workers more flexibility, allowing them to use their skills more fully (OECD, forthcoming). Overall, the former hypothesis is confirmed for reading, numeracy, ICT and problem-solving skills use, all of which increase with firm size. The only exception is numeracy, which shows a slight U shape, with higher use at both ends of the firm-size scale (Figure 4.11).

Figure 4.11 ▪ **Information-processing skills used at work, by firm size**

Average use of information-processing skills by firm size

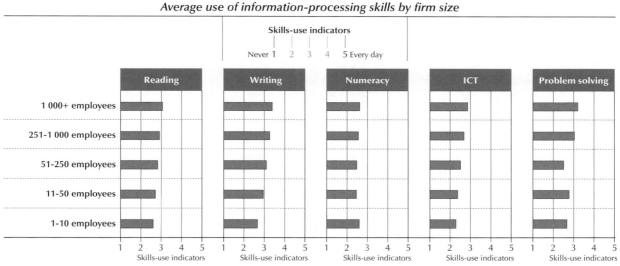

Notes: The data correspond to the average of OECD countries/economies participating in the Survey of Adult Skills (PIAAC). For reading, writing, numeracy and ICT skills, skills-use indicators are are scaled between 1 "Never" and 5 "Every day". Problem-solving skills use refer to repondents' answers to "How often are you usually confronted with more complex problems that take at least 30 minutes to find a good solution?". The set of possible answers also ranges between 1 "Never" and 5 "Every day". Firm size is measured by asking workers about the size of the establishment for which they work.

Source: Survey of Adult Skills (PIAAC) (2012, 2015), Table A4.11.

StatLink ⟦⟧ http://dx.doi.org/10.1787/888933366254

Type of contract

Contract type may also influence the extent of skills use at work through several mechanisms, including different degrees of attachment to the firm because of varying job security, willingness and flexibility to adapt job content to workers' skills or simply different job descriptions. This is an important issue as the use of temporary contracts has become pervasive in several OECD countries in recent years.[14] When combined with low rates of transition to permanent contracts and the fact that young people represent a disproportionate share of workers on temporary contracts, greater use of these contracts could have adverse effects on both individual workers and the economy as a whole.

For example, it has been extensively documented that workers on temporary contracts receive less training from their employers (Autor, 2001; OECD, 2006) when compared to workers in permanent contracts. Further, workers in temporary contracts have fewer opportunities to accumulate job-specific skills, thus potentially reducing their opportunities for career development and jeopardising the growth of labour productivity among younger generations. Understanding the differences in the skills used by workers on temporary and permanent contracts would shed further light on an additional mechanism of skills accumulation.

With very few exceptions, workers on fixed-term contracts use their information-processing skills less intensively than their colleagues in permanent employment (Figure 4.12).[15] The largest differences are found in Spain, but Greece and Turkey, among Round-2 countries/economies, also show a clear disadvantage among fixed-term workers, compared to those on permanent contracts, when it comes to using skills at work, particularly writing, numeracy and ICT skills.

Figure 4.12 ▪ **Information-processing skills used at work, by contract type**

Adjusted and unadjusted differences in the mean use of skills, by type of contract,
in percentage of the average use of skills by employees with a fixed-term contract

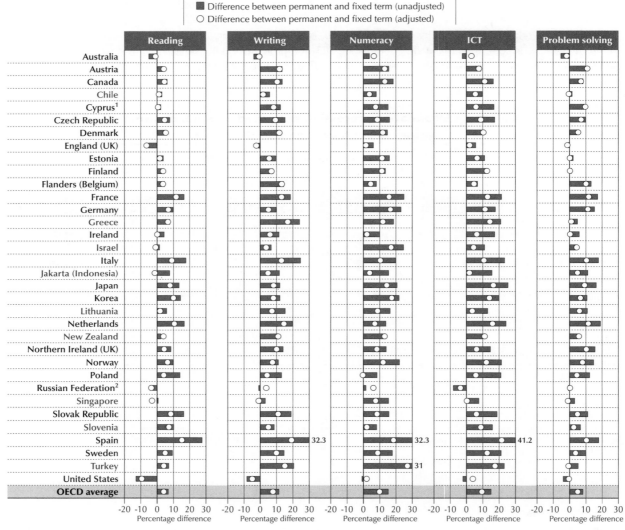

Note: Adjusted estimates are based on OLS regressions including controls for literacy and numeracy proficiency scores, hours worked and occupation dummies (ISCO 1-digit).

1. See note 1 under Figure 4.1.

2. See note at the end of this chapter.

Countries and economies are listed in alphabetical order.

Source: Survey of Adult Skills (PIAAC) (2012, 2015), Tables A4.12a and A4.12b.

StatLink ⟨⟩ http://dx.doi.org/10.1787/888933366263

At the other extreme, in Chile, differences are close to nil, similar to Australia, England (United Kingdom), the Russian Federation and the United States among Round-1 countries/economies.[16] Differences in the use of reading, writing and problem-solving skills between workers on different contract types are also small in Israel and Singapore.

In a number of countries, accounting for workers' skills proficiency, number of hours worked and occupation reduces the gap in skills use between contract types. However, while the correction reduces the differences, it does not eliminate them entirely, suggesting that other factors might be at play. For instance, in the Round-2 countries Greece, New Zealand and Turkey, the adjustment makes very little difference. The opposite is true for Jakarta (Indonesia) and Lithuania, where the adjustment reduces the difference in writing, numeracy and ICT skills use at work. Marked reductions in the gap in skills use are also observed in several Round-1 countries/economies, notably France, Italy, Poland and Spain.

The persistence of a gap in the use of skills between contract types could also be due to differences in management/ organisational practices. On the one hand, workers on temporary contracts might enjoy less flexibility in the way they carry out their tasks at work and have less voice in firms' decisions, reducing incentives to use their skills. On the other hand, employers may be less inclined to tailor job content and descriptions to the skills of their workers, exacerbating the effect of any qualification/skills mismatch on skills use.

Work organisation

The way work is organised and jobs are designed as well as the management practices adopted by the firm are likely to influence the extent to which skills are used in the workplace. In particular, it has been argued that better skills use and higher productivity can be achieved by implementing what are known as "High-Performance Work Practices" (HPWP), which include both aspects of work organisation – such as team work, autonomy, task discretion, mentoring, job rotation, applying new learning – and management practices – such as employee participation, incentive pay, training practices and flexibility in working hours (Bloom and Van Reenen, 2010; Johnston and Hawke, 2002).[17]

The Survey of Adult Skills collects information on a number of job aspects that are often associated with HPWP, including: whether workers have any flexibility in deciding on the sequence of tasks they perform, how they do the work, the speed of the work, and working time; how often they organise their own time and plan their own activities; how often they co-operate or share information with others; how often they instruct, teach or train other people; whether they participated in education/training in the previous 12 months; and whether they received a bonus payment. Figure 4.6 above confirms that these practices contribute substantially to the variation in adults' use of skills. The share of variation in skills use accounted for by HPWP ranges from 27% in reading to about 14% in problem solving. This makes HPWP the largest contributor to the variation in skills use in all domains except ICT, where occupation accounts for the largest share of this variation.

Figure 4.13 shows the use of information-processing skills by HPWP intensity. With only a few exceptions, workers who benefit from HPWP make greater use of reading, writing, numeracy, ICT and problem-solving skills than those who do not. Adults' use of their skills also tends to increase with HPWP intensity, i.e. skills use increases the more frequently workers engage in HPWP. Country-specific results follow similar patterns.

To get a sense of how widespread HPWP are across OECD countries, a scale aggregating the individual HPWP items shown in Figure 4.13 was constructed.[18] As shown in Figure 4.14, countries/economies vary in the intensity of HPWP at work. The figure shows the intensity of HPWP as well as the prevalence of its subcomponents: work organisation factors and management practices. Two measures of the overall prevalence of HPWP are shown in the figure: the average score and the share of jobs that adopt HPWP at least once a week. Countries and economies are ranked similarly on both measures, with HPWP being most prevalent in several Nordic countries, but also in New Zealand and, to a lesser extent, Israel among Round-2 countries/economies, and the least prevalent in Greece, Jakarta (Indonesia), Lithuania, the Russian Federation and Turkey.

Similar rankings are observed for work-organisation factors and for prevalence of training and flexible working hours. By contrast, the cross-country/economy distribution of the awarding of bonuses follows a different pattern, with bonuses widespread in Austria, Belgium and the Netherlands and least common in Australia, England (United Kingdom), Northern Ireland (United Kingdom) and Norway, and also in Lithuania, New Zealand and Turkey among Round-2 countries/economies. Additional analysis conducted for the *OECD Employment Outlook* (OECD, 2016a) confirms a strong correlation between HPWP and the use of information-processing skills at work.

Figure 4.13 ▪ **Skills use, by High-Performance Work Practices**

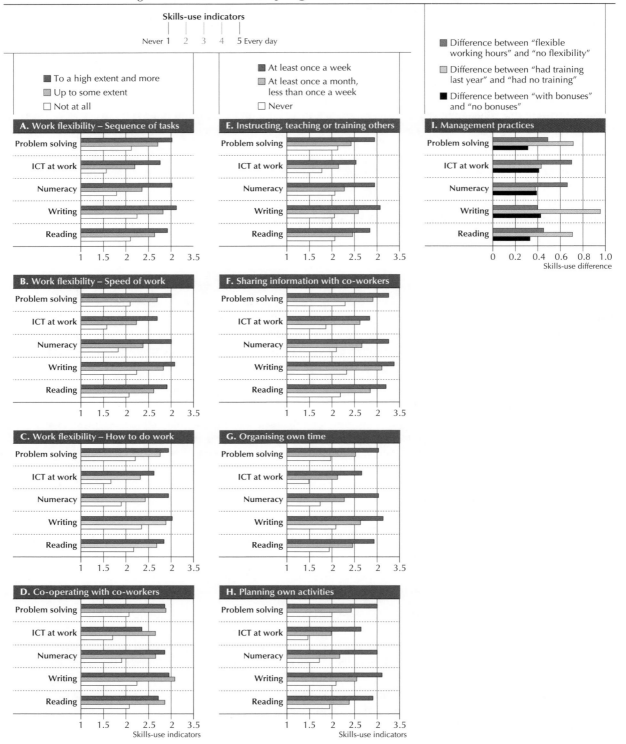

Notes: The data correspond to the average of OECD countries/economies participating in the Survey of Adult Skills (PIAAC). For reading, writing, numeracy and ICT skills, skills-use indicators are scaled between 1 "Never" and 5 "Every day". Problem-solving skills use refers to respondents' answers to "How often are you usually confronted with more complex problems that take at least 30 minutes to find a good solution?". The set of possible answers also ranges between 1 "Never" and 5 "Every day". Estimates for Panel I, "Management practices" show the difference in average skills use between: workers enjoying flexibility in working hours and those who do not; workers who participated in training over the previous year and those who did not; workers who receive annual bonus and those who do not.

Source: OECD (2016), Survey of Adult Skills (PIAAC) (2012, 2015), Table A4.13.

StatLink ⬛⬛ http://dx.doi.org/10.1787/888933366276

 SKILLS MATTER: FURTHER RESULTS FROM THE SURVEY OF ADULT SKILLS

Figure 4.14 ■ **High-Performance Work Practices, by type of practice**

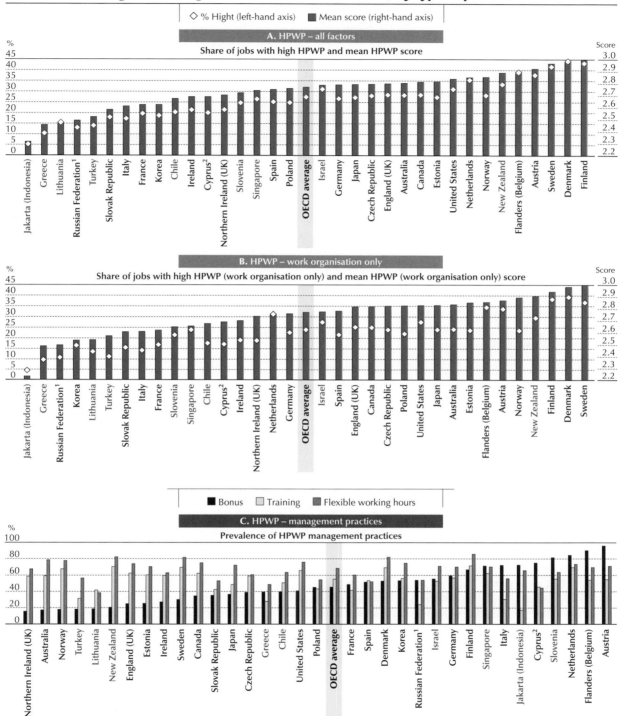

Notes: Panels A and B report the mean value of the HPWP indicator and the percentage of individuals in jobs above the 75th percentile in the respective pooled HPWP distribution. The HPWP index is obtained by summing the scales of all subcomponents shown in Figure 4.13 (Panel A) or summing the scales of work organisation subcomponents only (Panel B). Panel C reports the share of workers receiving annual bonuses, having participated in training over the previous year and those enjoying flexibility in working hours.

1. See note at the end of this chapter.

2. See note 1 under Figure 4.1.

Countries and economies are ranked in ascending order of the mean HPWP indicators in Panels A and B; in Panel C, countries/economies are ranked in ascending order of the prevalence of bonuses.

Source: Survey of Adult Skills (PIAAC) (2012, 2015), Table A4.14.

StatLink ᵐˢᵖ http://dx.doi.org/10.1787/888933366282

SUMMARY

Writing and problem solving are the skills most frequently used at work. Reading skills follow close behind while numeracy and ICT skills are least used. Among Round-2 countries/economies, New Zealand stands out as the one whose adults use almost all information-processing skills the most frequently at work, along with Australia and the United States from Round 1. Singapore also stands out as a country whose adults use their skills frequently at work, particularly ICT skills. Adults in Singapore show the most frequent use of ICT at work among all participating countries/economies. In Slovenia, the use of most information-processing skills is close to the average and, unsurprisingly, close to some other Eastern European countries, such as the Czech Republic, Estonia and the Slovak Republic. In addition, workers in Slovenia are among those who use their writing skills at work the most frequently. In all other Round-2 countries/economies, the use of information-processing skills at work is well below average and close to the bottom of the scale.

There appears to be a strong link between using skills at work and in everyday life, suggesting that adults' socio-demographic characteristics and personal dispositions play a role in defining their level of engagement with literacy, numeracy and ICT in their personal life.

Two themes emerge from the analysis that could have an impact on policy. First, countries and economies rank differently on the two dimensions of skills proficiency and skills use. Across all participating countries/economies, proficiency explains only about 5% of the variation in adults' use of numeracy skills at work across all participating countries/economies after accounting for workers' occupation and firm characteristics; it explains even less of the variation in adults' use of literacy skills. This is not to say that skills proficiency does not affect skills use; it does so indirectly through selection into occupations and firms. Put differently, the distribution of skills use among workers with different levels of proficiency overlap substantially. While the median use of both literacy and numeracy skills increases consistently as levels of proficiency increase, it is not uncommon that more proficient workers use their skills at work less intensively than less proficient workers do.

Second, in all the countries/economies covered in the Survey of Adult Skills, the type of jobs held by workers and the human-resource practices adopted in their job are the most important factors explaining the variation in skills use. High-Performance Work Practices – including work organisation and management practices – are positively related to the use of information-processing skills at work. They explain between 14% and 27% of the variation in skills use across adults. The way work is organised – the extent of team work, autonomy, task discretion, mentoring, job rotation and applying new learning – influences the degree of internal flexibility to adapt job tasks to the skills of new hires. Some management practices – bonus pay, training provision and flexibility in working hours – provide incentives for workers to use their skills at work more fully.

Many countries have put initiatives or policies in place to try to promote better skills use through workplace innovation. They recognise that adopting modern leadership and management practices in the workplace can create opportunities for workers to better use their skills, and that productivity gains can be achieved by engaging workers more fully. Concretely, many initiatives focus on raising awareness about the benefits of using skills more effectively, and present High-Performance Work Practices as a win-win option for both employers and workers. Countries have also focused on disseminating good practice and sharing good advice, such as by identifying model firms. In some instances, funding is available to develop diagnostic tools to help companies identify both bottlenecks and measures that will promote better use of their employees' skills. In the context of limited resources, small and medium-size enterprises with growth potential are often targeted on the grounds that employers of smaller firms tend to find it more difficult or costly to adopt innovative work-organisation practices (OECD, 2016a).

Notes

1. This information was originally included for the purpose of measuring the use of generic skills at work. See OECD (2013) and Quintini (2014) for analysis of these variables in Round-1 countries/economies.

2. Questions concerning the frequency of solving problems are only asked in the context of work.

3. It should be borne in mind that these data are self-reported by respondents, and that between-country/economy variations may be partly due to cultural differences in response behaviours. As discussed later in the chapter, cross-country/economy differences will also depend on demand-side factors, such as industry composition, the prevalence of certain contract types, the share of SMEs and the extent to which firms apply work-organisation and management practices that are likely to influence skills deployment at work.

4. These results could also suggest that skills learned and used more frequently in the workplace can transfer to skills use in everyday life.

5. The adjustment is based on multivariate regression analysis. First, both labour productivity and the average use of reading skills at work are separately regressed on average proficiency scores in literacy and numeracy, i.e. they are adjusted to control for the effect of literacy and numeracy proficiency. Then, the residuals of the two regressions are, in turn, regressed on one another. The adjusted results displayed in Figure 4.3 come from such a regression. This is a standard econometric procedure, commonly known as *partitioned regression*.

6. It is possible that the link between skills use at work and productivity may reflect the association between reading (or writing or problem solving) use and the use of other skills, or the link between use and the nature of the work environment (e.g. capital intensity).

7. Singapore provides an interesting example, where the apparently contradictory findings based on the skills-use data and the proficiency data could partly be due to the difference in language-specificity of the two sets of data. Specifically, while the literacy and numeracy proficiencies were measured only in the English language in Singapore, the skills used at work as reported by the respondents in the background questionnaire were non-language-specific.

8. The variance analysis presented here uses Fields (2004) regression-based decomposition technique. This approach is only one way of comparing the importance of a factor as a correlate of skill use. An alternative would be to use regression analysis. The advantage of the variance decomposition approach is that it allows for a comparison of factors that are measured on different scales. See also OECD (2014), Chapter 5.

9. Differences in the use of skills between part-time and full-time workers should be interpreted with caution, as they may simply relate to the fact that part-time workers are less often at work than full-time workers.

10. In the absence of panel data, this interpretation cannot be tested against the alternative possibility that there is a trend towards less-intensive use of certain skills over time. However, given the evolution of technology and labour demand towards more skills-intensive work this latter explanation does not seem particularly plausible.

11. Although the correction also includes contract type, proficiency has the strongest effect.

12. Less than upper secondary considers ISCED levels 0, 1, 2 and 3C short; completed upper secondary education includes ISCED levels 3A, 3B, 3C long or 4A, B, C; and tertiary education considers ISCED levels 5A, B or 6.

13. The adjustment is made using the workers' 1-digit ISCO occupational classification.

14. In the Survey of Adult Skills (PIAAC), approximately 12% of employees reported being employed under a fixed-term contract.

15. Self-employed workers are excluded from these calculations.

16. In the case of Australia, England (United Kingdom) and the United States, this could partly be because of the limited employment protection provided, regardless of the type of job. This is especially the case in the United States, where the distinction between temporary and permanent contracts is much more blurred, and where fixed-term contracts refer to a much more distinctive, and relatively uncommon, form of contract, than they do in other countries. On the other hand and rather surprisingly, this is not the case in New Zealand where differences are relatively large.

17. The literature on organisation capital – covering practices that are similar to those listed as High-Performance Work Practices – provides additional insights into the potential role of management practices on skills use (Squicciarini and Le Mouel, 2012). The *OECD Employment Outlook 2016* provides a more comprehensive analysis on the relationship between High-Performance Work Practices and skills use (OECD, 2016a).

18. To construct a single scale, items are standardised – across countries – to have mean of 2.79 and variance equal to one. The value of Cronbach's alpha for the resulting sum scale is 0.7, suggesting that the items are well-suited to form a single scale.

A note regarding the Russian Federation

The sample for the Russian Federation does not include the population of the Moscow municipal area. The data published, therefore, do not represent the entire resident population aged 16-65 in the Russian Federation but rather the population of the Russian Federation *excluding* the population residing in the Moscow municipal area.

More detailed information regarding the data from the Russian Federation as well as that of other countries can be found in the *Technical Report of the Survey of Adult Skills, Second Edition* (OECD, forthcoming).

References

Autor, D.H. (2001), "Why do temporary help firms provide free general skills training?", *Quarterly Journal of Economics*, Vol. 116/4, pp. 1409-1448.

Blau, F. and **L. Kahn** (2003), "Understanding international differences in the gender pay gap", *Journal of Labor Economics*, Vol. 21/1, pp. 106-144.

Blau, F. and **L. Kahn** (2000), "Gender differences in pay", *Journal of Economic Perspectives*, Vol. 14/4, pp. 75-99.

Bloom, N. and **J. Van Reenen** (2010), "Human resource management and productivity", *NBER Working Paper,* No. 16019.

Brown, C. and **J. Medoff** (1989), "The employer size-wage effect", *Journal of Political Economy*, Vol. 97/5, pp. 1027-1059.

Fields, G.S. (2004), *Regression-based Decompositions: A New Tool for Managerial Decision-making,* Department of Labor Economics, Cornell University, pp. 1-41.

Gibson, J. and **S. Stillman** (2009), "Why do big firms pay higher wages? Evidence from an international database", *The Review of Economics and Statistics*, Vol. 91/1, pp. 213-218.

Goldin, C. (1986), "Monitoring costs and occupational segregation by sex: A historical analysis." *Journal of Labor Economics*, Vol. 4/1, pp. 1-27.

Green, F., A. Felstead, D. Gallie and **H. Inanc** (2013), *Job-related Well-being in Britain, First Findings from the Skills and Employment Survey 2012,* Centre for Learning and Life Chances in Knowledge Economies and Societies, Institute of Education, London.

Johnston, R. and **G. Hawke** (2002), *Case Studies Of Organisations With Established Learning Cultures,* NCVER, Adelaide.

OECD (forthcoming), *Skills and Learning Strategies for Innovation in SMEs,* OECD Centre for SMEs, Entrepreneurship and Local Development, OECD Publishing, Paris.

OECD (2016a), *OECD Employment Outlook 2016*, OECD Publishing, Paris, http://dx.doi.org/10.1787/empl_outlook-2016-en.

OECD (2016b), *Survey of Adult Skills (PIAAC)* (Database 2012, 2015), www.oecd.org/site/piaac/publicdataandanalysis.htm.

OECD (2014), *OECD Employment Outlook 2014*, OECD Publishing, Paris, http://dx.doi.org/10.1787/empl_outlook-2014-en.

OECD (2013), *OECD Skills Outlook 2013: First Results from the Survey of Adult Skills*, OECD Publishing, Paris, http://dx.doi.org/10.1787/9789264204256-en.

OECD (2012), *Closing the Gender Gap: Act Now*, OECD Publishing, Paris, http://dx.doi.org/10.1787/9789264179370-en.

OECD (2006), *OECD Employment Outlook 2006*, OECD Publishing, Paris, http://dx.doi.org/10.1787/empl_outlook-2006-en.

Quintini, G. (2014), "Skills at work: How skills and their use matter in the labour market", *OECD Social, Employment and Migration Working Papers*, No. 158, OECD Publishing, Paris, http://dx.doi.org/10.1787/5jz44fdfjm7j-en.

Squicciarini, M. and **M. Le Mouel** (2012), "Defining and measuring investment in organisational capital: Using US microdata to develop a task-based approach", *OECD Science, Technology and Industry Working Papers*, No. 2012/05, OECD Publishing, Paris, http://dx.doi.org/10.1787/5k92n2t3045b-en.

UKCES (2014), *The Labour Market Story: Skills Use at Work, Briefing Paper,* UK Commission for Employment and Skills.

Wright J. and **P. Sissons** (2012), *The Skills Dilemma – Skills Under-Utilisation and Low-Wage Work – A Bottom Ten Million Research Paper*, The Work Foundation, Lancaster University, www.theworkfoundation.com/DownloadPublication/Report/307_Skills%20Dilemma.pdf.

5

The outcomes of investment in skills

This chapter looks at the extent to which proficiency in literacy, numeracy and problem solving in technology-rich environments makes a difference to the well-being of individuals and nations. The answer that emerges is clear: proficiency is positively linked to a number of important economic and social outcomes.

To what extent does proficiency in information-processing skills make a difference to the labour-market outcomes and well-being of individuals and nations? Previous chapters of this report have examined the level and distribution of these skills among countries and different groups in the population, as revealed through the Survey of Adult Skills, a product of the OECD Programme for the International Assessment of Adult Competencies (PIAAC). They have also discussed the relationship between proficiency and factors that are thought to help adults develop and maintain their proficiency. This chapter examines the relationship between proficiency and some aspects of individual and social well-being: employment, earnings, and individual and social outcomes like health, participation in associative or volunteer activities, and the sense of influence on the political process.

Among the main findings discussed in this chapter:

- In most countries and economies, proficiency in information-processing skills is positively associated with the probability of being employed and earning higher wages. In practically all countries/economies, proficiency in literacy is valued independently of educational qualifications or experience.

- After the effects of educational attainment are taken into account, a 48 score-point increase in an individual's literacy proficiency (equivalent to one standard deviation) is associated with a 0.8 percentage-point increase in the likelihood of being employed as opposed to being unemployed. For salaried employees, an increase of one standard deviation in literacy proficiency is associated with a 6% increase in hourly wages, on average across OECD countries/economies that participated in the survey.

- In England (United Kingdom), Ireland, Lithuania, New Zealand, the Slovak Republic, Spain and Sweden, proficiency in literacy is a comparatively accurate predictor of employment. In England (United Kingdom), Israel, New Zealand, Singapore and the United States, proficiency in literacy is a comparatively strong predictor of higher wages. In Chile, Jakarta (Indonesia), Singapore, Slovenia and Turkey, educational qualifications are most strongly related to wages.

- Mismatches between skills and what is required or expected at work are pervasive, but only when workers are overqualified do they suffer a strong wage penalty. On average across OECD countries/economies that participated in the survey, about 22% of workers reported that they are overqualified – that they have higher qualifications than required to get their jobs – and 13% reported that they are underqualified for their jobs – that they have lower qualifications than required to get their jobs. Moreover, 11% have higher literacy skills than those typically required in their job, and 4% are underskilled. Some 40% of workers work in an occupation that is unrelated to their field of study.

- Overqualification has a significant impact on wages, even after adjusting for proficiency. Mismatch by field of study does not have a strong impact on wages; in many countries, the impact is not necessarily negative. Only when workers work outside their field and become overqualified do field-mismatched workers suffer a significant wage penalty.

- Proficiency in literacy, numeracy and problem solving in technology-rich environments is positively associated with other aspects of well-being. Adults who scored at lower levels of proficiency on the literacy scale were more likely than those who scored at high levels to have reported poor health, that they have little impact on the political process, and that they do not participate in associative or volunteer activities. Individuals with lower proficiency were also more likely than those with higher proficiency to have reported less trust in others.

The results, which focus primarily on literacy proficiency, suggest that, independent of policies designed to increase participation in education and training, improvements in adults' skills proficiency may provide potentially significant economic and social returns for individuals and society a whole.[1] Adults' proficiency can be improved through formal schooling, programmes for adults with poor literacy and numeracy skills or with limited familiarity with ICTs, training in the workplace, and better use of skills in and outside of work.

SKILLS PROFICIENCY, LABOUR MARKET STATUS AND WAGES[2]

To the extent that workers' productivity is related to the knowledge and skills they have, and that wages reflect such productivity, albeit imperfectly, individuals with more skills should expect higher returns from labour market participation and would thus be more likely to participate in the labour market. Most studies use educational qualifications attained in the past as a proxy for individuals' current productive potential when investigating the returns to investments in human capital. Until the Survey of Adult Skills (PIAAC), only a few studies examined the returns to actual skills (e.g. Leuven, Oosterbek and van Ophem, 2004; Tyler, 2004). PIAAC provides more precise, recent and comparative information on how a person's current skills proficiency positively influences his or her likelihood to work and his or her wages (e.g. Hanushek et al., 2013; OECD, 2013; Vignoles, 2016).[3]

Analyses for the 24 countries and economies that participated in the Survey of Adult Skills in 2011-12 (Round-1 countries/ economies) concluded that, after the effects of educational attainment are taken into account, an increase of one standard deviation in an individual's literacy proficiency (46 score points[4]) is associated with a 20% increase in the probability of being employed as opposed to being unemployed. In this group of countries, and for salaried employees, an increase of one standard deviation in literacy proficiency is also associated with an 8% increase in hourly wages (OECD, 2013). As will be shown in the following sections, similar findings hold when considering countries and economies that participated in the survey in 2014-15 (Round-2 countries/economies).

Proficiency and employment

When the total population is divided into the three standard labour market groups – i.e. employed, unemployed and inactive – the average proficiency in literacy among employed adults is generally higher than that among unemployed and inactive adults (Figure 5.1). However, the differences in proficiency are surprisingly small.[5] Across the OECD countries/ economies that participated in the Survey of Adult Skills, the average literacy score of employed adults is about 11 score points higher (about 4%) than that of unemployed adults, which, in turn, is almost identical to that of inactive adults.

Figure 5.1 ■ Mean proficiency in literacy, by labour force status

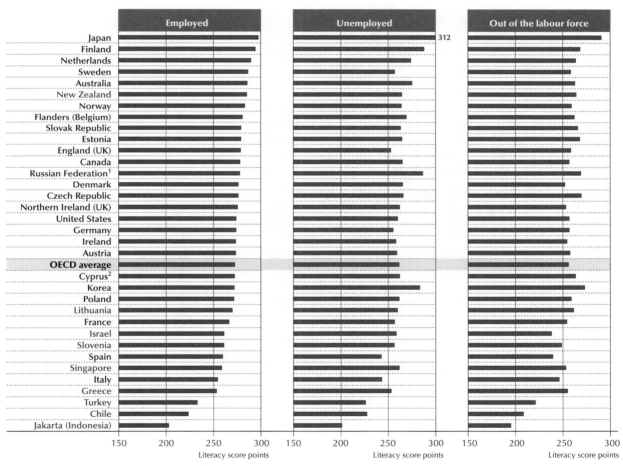

Note: Proficiency in literacy ranges between 0 and 500 score points.

1. See note at the end of this chapter.

2. *Note by Turkey:* The information in this document with reference to "Cyprus" relates to the southern part of the Island. There is no single authority representing both Turkish and Greek Cypriot people on the Island. Turkey recognises the Turkish Republic of Northern Cyprus (TRNC). Until a lasting and equitable solution is found within the context of the United Nations, Turkey shall preserve its position concerning the "Cyprus issue".

Note by all the European Union Member States of the OECD and the European Union: The Republic of Cyprus is recognised by all members of the United Nations with the exception of Turkey. The information in this document relates to the area under the effective control of the Government of the Republic of Cyprus.

Countries and economies are ranked in descending order of workers' mean literacy score.

Source: Survey of Adult Skills (PIAAC) (2012, 2015), Table A5.1 (L).

StatLink ⧉ http://dx.doi.org/10.1787/888933366299

This relatively small difference can be partly attributed to the high rate of unemployment among young people and the fact that many are inactive as they remain in education. Given that proficiency peaks at the age of 30, as described in Chapter 3, young people may be more proficient than their older counterparts, driving up the average literacy score of unemployed or inactive adults. In addition, the difference in proficiency between employed and unemployed adults is much larger when only those individuals who have been unemployed for longer than 12 months – the long-term unemployed – are used in the comparison.

Overall, while there is a relatively large pool of highly proficient adults who are out of work, either unemployed or inactive, some caveats are in order. First, it is important to keep in mind that while some unemployed adults may have scores in literacy, numeracy and problem solving in technology-rich environments that are similar to those of employed adults, they may lack other key skills needed to get a job, for example, job-specific skills or generic skills frequently required at work, such as self-organising skills.

Second, some inactivity might be voluntary and temporary, such as among young people who are still engaged in full-time education or skilled men and women who are caring for family members (Leaker, 2009). Differences in skills proficiency between unemployed and employed adults may be small in countries that offer little unemployment protection as it is those individuals with higher skills and better-paying jobs who can save and afford to spend time unemployed while looking for a job; low-skilled workers are often forced to find a job, any job, as quickly as possible to maintain some income and avoid falling into poverty (OECD, 2014a).

At the same time, the relatively high proficiency found among unemployed adults is important for labour market policy in identifying well-targeted skills-development programmes. Mismatches between people's skills and the skill requirements for jobs, in addition to various institutional constraints, are likely to prevent skilled people from engaging in employment or looking for work.

The skills proficiency among different groups of workers, based on their employment status, highlights the importance of taking stock of the skills held by unemployed individuals at the start of a period of unemployment, both in the domains assessed by the Survey of Adult Skills and in other key areas relevant to labour market needs, including job-specific and generic skills. This would help public employment services to identify the most appropriate course of action for each job-seeker, and to target interventions to ensure that unemployed adults remain motivated, gain relevant skills and do not suffer from skills obsolescence by not putting skills to use (OECD, 2015a).

Literacy proficiency, education and employment

Are workers' actual information-processing skills or their educational attainment better predictors of employment? The relationship between skills proficiency and the likelihood of employment could be the result of compositional effects. Proficiency could simply be the reflection of higher educational attainment, which, in turn, affects the likelihood of employment. This is generally not the case, however. Proficiency plays an important and independent role as a determinant of success in the labour market, over and above the role played by formal education. Although it may be intuitive that adults with higher skills proficiency are more likely to be employed, the direction of cause and effect is unclear. For example, employment may itself favour skills acquisition or prevent the depreciation of workers' skills that are not put to use when adults are unemployed.

Across the OECD countries/economies that participated in the Survey of Adult Skills, an individual who scores 48 points higher than another on the literacy scale (the equivalent to one standard deviation) is 0.8 percentage point more likely to be employed than unemployed (see Figure 5.2). An increase of 3.2 years in formal education (the equivalent of one standard deviation) is related to a 3.1 percentage-point increase in the likelihood of being employed. The relationship between skills proficiency and the likelihood of employment is strongest in England (United Kingdom), Ireland, Lithuania, New Zealand, the Slovak Republic, Spain and Sweden.

The relationship between years of education and the likelihood of employment is strongest in the Czech Republic, Ireland, Lithuania, Poland, the Slovak Republic and Slovenia, where an individual with an additional 3.2 years of education is at least 5 percentage-points more likely to be employed. In Chile, Korea, Northern Ireland (United Kingdom) and Turkey, neither skills proficiency nor years of education are predictive of workers' employment status. Among Round-2 countries/economies, in New Zealand and Lithuania, both years of education and proficiency in literacy predict workers' likelihood of being employed.

The effect of literacy proficiency is computed by comparing the likelihood of being employed among adults with different proficiency in literacy, but who have spent the same number of years in education. Similarly, the effect of years of education is computed by comparing adults with similar proficiency in literacy but who have spent a different number of years in education. Such a calculation is possible because of the imperfect overlap of education and proficiency, as discussed in previous chapters.

Figure 5.2 ▪ **Effect of education and literacy proficiency on the likelihood of being employed**

Marginal effects (as percentage point change) of a one standard deviation increase in years of education or literacy on the likelihood of being employed among adults not in formal education

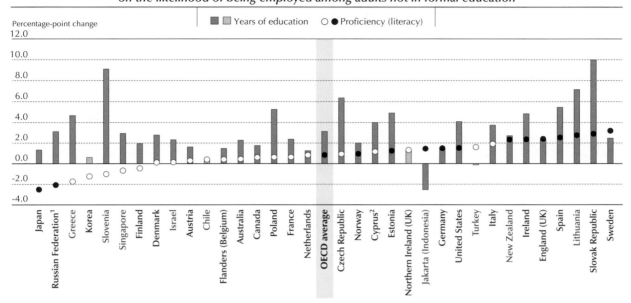

Notes: The reference category is «unemployed». Results are adjusted for gender, age, marital and foreign-born status. One standard deviation in proficiency in literacy for the working population is 48 score points. One standard deviation in years of education is 3.2 years for the working population. Statistically significant values (at the 10% level) are shown in a darker tone.
1. See note at the end of this chapter.
2. See note 2 under Figure 5.1.
Countries and economies are ranked in ascending order of the effect of proficiency on the likelihood of being employed.
Source: Survey of Adult Skills (PIAAC) (2012, 2015), Table A5.2.
StatLink http://dx.doi.org/10.1787/888933366304

Educational attainment is a better predictor of employment than skills proficiency. Since it is difficult for employers to judge workers' actual skills proficiency before or outside of work, they are more likely to rely on readily available, albeit potentially imperfect, signals, such as educational qualifications. Skills thus become a stronger predictor of labour market outcomes when workers have more experience and have shown in work what they are capable of doing, a phenomenon called "employer learning" (OECD, 2014b).

An important result of this analysis, which is confirmed in 14 of the 33 participating countries and economies is that proficiency in literacy plays a role in the likelihood that an adult in the labour force will be employed. This highlights the importance of job-matching policies to ensure that workers' skills are recognised and pay off. In these countries, skills proficiency is recognised and valued in finding employment, highlighting the importance of skills development in active labour market policies to help unemployed adults find work. These results suggest that in these countries there may be more direct rewards to lifelong learning and the development of skills beyond school.

These findings suggest that improving literacy, numeracy and problem-solving skills, together with the ability of employers to identify and recognise these skills, may have a significant impact on the likelihood of being employed, beyond encouraging participation in education and training. Improving the quality of instruction in reading and mathematics in schools, for example, could have long-term beneficial effects, as could improving the quality, targeting and the availability of adult learning opportunities and ensuring that adults' skills are put to use to avoid depreciation.

Proficiency and wages

Hourly wages are strongly associated with skills proficiency (Figure 5.3).[6] On average across the OECD countries/ economies that participated in the Survey of Adult Skills, the median hourly wage of salaried employees scoring at Level 4 or 5 on the literacy scale is 65% higher than that of workers scoring at or below Level 1. Differences in returns to proficiency vary across countries and economies, more so than for employment status. In Greece, as in Denmark, Finland, Norway and Sweden, the distribution of wages appears to be compressed:[7] the median worker scoring at Level 4 or 5 on the literacy scale earns no more than 40% more than the median worker scoring at or below Level 1.

Figure 5.3 [1/2] ▪ **Distribution of wages, by literacy proficiency level**

25th, 50th and 75th percentiles of the wage distribution

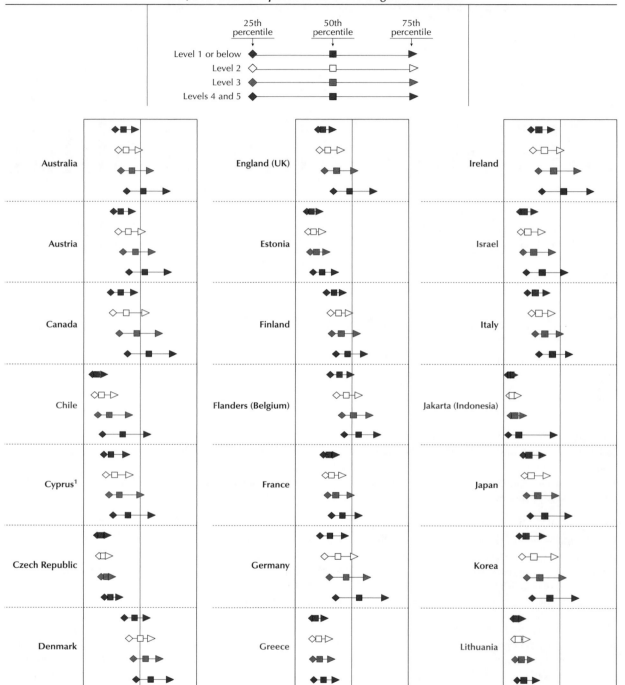

Notes: Employees only. Hourly wages, including bonuses, in purchasing-power-parity-adjusted USD (2012). The analysis excludes the Russian Federation because wage data obtained through the survey do not compare well with those available from other sources. Hence further checks are required before wage data for this country can be considered reliable.

1. See note 2 under Figure 5.1.

Countries and economies are listed in alphabetical order.

Source: Survey of Adult Skills (PIAAC) (2012, 2015), Table 5.3 (L).

StatLink ᴀᴬᴴ᳘ http://dx.doi.org/10.1787/888933366318

Figure 5.3 [2/2] ■ **Distribution of wages, by literacy proficiency level**

25th, 50th and 75th percentiles of the wage distribution

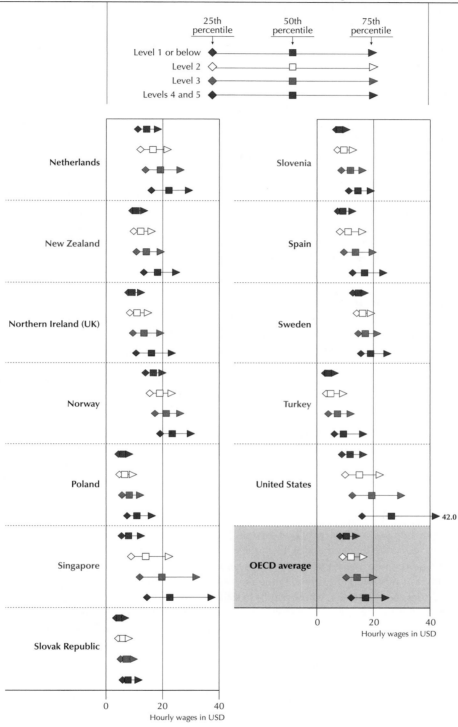

Notes: Employees only. Hourly wages, including bonuses, in purchasing-power-parity-adjusted USD (2012). The analysis excludes the Russian Federation because wage data obtained through the survey do not compare well with those available from other sources. Hence further checks are required before wage data for this country can be considered reliable.

Countries and economies are listed in alphabetical order.

Source: Survey of Adult Skills (PIAAC) (2012, 2015), Table 5.3 (L).

StatLink ⟶ http://dx.doi.org/10.1787/888933366318

At the other extreme, returns to greater proficiency in literacy appear to be extremely large in Jakarta (Indonesia), Korea, Turkey and the United States, where the median worker scoring at Level 4 or 5 earns more than double that of the median worker scoring at or below Level 1. In Chile and Singapore, the median worker in the highest proficiency levels earns almost three times more than the median worker scoring at or below Level 1.

There is significant overlap in the distribution of wages by proficiency level within and across countries. For instance, on average across the OECD countries/economies that participated in the Survey of Adult Skills, the top 25% best-paid workers scoring at Level 2 earn about the same as the median worker scoring at Level 4 or 5, a result that is also observed in Israel, Singapore and Turkey. In Greece and Lithuania, the top 25% best-paid workers scoring at Level 2 in literacy earn 19% and 13% more, respectively, than the median hourly wage of those scoring at Level 4 or 5 (Figure 5.3), suggesting that although literacy is an important and valued skill in the labour market, other skills or attributes are rewarded as well. In Chile, the median worker scoring at proficiency Level 4 or 5 earns almost 30% more than the top earners in Level 2, suggesting that literacy skills are accurate predictors of higher wages.

The assessment allows for a comparison of the earnings of workers with similar proficiency across countries/economies. The median worker scoring at Level 2 in New Zealand and Singapore earns higher hourly wages than the median worker scoring at Level 4 or 5 in the Czech Republic, Estonia, Greece, Jakarta (Indonesia), Lithuania, Poland, the Slovak Republic and Turkey. Put another way, the bottom 25% of earners among workers scoring at Level 4 or 5 in New Zealand and Singapore earn more than the top 25% of earners scoring at the same level in the Czech Republic, Lithuania and the Slovak Republic. These international comparisons raise interesting questions concerning the variation in how literacy skills determine workers' wages and productivity.

Literacy proficiency, education and wages

The relationship between wages and skills proficiency is explored in more detail by adjusting for several individual characteristics, including years of education. Cause and effect between skills proficiency and wages is unclear. Higher wages may be characteristic of occupations that favour workers' skills acquisition through formal training, for example. Distinguishing years of education from skills proficiency in the returns to skills helps determine whether returns to skills merely reflect the fact that high-educated individuals tend to have – but not always do have – higher skills proficiency. This section shows that skills proficiency plays an important and independent role in determining wages, over and above the role played by formal education.

Proficiency and schooling have significant and distinct effects on hourly wages.[8] The increase in wages associated with a one standard deviation increase in literacy proficiency (around 48 points for the working population) ranges from less than 4% in Finland, Greece, Italy, Lithuania and Spain, to 10% or more in England (United Kingdom), Israel, Singapore and the United States (Figure 5.4). The increase in wages associated with a one standard deviation rise in years of education (around 3.4 years for the working population) is larger, ranging from less than 7% in Sweden to more than 20% in Chile, Jakarta (Indonesia), Slovenia, Turkey and the United States, and to more than 30% in Singapore.

Part of the effect of proficiency on hourly wages may be based on the type of tasks and responsibilities that are part of a worker's job. In addition to years of education and skills proficiency, Figure 5.4 considers the use of reading skills at work. Workers in jobs that require more intense use of reading also earn higher wages, pointing to the fact that wages do not just reflect the supply of skills (workers), but also the demand for skills (employers). This is especially true in England (United Kingdom), Estonia and Lithuania, where returns to skills use are the highest among participating countries. Including skills use at work in the models also serves to show that the effect of skills use proficiency is not driven by selection. It is not that more proficient workers earn more because they are selected for more skills-intensive jobs, but rather that they earn higher wages even when compared to workers in jobs with similar skill requirements.

One can also adjust the estimates by other indicators of skills use at work. Not surprisingly, the inclusion of skills-use variables weakens the effect of both education and proficiency on wages by about a third, on average.[9] In about half of the participating countries/economies, co-operative skills, influence and task discretion, are positively and significantly correlated with wages, while dexterity is negatively and significantly correlated with wages. In most countries/economies, the use of physical skills is negatively and significantly correlated with wages, while the use of information-processing skills, such as writing, familiarity with ICTs and problem solving, is positively and significantly correlated with wages. The fact that skills use, over and above general proficiency and education, influences wages strengthens the findings on skills mismatch presented below.

Overall, the number of years spent in education tends to have a smaller impact on wages in countries/economies with a more compressed wage distribution, such as the Nordic countries, Flanders (Belgium) and Italy (see OECD, 2015a).

By contrast, greater proficiency and educational attainment are associated with significantly higher wages in Chile, Israel, Jakarta (Indonesia), Singapore and the United States, all of which have relatively high earnings inequality. However, this only suggests a link between the earnings distribution and returns to education, as other factors affect the ranking of countries/economies. For instance, Slovenia, where earnings inequality by proficiency level is relatively low, shows relatively high returns to education.

Figure 5.4 ▪ **Effect of education, literacy proficiency and use of reading at work on wages**

Percentage change in wages associated with a one standard deviation increase in years of education, proficiency in literacy and use of reading at work

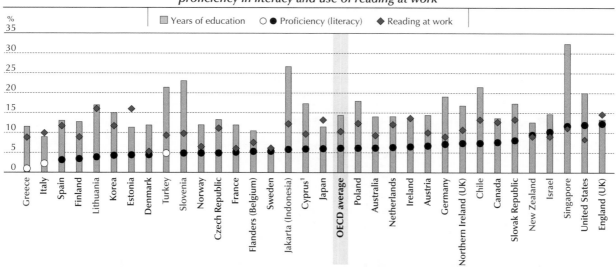

Notes: Hourly wages, including bonuses, in PPP-adjusted USD (2012). Coefficients from the OLS regression of log hourly wages on years of education, proficiency and use of reading skills at work, directly interpreted as percentage effects on wages. Coefficients adjusted for age, gender, foreign-born status and tenure. The wage distribution was trimmed to eliminate the 1st and 99th percentiles. One standard deviation in proficiency in literacy is 48 points. One standard deviation in years of education is 3.2 years. The analysis excludes the Russian Federation because wage data obtained through the survey do not compare well with those available from other sources. Hence further checks are required before wage data for this country can be considered reliable. Statistically significant values (at the 10% level) are shown in a darker tone.
1. See note 2 under Figure 5.1.
Countries and economies are ranked in ascending order of the effect of literacy proficiency on wages.
Source: Survey of Adult Skills (PIAAC) (2012, 2015), Table A5.4.
StatLink ⫘ http://dx.doi.org/10.1787/888933366323

Finally, all of the above analyses assume that the effects of educational attainment and proficiency on wages are independent; but some recent research suggests that this may not be the case. In the recent past, several OECD countries have reported a sharp increase in wage inequality at the very top of the earnings distribution (OECD, 2015a, 2015b, 2013). One explanation for this is that the returns to skills are significantly larger for the most-educated individuals. Analysis of results from the Survey of Adult Skills confirms this hypothesis. In over half of the countries, estimates of returns to proficiency increase with qualifications, pointing to larger returns to skills acquisition for those who are already highly qualified.

Educational attainment and proficiency in information-processing skills contribute independently to explaining individuals' wages. But what is the relative contribution of each? And what is their relative contribution compared to other human-capital wage determinants, like experience or individual characteristics? The answer to these questions is complicated by the fact that educational attainment and proficiency are measured according to different metrics: years of education and assessment scores, respectively. One way of overcoming this restriction is by analysing how much a standard deviation in educational attainment (or skills proficiency) relates to wages. Another is to look at how much of the variation in wages is explained by each variable (OECD, 2014b).

Human capital components, that is experience, years of education, field of study and proficiency in literacy and numeracy, account for almost 30% of the variation in wages, on average across countries/economies. Information-processing skills contribute 5%, educational attainment accounts for 13%, field of study 1% and experience accounts for 9%, on average across the OECD countries and economies that have participated in the Survey of Adult Skills. Individual characteristics, like gender, immigrant background, marital status and language spoken at home, account for 4% combined. More than 60% is related to other individual and human capital characteristics. Skills use, occupation, industry and firm characteristics also determine individual wages.[10]

Proficiency in literacy and numeracy, education, field of study and experience can all be considered different aspects of workers' human capital. The contribution of literacy and numeracy skills, relative to educational attainment, field of study and experience, is greatest in England (United Kingdom), Estonia and Israel, where workers' proficiency explains a third of the overall contribution of the different components of human capital. In Chile, Jakarta (Indonesia), Japan, New Zealand and Slovenia, the relative importance of skills proficiency is also high, explaining more than one-fifth of the variation in wages. These are countries where the returns to skills are more important in understanding the returns to human capital.

Years of education are most relevant, *vis-a-vis* information-processing skills and experience, in the Czech Republic, Lithuania and Poland, where they account for more than two-thirds of the overall variation in wages explained by components of human capital. These are countries where educational credentials have more power in explaining the wage distribution. As a component of human capital, experience accounts for a larger share in Flanders (Belgium), Greece, Ireland and the Netherlands (Figure 5.5).

Figure 5.5 ▪ **Contribution of education, literacy and numeracy to the variation of hourly wages**
Contribution of each factor to the percentage of the explained variance (R-squared) in hourly wages

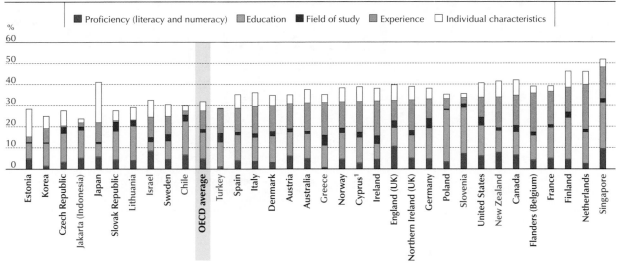

Notes: Results obtained using a regression-based decomposition following the methods in Fields (2004). Each bar summarises the results from one regression and its height represents the R-squared of that regression. The sub-componets of each bar show the contribution of each factor (or set of regressors) to the total R-squared. The Fields decomposition is explained in more detail in Box 5.4 of the *OECD Employment Outlook 2014* (OECD, 2014b).

The dependent variable in the regression model is the log of hourly wages, including bonuses in PPP-adjusted USD (2012). The regressors for each factor are: years of working experience and its squared term for "Experience"; proficiency in literacy and numeracy for "Proficiency"; years of education for "Education"; and gender, marital status, migration status and language spoken at home for "Individual characteristics".

The analysis excludes the Russian Federation because wage data obtained through the survey do not compare well with those available from other sources. Hence, further checks are required before wage data for this country can be considered reliable.

1. See note 2 under Figure 5.1.

Countries and economies are ranked in ascending order of the sum of the contributions of education, proficiency, field of study and experience.

Source: Survey of Adult Skills (PIAAC) (2012, 2015), Table A5.5.

StatLink ▪ http://dx.doi.org/10.1787/888933366332

The phenomenon of employer learning is most clearly illustrated in Figure 5.6. Information-processing skills and experience explain a larger share of the variation in wages among prime-age (30-49 years) and older workers (50-65 years) than among younger workers (16-29 years), on average across participating OECD countries/economies. The components of human capital (years of education, proficiency in literacy and numeracy, field of study and experience) explain a larger share of the variation in wages among prime-age and older workers. Across all participating countries/economies, and net of differences between them, proficiency in numeracy and literacy accounts for 3% of the variation in wages among younger adults, 6% among prime-age workers and 5% among older workers. Experience accounts for a larger part among young adults than prime-age workers, highlighting the importance of work-experience training schemes and the value of work-related skills for youth.

There are gender differences in the extent to which different components account for wages. Proficiency in numeracy and literacy and experience account for a larger share of the variation in wages among men than women, but educational attainment accounts for a greater share of wage variation among women than among men.

Figure 5.6 ▪ Contribution of education, literacy and numeracy to the variation of hourly wages, by age group and gender

Contribution of each factor to the percentage of the explained variance (R-squared) in hourly wages in OECD countries/economies participating in the Survey of Adult Skills (PIAAC)

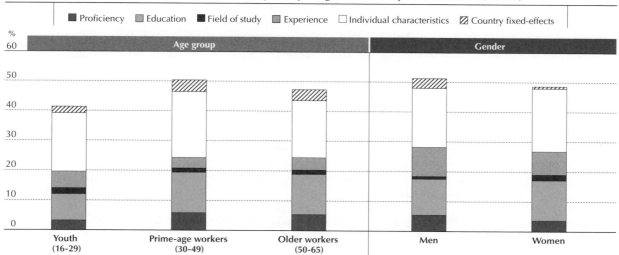

Notes: The dependant variable is the log of hourly wages, including bonuses, in PPP-adjusted USD (2012). The factors are: years of work experience and a squared term; proficiency in literacy and numeracy; years of education; and demographic variables (gender, marital status, immigrant background and the language spoken at home).

Results obtained using regression-based decomposition through the formulae proposed by Fields (2004). Each bar summarises the results from one regression and the height of each bar represents the total R-squared for that regression. The subcomponents of each bar show the contribution of each factor (or set of regressors) to the R-squared. The Fields decomposition is explained in more detail in Box 5.4 of the *OECD Employment Outlook 2014* (OECD, 2014b).

Source: Survey of Adult Skills (PIAAC) (2012, 2015), Tables A5.6a and A5.6b.

StatLink ᴍᴰᴾ http://dx.doi.org/10.1787/888933366349

These results suggest that educational attainment, experience and proficiency in literacy and numeracy reflect different aspects of individuals' human capital, each of which has independent and statistically significant effects on wages. Educational attainment, either in itself or expressed as years of education, represents a wider set of knowledge and skills, including job- and domain-specific competencies, as well as personal attributes, than does proficiency in the domains assessed in the Survey of Adult Skills. Since it is more difficult for a prospective employer to assess skills than qualifications, the relative strength of the influence of years of education and proficiency on wages may also reflect the fact that wage negotiations that occur during hiring are based on the observable characteristics of individuals, i.e. formal qualifications, and have a lasting impact on wages.

In the course of the employment relationship, employers may learn about the competencies of their employees, which is then translated into a larger effect of proficiency on wages (Pinkston, 2009). Evidence of this phenomenon of employer learning has been found in the Survey of Adult Skills (OECD, 2014b). However, the fact that proficiency has an independent influence on wages, beyond that of educational attainment, confirms the importance of maintaining and acquiring skills throughout a lifetime. Differences across countries and economies in the magnitude of the effects are heavily influenced by how wages are distributed across occupations and, in turn, by the labour market institutions, such as minimum wages and unions, that affect that distribution.

MISMATCH BETWEEN WORKERS' SKILLS AND JOB REQUIREMENTS, AND ITS IMPACT ON WAGES

Ensuring a good match between the skills acquired in education and on the job and those required in the labour market is essential if countries want to make the most of their investments in human capital and promote strong and inclusive growth. It is also a desirable outcome for individuals who have, themselves, invested in education. A mismatch between workers' skills and the demands of their job has potentially significant economic implications. At the individual level, it affects job satisfaction and wages. At the firm level, it increases the rate of turnover and may reduce productivity. At the macro-economic level, it increases unemployment and reduces GDP growth through the waste of human capital and/or a reduction in productivity (e.g. Adalet McGowan and Andrews, 2015).

Because of the difficulty of measuring the relationship directly, studies infer the consequences of mismatch on productivity either by relying on human capital theory, equating wages to productivity, or by studying the effect of mismatch on job satisfaction. Using these approaches, most studies conclude that, by comparing workers with similar credentials/skills but in jobs for which they are well-matched or overqualified/overskilled, mismatch has a negative impact on productivity: overqualified/overskilled workers earn less than their well-matched peers with similar credentials or skills proficiency.

Adalet McGowan and Andrews (2015) analyse productivity directly and find strong negative effects of mismatch. However, when comparing workers performing a similar job, those who are overqualified are more productive, as they have more human capital than their colleagues (Kampelmann and Rycx, 2012). Thus, at the firm level, mismatch can lead to higher productivity; but, on the aggregate level, this may not be the case.

Yet some level of mismatch is inevitable. Requirements regarding skills and qualifications are never fixed. The task content of jobs changes over time in response to technological and organisational change, the demands of customers, and in response to the evolution of the supply of labour. Young people leaving education and people moving from unemployment into employment, for example, may take jobs that do not necessarily fully match their qualifications and skills. Thus, for a number of reasons, some workers are likely to be employed in jobs for which they are too qualified and others may be in jobs, at least temporarily, for which they lack adequate schooling.

Mismatch, understood as a poor fit between an individual worker's qualifications or skills and those demanded or required by his or her job, needs to be distinguished from aggregate balances or imbalances in the supply of and demand for different types of qualifications and skills in the labour market, such as skill shortages or the oversupply or undersupply of people with different educational qualifications or skills. Although these two phenomena are distinct, they are, nevertheless, related.

Imbalances (e.g. shortages or oversupply of individuals with particular qualifications or skills) have an effect on the prevalence and type of mismatches observed at the individual level (Montt, 2015). But that relationship is not automatic. A balance between the supply of and demand for workers at a given qualification does not guarantee that individual workers will be matched to jobs that require the level of education they have attained. A high level of mismatch at the individual level does not imply any particular level of imbalance between aggregate supply and demand.

The discussion of qualification, field-of-study and skills mismatch that follows focuses on the question of mismatch at the individual level, that is, on the outcomes of allocating individuals to jobs and adapting job tasks to workers' skills. It does not address the extent of the balance or imbalance in the supply of and demand for individuals with particular educational qualifications or skills. From this perspective, any evidence of mismatch between workers' qualifications and skills and those required by their jobs should be interpreted primarily as suggesting that there are economic benefits (and benefits in terms of the well-being of workers) to be gained from better management of human resources. The evidence should not be interpreted as indicating the existence of "overeducation" or "overskilling" in the economy as a whole.

Mismatch in the Survey of Adult Skills

The Survey of Adult Skills provides a rare opportunity to simultaneously measure qualification, field-of-study and skills mismatch. Some workers may be overqualified or underqualified for their jobs. Others may be working in a sector of the economy (or in a job) that is unrelated to their field of study. And other workers may be mismatched in a particular type of skill, like numeracy, if their ability to deal with numbers, calculation and other numeracy tasks exceeds (or is insufficient for) those required by the job. (Box 5.1 provides more details on measuring these forms of mismatch in the Survey of Adult Skills).

Because qualifications do not accurately reflect actual skills held by individuals – not even those acquired in initial education – and occupations do not accurately describe the specific job held by an individual, the resulting measures of qualification and field-of-study mismatch do not precisely describe how a worker's skills set matches the skills needed to carry out his or her tasks at work. Skills mismatch refers more precisely to a worker's actual skills and to the skills needed in his or her specific job.

Despite these important differences, the three measures of mismatch overlap to some extent, in the same way as education and skills do. Some researchers use the term "genuine mismatch" to indicate when a worker is both overqualified <u>and</u> overskilled (or both underqualified <u>and</u> underskilled) for his or her job. The term "apparent qualification mismatch"[11] is used to refer to workers who are overqualified (underqualified) but not overskilled (underskilled).

For instance, workers may hold a tertiary qualification but not have the skills expected of a tertiary graduate, making them overqualified but not overskilled for a job normally requiring an upper secondary qualification. Similarly, field-of-study mismatch is generally accompanied by overqualification. Workers who find jobs outside their field may not have their highest qualification recognised and must settle for a job that requires lower educational attainment. As such, they may be also overskilled if they do not use all their skills in their mismatched job.

Although qualifications are an imperfect proxy for skills, qualification and field-of-study mismatch should not be simply dismissed as a "bad" measure of skills mismatch. First, by uncovering the causes of "apparent" qualification mismatch, for example when there is a mismatch between the skills learned in school and those required in the labour market, the areas requiring policy intervention are revealed. Second, workers have many different skills, ranging from information-processing skills, to occupation-specific/sector-specific knowledge and abilities, to generic skills. As a result, any concept of mismatch based on an individual's skills offers only a partial view of the match between a worker and his or her job.

Qualifications reflect several different skills, including both information-processing and job-specific competencies, and could complement narrower, though more precise, skills measures. Field-of-study, if associated with qualifications mismatch, may reflect the difficulty workers face in having their credentials recognised and valued in other fields. In addition, skills use depends, at least partly, on the effort that workers invest in their jobs, making it difficult to define precise skills requirements. Qualification requirements are easier to define.

Thus, several measures of qualifications and skills mismatch can be derived using the data available from the Survey of Adult Skills on qualifications, field of study, occupation skill requirements and skills use (Table 5.1 and Box 5.1). Analysing them simultaneously and seeing how they overlap offers insights into the linkages between education and the labour market, and sheds light on appropriate policy responses (e.g. Montt, 2015; OECD, 2016a).

Table 5.1 **Glossary of key terms related to mismatch**

	Mismatch concept	Measure used in this chapter
Qualification mismatch	Overqualification	A worker is classified as overqualified when the difference between his or her qualification level and the qualification level required in his or her job is positive.
	Underqualification	A worker is classified as underqualified when the difference between his or her qualification level and the qualification level required in his or her job is negative.
	Required qualification	Based on respondents' answers to the question "If applying today, what would be the usual qualifications, if any, that someone would need to get this type of job?" Qualifications were translated into years of education based on the structure of each country's education system.
Skills mismatch in literacy, numeracy or problem solving	Overskilling in literacy, numeracy or problem solving	When a worker's proficiency is above the maximum required by his or her job.
	Underskilling in literacy, numeracy or problem solving	When a worker's proficiency is below the minimum required by his or her job.
	Skill requirements	The minimum and maximum levels required correspond to the minimum and maximum observed proficiency of workers who answer negatively to both questions used to identify self-reported over- and underskilling.
Field-of-study mismatch	Mismatch by field of study	A worker is classified as mismatched by field of study if the area of study of his or her highest qualification is not related to the field that is most relevant to the worker's job following the coding used by Wolbers (2003), Quintini (2011) and, for ISCO 08 occupations, Montt (2015).
	Matched by field of study	A worker's area of study of his or her highest qualification matches the field of study that is most relevant for his or her job.

Sources: Montt, G. (2015), "The causes and consequences of field-of-study mismatch: An analysis using PIAAC", *OECD Social, Employment and Migration Working Papers,* No. 167; Quintini, G. (2011), "Right for the job: Over-qualified or under-skilled?", *OECD Social, Employment and Migration Working Papers,* No. 120; Wolbers, M. (2003), "Job mismatches and their labour market effects among school-leavers in Europe", *European Sociological Review,* Vol. 19, pp. 249-266.

The key way of determining the extent of qualifications mismatch is to measure the level of education required at work.[12] The most frequently used measure is the modal qualification of workers in each occupation and country/economy. However, this measure combines current and past qualification requirements as it reflects the qualifications of people who were hired at different times.

The Survey of Adult Skills asks workers to report the qualifications they consider necessary to get their job today. The comparison between workers' qualifications and this self-reported requirement shows that, on average, 22% of workers are overqualified while about 13% are underqualified (Figure 5.7). The prevalence of qualifications mismatch varies significantly across countries. The share of overqualified workers ranges from less than one in seven workers in Italy, Jakarta (Indonesia), Slovenia and Turkey, to around one in three workers in France, Israel, Japan and New Zealand.

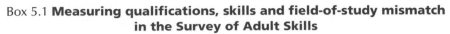

Box 5.1 **Measuring qualifications, skills and field-of-study mismatch in the Survey of Adult Skills**

There are several ways to measure every type of mismatch. Surveys can ask respondents about their own appraisal of potential mismatch (subjective measures), or compare a respondent to what is common in his or her country (statistical approach) or to what is appropriate (normative approach). Each type of measure has its advantages and disadvantages (OECD, 2016a).

Qualifications mismatch arises when workers have an educational attainment that is higher or lower than that required by their job. If their qualification level is higher than that required by their job, workers are classified as overqualified; if the opposite is true, they are classified as underqualified. In the Survey of Adult Skills, workers are asked what would be the usual qualifications, if any, "that someone would need to get (their) type of job if applying today". The answer to this question is used as each worker's qualification requirements and compared to their actual qualifications to identify mismatch. While biased by individual perceptions and period or cohort effects, self-reported qualification requirements along these lines have the advantage of being job-specific rather than assuming that all jobs with the same occupational code require the same level of qualifications.

Skills mismatch arises when workers have higher or lower skills proficiency than that required by their job. If their skills proficiency is higher than that required by their job, workers are classified as overskilled; if the opposite is true, they are classified as underskilled. For the purpose of this chapter, skill requirements at work, the key term in the measurement of skills mismatch, are derived following Pellizzari and Fichen (2013). Though a robust measure, it does not measure mismatch on all possible domains as it focuses on information-processing skills (for other approaches to measuring skills mismatch, see Perry, Wiederhold and Ackermann-Piek, 2014).

Field-of-study mismatch arises when workers are employed in a different field from that in which they have specialised. The matching is based on a list of occupations (at the 3-digit ISCO classification) that are considered as an appropriate match for each field of study. Workers who are not employed in an occupation that is considered a good match for their field are counted as mismatched. The list of fields and occupations used in this chapter can be found in Annex 5 of the *OECD Employment Outlook 2014* (OECD, 2014b). The list is largely based on that developed by Wolbers (2003) but has been adapted to the ISCO08 classification (Montt, 2015).

Sources:

Montt, G. (2015), "The system-level causes and consequences of field-of-study mismatch: An analysis using PIAAC", *OECD Social, Employment and Migration Working Papers*, No. 167, http://dx.doi.org/10.1787/1815199x.

OECD (2016a), *Getting Skills Right: Assessing and Anticipating Changing Skill Needs*, OECD Publishing, Paris. http://dx.doi.org/10.1787/9789264252073-en.

OECD (2014b), *OECD Employment Outlook 2014*, OECD Publishing, Paris, http://dx.doi.org/10.1787/19991266.

Pellizzari, M. and A. Fichen (2013), "A new measure of skills mismatch: Theory and evidence from the Survey of Adult Skills (PIAAC)", *OECD Social, Employment and Migration Working Papers*, No. 153, http://dx.doi.org/10.1787/5k3tpt04lcnt-en.

Perry, A., S. Wiederhold and D. Ackermann-Piek (2014), "How can skill mismatch be measured? New approaches with PIAAC", *Methods, data, analyses*, Vol. 8/2, pp. 137-174, http://dx.doi.org/10.12758/mda.2014.006.

Wolbers, M. (2003), "Job mismatches and their labour market effects among school-leavers in Europe" *European Sociological Review*, Vol. 19, pp. 249-266.

The prevalence of underqualification is lowest in the Czech Republic, Japan and the Slovak Republic. It varies between less than 10% in Lithuania and Israel among Round-2 countries/economies to more than one in six workers in Chile, Italy, the Netherlands and Sweden. This might reflect the rapid growth in educational attainment and the fact that workers today need higher qualifications to enter jobs that were previously accessible to workers with lower qualifications. If this were the case, workers – especially older workers – may have difficulties transitioning to other jobs if their experience is not recognised.[13] The prevalence of overqualification may also be the result of economic cycles: under favourable labour market conditions or full employment, employers seeking employees may recruit less-qualified workers to meet the demand at a given wage rate.

The survey asked workers whether they feel they "have the skills to cope with more demanding duties than those they are required to perform in their current job" and whether they feel they "need further training in order to cope well with their present duties". According to the survey's measure of skills mismatch, workers are classified as well-matched in a domain if their proficiency score in that domain is between the minimum and maximum score observed among workers who answered "no" to both questions in the same occupation and country.[14] Workers are overskilled in a domain if their score is higher than the maximum score of the self-reported well-matched worker; they are underskilled in a domain if their score is lower than the minimum score of the self-reported well-matched worker.

The survey's measure of skills mismatch may be an improvement over existing indicators as it is more robust with respect to reporting bias, such as overconfidence, and it does not impose the strong assumptions needed when directly comparing skills proficiency and skills use.[15] However, this approach does not measure all forms of skills mismatch; it focuses on mismatch in the proficiency domains assessed by the Survey of Adult Skills, leaving out mismatch related to job-specific skills or that involve generic skills. (A detailed discussion of the survey's measure of skills mismatch, its advantages and disadvantages as well as its underlying theoretical framework is presented in Fichen and Pellizzari [2013]).

Figure 5.7 ■ Qualification, literacy and field-of-study mismatch
Percentage of mismatched workers, by type of mismatch

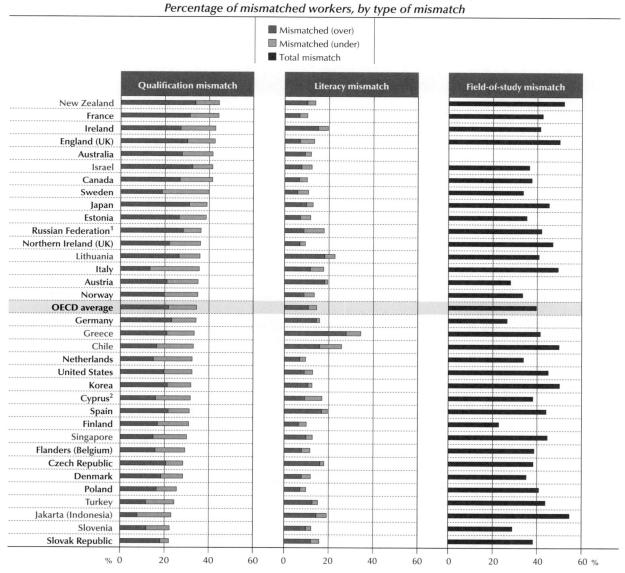

Note: Field-of-study mismatch is unavailable for Australia due to the unavailability of ISCO 3-digit information for Australian workers in the Survey of Adult Skills (PIAAC).

1. See note at the end of this chapter.
2. See note 2 under Figure 5.1.

Countries and economies are ranked in descending order of the prevalence of qualification mismatch (overqualification or underqualification).

Source: Survey of Adult Skills (PIAAC) (2012, 2015), Table A5.7.

StatLink ⟐ http://dx.doi.org/10.1787/888933366353

On average across the OECD countries/economies that participated in the Survey of Adult Skills, about 11% of workers are overskilled while about 4% are underskilled in literacy (Figure 5.7). Austria, Greece and Lithuania show the highest prevalence of overskilling in literacy, while among Round-2 countries, Israel and Singapore are below the average for OECD countries/economies. The prevalence of overskilling is lowest in Canada, Finland, France and Sweden. By contrast, the highest prevalence of underskilling in literacy is observed in Chile, England (United Kingdom), Greece and the Russian Federation, while the lowest prevalence is found in Austria, the Czech Republic, Germany, Korea and Slovenia.

Survey respondents were also asked to describe their occupation and to point out the field of specialisation of their highest qualification.[16] Mismatch by field of study is gauged by identifying each occupation's most relevant field of study (or fields of study, if more than one field is best related to the occupation) and comparing it to workers' actual field of study. Workers can report one of nine possible fields: i) general programmes; ii) teacher training and education science; iii) humanities, languages and arts; iv) social sciences, business and law; v) science, mathematics and computing; vi) engineering, manufacturing and construction; vii) agriculture and veterinary medicine; viii) health and welfare; and ix) services. The matching of field(s) most relevant to each occupation follow(s) the coding used by Wolbers (2003), Quintini (2011) and Montt (2015).

As shown on the right-most panel of Figure 5.7, and on average across OECD countries/economies that participated in the Survey of Adult Skills, 40% of workers are mismatched by field of study. Field-of-study mismatch is largest in Chile, England (United Kingdom), Italy, Jakarta (Indonesia), Korea and New Zealand, with values showing that around one in two workers is mismatched by field of study. By contrast, the least prevalence of mismatch is found in Austria, Finland, Germany and Slovenia, where fewer than one in three workers is mismatched by field of study.

Field-of-study mismatch does not necessarily lead to wage penalties for individuals if the skills are transferable and recognised as workers transition from one field to another. It can translate into lower wages when this transferability does not take place and workers must downgrade – become overqualified – to find a job in another field (Montt, 2015).

Overlap between skills, field-of-study and qualifications mismatch

These different forms of mismatch overlap (Figures 5.8a and 5.8b). Workers can be simultaneously overqualified, overskilled and mismatched by field of study. These are workers who are not using all their skills, and their qualifications are not being recognised when working outside their field. By contrast, workers working outside their field can be well-qualified and well-matched if their qualifications are recognised and valued outside their field. Those working within their own field can be overqualified but not overskilled if their qualification does not necessarily reflect their actual skills level. Different combinations of these forms of mismatch point to different challenges to align the credentials, skills and the demands of the labour market.

Who are the overqualified? Are they genuinely or apparently mismatched? Overall, only a subset of overqualified workers has literacy skills that exceed those required for their jobs, so only a part of the overqualified population is "genuinely" overqualified (Figure 5.8a). Across the OECD countries/economies that participated in the Survey of Adult Skills, 14% of overqualified workers (working in or out of their field of study) are also overskilled, meaning that a majority of overqualified workers is well-matched in terms of the literacy skills required at work (or what is sometimes referred to as "apparent" mismatch). This suggests that qualifications are an imperfect proxy for skills, and also suggests that overqualification may reflect the underuse of skills other than literacy.

In all countries, the majority of workers who are overqualified are also mismatched along another dimension. Overqualified workers are either overskilled, mismatched by field of study or both, as depicted by the white, light blue and blue bars, respectively, in Figure 5.8a. In Greece and Ireland, more than one in four overqualified workers is also overskilled – pointing to a comparatively large share of genuine mismatch. Overqualification tends to be associated with field-of-study mismatch in Chile, England (United Kingdom), Israel, Italy, Korea, Singapore and Turkey. In these countries, more than one in two overqualified workers are also mismatched by field of study, but well-matched by skills. This raises questions about the capacity of workers to find jobs in their field and to transfer their skills to other sectors. In these countries/economies, the skills of workers who transition out of their field may not be recognised, and so the workers must downgrade in order to find work (Montt, 2015).

Figure 5.8b shows workers who are mismatched by field of study. Are these workers also likely to be overqualified and overskilled, meaning that their highest credentials and skills proficiency are not recognised when they find work in another field? On average across countries, workers mismatched by field of study also tend to be overqualified or overskilled. Almost 40% of workers who are mismatched by field of study are either overskilled or overqualified or both. This is most markedly the case in Greece, Ireland, Lithuania and Spain, where around half of workers who work outside their field are also overqualified or overskilled. In Singapore, by contrast, workers are more likely to work outside their field and their highest credentials and literacy skills are recognised (Figure 5.8b).

Figure 5.8a ▪ **Overqualified workers who are mismatched by literacy or field of study**

Percentage of overqualified workers in each category of literacy and field-of-study mismatch

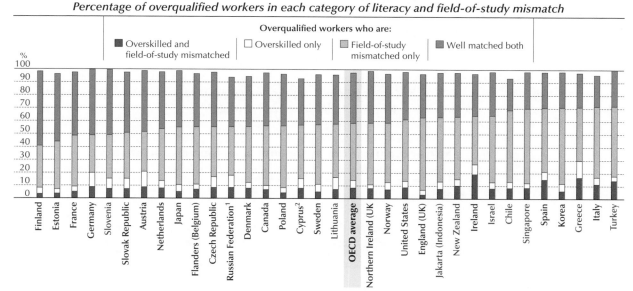

Notes: Overqualified workers who are "underskilled and field-of-study mismatched" or "underskilled and field-of-study well-matched" are omitted from the figure and together correspond to the remaining part of the total 100%. Field-of-study mismatch is unavailable for Australia due to the unavailability of ISCO 3-digit information for Australian workers in the Survey of Adult Skills (PIAAC).

1. See note at the end of this chapter.

2. See note 2 under Figure 5.1.

Countries and economies are ranked in ascending order of the percentage of overqualified workers who are overskilled in literacy and/or mismatched by field of study.

Source: Survey of Adult Skills (PIAAC) (2012, 2015), Table A5.8a.

StatLink ⧉ http://dx.doi.org/10.1787/888933366362

Figure 5.8b ▪ **Field-of-study mismatched workers who are mismatched by qualification or literacy**

Percentage of field-of-study mismatched workers in each category of qualification and literacy mismatch

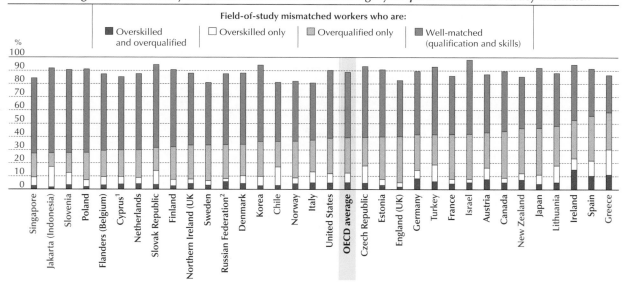

Notes: Field-of-study mismatched workers who are underskilled or underqualified are omitted from the figure and together correspond to the remaining part of the total 100%. Field-of-study mismatch is unavailable for Australia due to the unavailability of ISCO 3-digit information for Australian workers in the Survey of Adult Skills (PIAAC).

1. See note 2 under Figure 5.1.

2. See note at the end of this chapter.

Countries and economies are ranked in ascending order of the percentage of field-of-study mismatched workers who are overqualified and/or overskilled in literacy.

Source: Survey of Adult Skills (PIAAC) (2012, 2015), Table A5.8b.

StatLink ⧉ http://dx.doi.org/10.1787/888933366377

How mismatch interacts with proficiency and other individual and job characteristics

Mismatch and proficiency

Several studies show that there are significant differences in skills proficiency among workers with the same qualifications (Quintini, 2011). In the context of qualifications mismatch, the best-skilled individuals in a given qualification category may get jobs that require higher formal qualifications while the least skilled will only be able to get jobs requiring lower formal qualifications. Hence, individuals in the former group will appear as underqualified, despite having the skills required for their jobs, while those in the latter group will appear as overqualified, even though they lack some of the key skills needed to get and do a job with higher qualification requirements.[17]

Figure 5.9 [1/2] ▪ **Overqualification, by individual and job characteristics**
Marginal effects (as percentage-point change) on the likelihood of a worker being overqualified

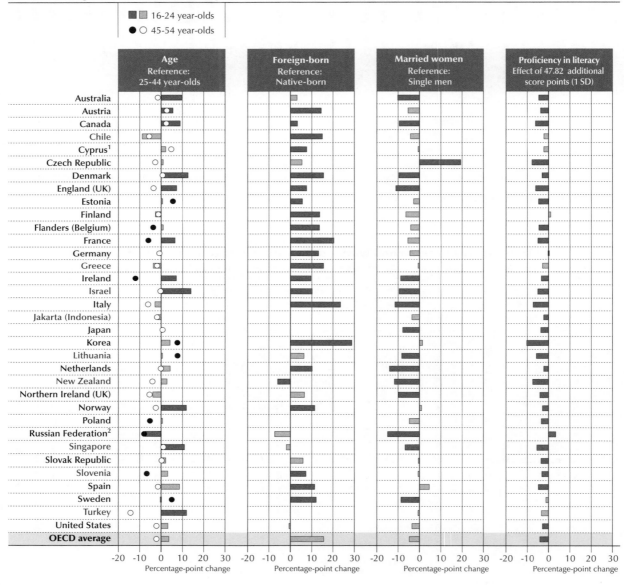

Note: Statistically significant values (at the 10% level) are shown in a darker tone.

1. See note 2 under Figure 5.1.

2. See note at the end of this chapter.

Countries and economies are listed in alphabetical order.

Source: Survey of Adult Skills (PIAAC) (2012, 2015), Table A5.9.

StatLink ⟡ http://dx.doi.org/10.1787/888933366386

In addition, lower-skilled workers in a particular qualification level may prefer to work outside their field of study to secure higher wages.[18] Alternatively, in tight labour markets, workers unable to find a job in their field may have to settle for a job outside their field of study, often having to downgrade and become overqualified in the process (Montt, 2015).

On average, and in most countries, overqualified and field-mismatched individuals score lower in literacy proficiency than their well-matched counterparts (Figures 5.9 and 5.11). This supports the theory that differences in proficiency within qualification levels and fields of study explain some qualifications mismatch, a phenomenon also referred to as "skills heterogeneity" (Quintini, 2011). Less-proficient workers may become overqualified because their qualifications do not adequately reflect their skills proficiency. They are also more likely to be mismatched by field of study, suggesting that workers work in occupations outside their field of study because they may find better wage or employment opportunities there.

Figure 5.9 [2/2] ▪ Overqualification, by individual and job characteristics
Marginal effects (as percentage-point change) on the likelihood of a worker being overqualified

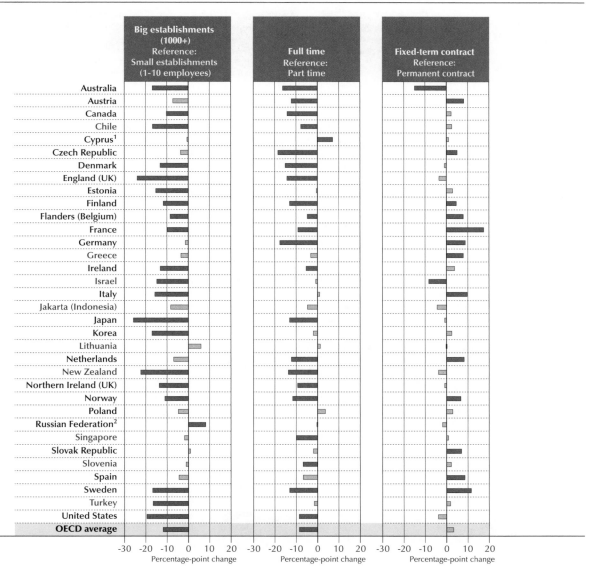

Note: Statistically significant values (at the 10% level) are shown in a darker tone.
1. See note 2 under Figure 5.1.
2. See note at the end of this chapter.
Countries and economies are listed in alphabetical order.
Source: Survey of Adult Skills (PIAAC) (2012, 2015), Table A5.9.
StatLink http://dx.doi.org/10.1787/888933366386

Socio-demographic and job characteristics and mismatch

Individual and job characteristics may influence the likelihood of mismatch too (Figures 5.9, 5.10 and 5.11). For example, it may take young people, as new entrants into the labour market, some time to sort themselves into well-matched jobs. Or, some workers may choose to accept a job for which they are overqualified. This can happen when workers wish to remain close to their families or better reconcile work and family life and accept part-time jobs or jobs outside their field of study. It can also happen during economic downturns and an overqualified job is preferred over unemployment.

Figure 5.10 [1/2] ■ **Overskilling in literacy, by individual and job characteristics**
Marginal effects (as percentage-point change) on the likelihood of a worker being overskilled in literacy

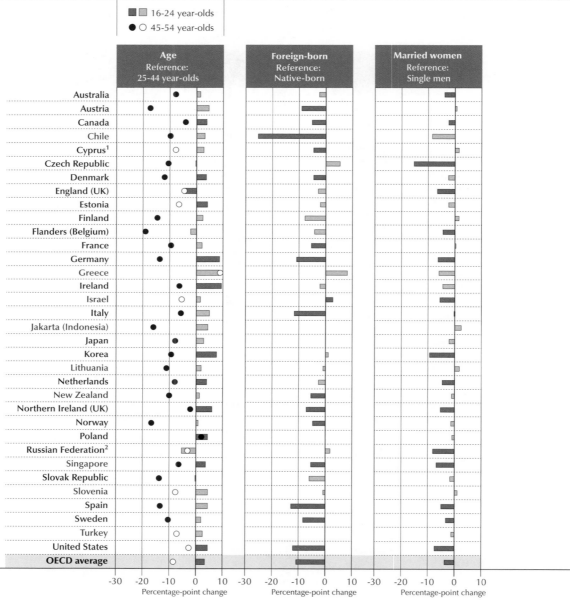

Note: Statistically significant values (at the 10% level) are shown in a darker tone.
1. See note 2 under Figure 5.1.
2. See note at the end of this chapter.
Countries and economies are listed in alphabetical order.
Source: Survey of Adult Skills (PIAAC) (2012, 2015), Table A5.10.
StatLink ⌗ http://dx.doi.org/10.1787/888933366397

Figure 5.10 [2/2] ▪ **Overskilling in literacy, by individual and job characteristics**

Marginal effects (as percentage-point change) on the likelihood of a worker being overskilled in literacy

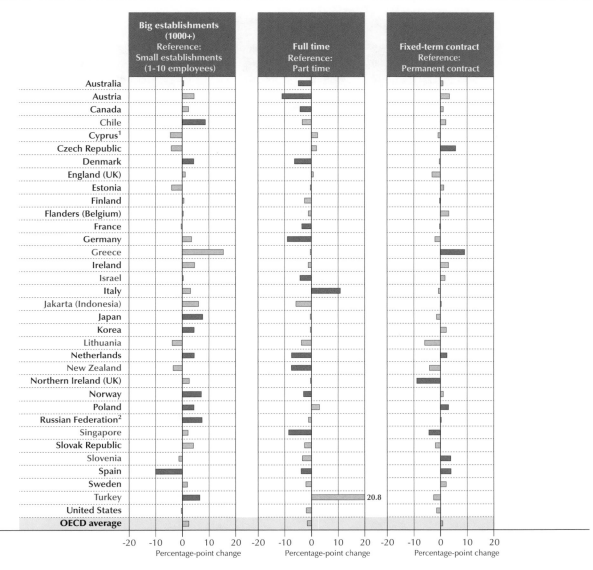

Note: Statistically significant values (at the 10% level) are shown in a darker tone.
1. See note 2 under Figure 5.1.
2. See note at the end of this chapter.
Countries and economies are listed in alphabetical order.
Source: Survey of Adult Skills (PIAAC) (2012, 2015), Table A5.10.
StatLink ᵐˢᵖ http://dx.doi.org/10.1787/888933366397

An analysis of the relationship between socio-demographic characteristics and mismatch shows clearly that foreign-born workers are more likely to be overqualified (even if they have the same proficiency in literacy) and mismatched by field of study than their native-born counterparts (Figures 5.9 and 5.11). This could be because qualifications acquired outside the host country are not recognised, and so highly qualified migrants are relegated to working in lower-skilled jobs.

However, foreign-born workers are less likely to be overskilled in literacy, possibly pointing to the barriers facing foreign-born adults who are not fluent in the host country's language. This finding also underscores the importance of offering language programmes so that host countries and immigrants themselves can fully benefit from immigrants' skills.

Figure 5.11 [1/2] ▪ Field-of-study mismatch, by individual and job characteristics
Marginal effects (as percentage-point change) on the likelihood of a worker being field-of-study mismatched

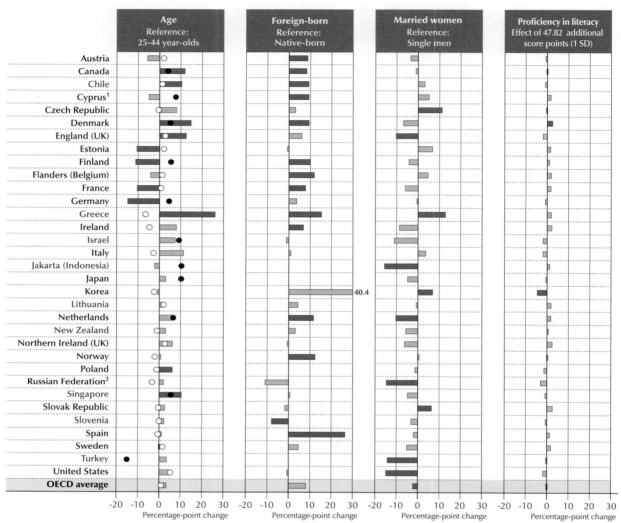

Notes: Statistically significant values (at the 10% level) are shown in a darker tone. Field-of-study mismatch is unavailable for Australia due to the unavailability of ISCO 3-digit information for Australian workers in the Survey of Adult Skills (PIAAC).

1. See note 2 under Figure 5.1.
2. See note at the end of this chapter.

Countries and economies are listed in alphabetical order.

Source: Survey of Adult Skills (PIAAC) (2012, 2015), Table A5.11.

StatLink ⟨⟩ http://dx.doi.org/10.1787/888933366405

In addition, in some countries 16-24 year-olds are more likely to be overqualified than 25-44 year-olds,[19] although the relationship is often not statistically significant; and older workers are less likely to be overskilled. Contrary to the assumption that women are more likely to be overqualified because of family constraints, once socio-demographic and job characteristics are accounted for, married women are slightly less likely to be overqualified than their single male counterparts, and are also less likely to be overskilled in many countries.[20]

Workers in larger firms and workers working full time are less likely to be overqualified and also less likely to be mismatched by field of study than workers in smaller firms or part-time workers (Figure 5.9). One possible explanation for this is that establishment size is a proxy for the quality of human-resource policies, with larger establishments being better at screening candidates and at understanding how overqualification may affect satisfaction at work and, ultimately, productivity.

Figure 5.11 [2/2] ▪ **Field-of-study mismatch, by individual and job characteristics**
Marginal effects (as percentage-point change) on the likelihood of a worker being field-of-study mismatched

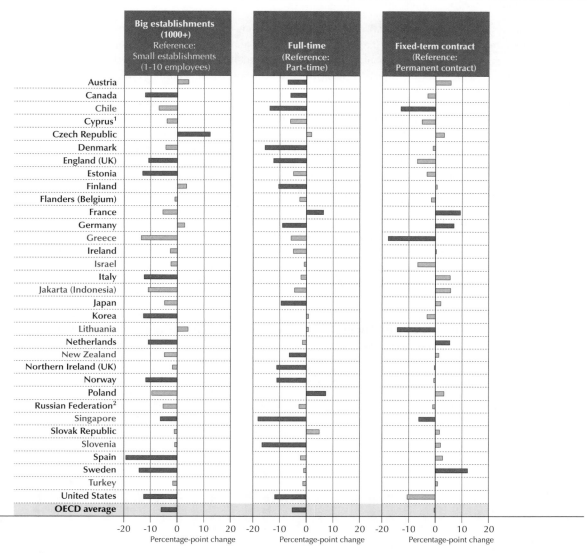

Notes: Statistically significant values (at the 10% level) are shown in a darker tone. Field-of-study mismatch is unavailable for Australia due to the unavailability of ISCO 3-digit information for Australian workers in the Survey of Adult Skills (PIAAC).

1. See note 2 under Figure 5.1.

2. See note at the end of this chapter.

Countries and economies are listed in alphabetical order.

Source: Survey of Adult Skills (PIAAC) (2012, 2015), Table A5.11.

StatLink ᴍꜱ⬛ http://dx.doi.org/10.1787/888933366405

Large establishments may also have larger internal labour markets through which workers can be transferred to better matching tasks and jobs inside the firm. Part-time jobs may have lower skills content, but they attract qualified workers because they are more compatible with personal/family life or a preferred option over unemployment during economic downturns. Fixed-term contract jobs could be expected to have lower qualification requirements than permanent jobs, but they often attract tertiary-educated workers who cannot find a permanent position. This hypothesis is supported by the data in most countries.

The effect of mismatch on wages

Overqualification has a stronger negative impact on hourly wages than overskilling or field-of-study mismatch, when workers are compared with their equally-qualified and equally-proficient well-matched counterparts (Figure 5.12).

On average across countries and economies, overqualified workers earn about 14% less than well-matched workers with the same qualifications and skills proficiency. The wage penalty associated with overqualification is 20% or more in Canada, Israel, Singapore, Turkey and the United States.

The effect of overskilling on wages is small and often not statistically significant, and remains so even when the controls for qualification mismatch are removed (Figure 5.12). The largest and statistically significant differences are observed in Israel, where overskilled workers earn about 16% less than their equally skilled, well-matched counterparts. This relatively large negative effect is in addition to the sizeable adverse effect of overqualification on wages.

After accounting for overqualification and overskilling, field-of-study mismatch entails a small wage penalty of less than 3%, on average across countries and economies. It entails a wage penalty of more than 6% in Estonia, Germany, Ireland, Israel, Italy, Jakarta (Indonesia), Lithuania and Northern Ireland (United Kingdom). Though field-of-study mismatch may not be linked to a wage penalty (or only a minimal one), this is only the case when workers are mismatched by field of study but are well-matched in terms of qualifications. Figure 5.8b, however, shows that a large part of field-mismatched workers are also overqualified. To the extent that workers who venture outside their field need to downgrade in order to find a job, field-of-study mismatch will result in a penalty that is largely related to their overqualification (Figure 5.12).

This evidence should not be interpreted as suggesting that having skills in excess of those required at work is not valued at all on the labour market. On average across countries and economies, overqualified workers earn about 4% more than well-matched workers in similar jobs. In other words, a tertiary graduate who holds a job requiring only an upper secondary qualification will earn less than if he or she were in a job requiring a tertiary qualification, but more than an upper secondary graduate in a job requiring upper secondary qualifications.

Figure 5.12 ■ **Effect of qualification, literacy and field-of-study mismatch on wages**
Percentage difference in wages between overqualified, overskilled or field-of-study mismatched workers and their well-matched counterparts

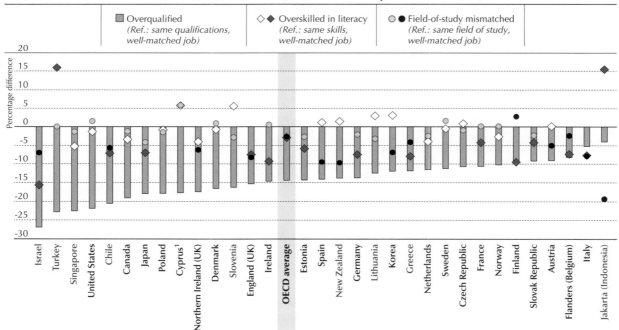

Notes: Coefficients from OLS regression of log hourly wages on mismatch directly interpreted as percentage effects on wages. Coefficients adjusted for years of education, age, gender, marital status, working experience, tenure, foreign-born status, establishment size, contract type, hours worked, public sector dummy, proficiency in literacy and use of skills at work. The wage distribution was trimmed to eliminate the 1st and 99th percentiles. Statistically significant values (at the 10% level) are shown in a darker tone. The regression sample includes only employees. The analysis excludes the Russian Federation because wage data obtained through the survey do not compare well with those available from other sources. Hence further checks are required before wage data for this country can be considered reliable.

1. See note 2 under Figure 5.1.

Countries and economies are ranked in ascending order of the effect of overqualification on wages.

Source: Survey of Adult Skills (PIAAC) (2012, 2015), Table A5.12.

StatLink ᵃᵍᵖ http://dx.doi.org/10.1787/888933366414

Qualifications mismatch and skills mismatch might each have distinct effects on wages, even after adjusting for both qualifications level and proficiency scores, because jobs with similar qualification requirements may have different skill requirements. This may happen because employers can evaluate qualifications but they cannot measure skills directly. In addition, the kinds of mismatch in skills captured by the two indicators are different. The survey's indicators of skills mismatch are based on numeracy, literacy and problem solving, while skills mismatch captured by qualification-based indicators may be interpreted as more general mismatch with the job or may also include, for example, mismatch that relates to job-specific skills.

Box 5.2 The STEP Skills Measurement Study: A skills survey in low- and middle-income countries

The framework for analysing and measuring adult skills by the Survey of Adult Skills has also been applied in low- and middle-income countries. The World Bank's STEP Skills Measurement Study was launched in 2010 to gather more evidence on the level and distribution of skills – including socio-emotional skills – relevant to the labour market in the adult populations of developing countries. The study consisted of one survey for individuals and one for employers. The individual survey contained three modules focused on cognitive skills, technical (job-specific) skills and socio-emotional skills. In addition to collecting self-reported information regarding certain cognitive skills, the cognitive module involved administering a direct assessment of reading literacy based on the Survey of Adult Skills instruments.

Eight countries participated in the first wave of data collection, which took place in 2011: Plurinational State of Bolivia (hereafter "Bolivia"), Colombia, Ghana, Lao People's Democratic Republic (hereafter "Lao PDR"), Sri Lanka, Ukraine, Viet Nam, and the Yunnan province of the People's Republic of China (hereafter "China"). The second wave, which took place in 2012-13, involved five countries: Armenia, Azerbaijan, Former Yugoslav Republic of Macedonia (FYROM), Georgia, and Kenya.

Some relevant findings:

- **Over 80% of adults pass the literacy threshold in most countries.** In four of the five countries surveyed in 2012-13, more than 80% of adults passed the core test (i.e. responded correctly to at least three out of eight items). In Lao PDR, only 67% of adults reached the literacy threshold.

- **The relationship between reading literacy and gender varies by country.** In Sri Lanka, Viet Nam and Yunnan province (China), the proportion of men and women who passed the core module is similar. However, in the case of Lao PDR and Bolivia, men had higher pass rates than women.

- **Educational attainment is positively related to performance.** In all countries except Yunnan province (China), adults with primary education or less were more likely to answer fewer than three responses correctly. Interestingly, there is little difference in performance between adults who completed secondary and post-secondary education, probably because the core assessment is designed to screen adults with low literacy.

- **As respondents' age increases, there is an increase in conscientiousness and stability, a decrease in openness, and no change in agreeableness and extraversion.** A correlation was found between personality traits and age. In three of the five countries surveyed in 2012-13, conscientiousness and stability increased with age, while in Bolivia and Yunnan province (China), these two traits remained stable across all age groups.

- **Cognitive skills are associated with higher earnings, especially for wage workers.** Greater use of cognitive skills (reading and numeracy) is associated with higher earnings for both wage earners and self-employed workers. In most countries, more frequent reading and using mathematics at an advanced level are associated with higher earnings. Interestingly, the basic reading literacy assessment score is positively correlated with employees' wages in all five countries, but is statistically significant only in Lao PDR and Sri Lanka.

- **Socio-emotional skills are correlated with educational attainment.** In all STEP countries, greater openness and higher levels of conscientiousness are correlated with a higher level of education; neuroticism seems negatively correlated. Extraversion and agreeableness are not significantly correlated with education.

- **Higher scores on socio-emotional skills scales are correlated with greater earnings, but no particular skill can be singled out as being important in all countries.** Openness to experience is associated with greater earnings for wage earners in Bolivia and Lao PDR and for self-employed workers in Sri Lanka and Viet Nam. More grit is associated with higher wages in Bolivia, Viet Nam and Yunnan province (China), but not at all with the earnings of self-employed workers. Conscientiousness is significantly associated with earnings for self-employed workers in Bolivia and Yunnan province (China), but not with the earnings of wage earners.

SKILLS AND NON-ECONOMIC OUTCOMES

While employability and wages are important for individual well-being, individuals and policy makers are becoming aware that non-economic factors also contribute to individual well-being and to the smooth functioning of societies as a whole. The report by the Commission on the Measurement of Economic Performance and Social Progress (Stiglitz, Sen and Fitoussi, 2009) is one example of the interest in developing broader measure of well-being, going beyond traditional measures of economic success like wages (at the individual level) and GDP (at the country level).

The Survey of Adult Skills collects information on four non-economic outcomes: the level of trust in others; participation in associative, religious, political, or charity activities (volunteering); the sense of being able to influence the political process (i.e. political efficacy); and self-assessed health conditions. Trust, volunteering, and political efficacy are variables collected in many surveys, such as the World Value Survey and the European Social Survey. They are often used as proxies to measure social capital in the large economic and sociological literature that, starting from the seminal contribution of Putnam (1993), has investigated the link between social capital (and cultural traits) and long-term economic development.[21]

There is a large body of empirical literature documenting the relationship between economic and non-economic outcomes. The mechanisms linking the two, as well as the individual determinants of non-economic outcomes (and, ultimately, of individual well-being) have been much less investigated, partly because of lack of data, and partly because of the inherent difficulty in determining causal relationships. In this respect, the Survey of Adult Skills offers a unique opportunity to better understand the relationship among education, skills proficiency, and widely used measures of social capital and individual well-being. Depending on the subjective value one attaches to the various non-economic outcomes, they can be seen as either interesting outcomes *per se*, or, in light of the vast literature on the relationship between social capital and economic growth, as mediating variables in studying the relationship between skills proficiency and economic outcomes.

Proficiency in information-processing skills is positively associated with trust, volunteering, political efficacy and self-assessed health. These relationships hold even after accounting for the usual range of socio-demographic characteristics, like education, parents' educational attainment, age, gender and immigrant and language background. The strength of the association, however, differs across countries (Figure 5.13).

For each of these non-economic outcomes, Figure 5.13 shows adjusted and unadjusted differences in the likelihood of reporting positive outcomes between highly proficient adults and adults with low proficiency, defined, respectively, as people scoring at Level 4 or 5 or at or below Level 1 on the literacy scale.

Across countries and economies, there is a positive correlation between skills proficiency in literacy and trust, volunteering and political efficacy (with correlation coefficients in the order of 0.40). The strength of the relationship between literacy skills and self-assessed health is almost uncorrelated with the strength of the relationship with the other three social outcomes.

Trust

Interpersonal trust, especially generalised trust, is a strong predictor of economic prosperity (Fukuyama, 1995; Knack and Keefer, 1997; Putnam, 1993) and individual well-being (Helliwell and Wang, 2010), although recent research by Butler, Guiso and Giuliano (2009) also shows that, at the individual level, excessive trust can be detrimental.[22] Generalised trust develops out of a feeling of goodwill towards anonymous others, and enables smooth social and economic interactions in complex societies where people engage frequently in interactions with others whom they do not know and from whom they differ in many ways. In such contexts, the absence of trust can result in negative consequences for economic activity. In particular, the literature has identified a number of channels through which trust can affect economic performance (Algan and Cahuc, 2014): trust is thought to be essential for the smooth functioning of financial markets; it is likely to play an important role in economic activities that involve a high degree of uncertainty (like investments in research and development, which are the sources of technological innovations), or in which contracts are difficult to enforce; and by promoting co-operation, trust can improve firm organisation and the quality of labour relations.

While institutions, such as efficient judicial systems, are crucial in sustaining trust, education and skills policies are also likely to play an important role. Higher information-processing skills can help people to better understand the motives underlying others' behaviours, as well as the negative consequences of lack of co-operation. Education and cognitive skills help build the socio-emotional skills needed to engage in fruitful social relationships (Borgonovi and Burns, 2015). Indirectly, societies with larger shares of skilled individuals might function more efficiently, thus helping to sustain trust.

Figure 5.13 ▪ **Literacy proficiency and positive social outcomes**

Adjusted and unadjusted difference between the percentage of adults with high proficiency and the percentage of adults with low proficiency who reported high levels of trust and political efficacy, good to excellent health, or participating in volunteer activities

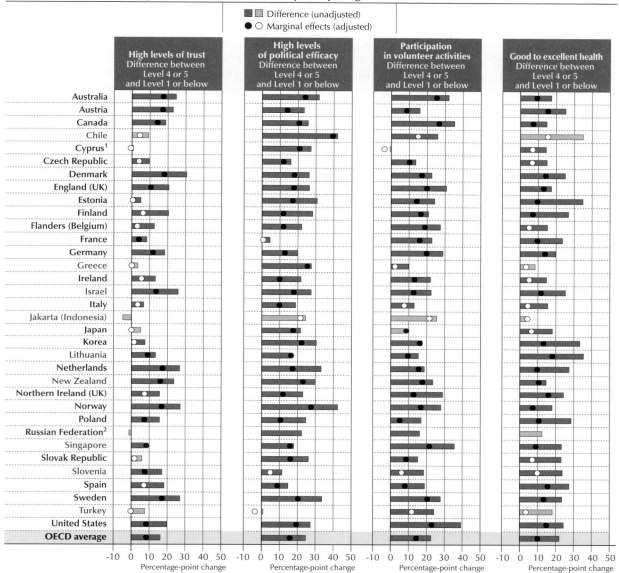

Notes: Statistically significant differences are marked in a darker tone. Adjusted differences are based on a regression model and take account of differences associated with the following variables: age, gender, education, immigrant and language background and parents' educational attainment. Adjusted differences for the Russian Federation are missing due to the lack of language variables.

1. See note 2 under Figure 5.1.

2. See note at the end of this chapter.

Countries and economies are listed in alphabetical order.

Source: Survey of Adult Skills (PIAAC) (2012, 2015), Tables A5.13(L) and A5.14(L).

StatLink ⟨ₘₛ⟩ http://dx.doi.org/10.1787/888933366425

The Survey of Adult Skills allows for the creation of a measure of interpersonal trust through the answers to the question: "Do you agree that only few people can be trusted?". For the purpose of the analysis carried out in this section, individuals who disagreed or strongly disagreed with this statement are classified as having high levels of trust.

Trust is the social outcome whose relationship with literacy proficiency varies the most across countries/economies. In Greece and Turkey, trust is less sensitive to adults' proficiency in skills. When moving from at or below Level 1 to Level 4 or 5 on the literacy scale, the probability of reporting high levels of trust increases by less than six percentage points, a difference that is not statistically different from zero. In Israel and New Zealand, by contrast, trust is comparatively more sensitive to proficiency: adults who scored at Level 4 or 5 in literacy were about 25 percentage points more likely to have reported high levels of trust when compared to adults who scored at or below Level 1. The relationship remains strong (at about 15 percentage points) even after accounting for socio-demographic characteristics.

Volunteering

Higher proficiency in literacy is associated with a greater likelihood of engaging in voluntary work for non-profit organisations (e.g. political, charity or religious organisations). Active participation in this kind of activity is likely to be a good proxy for altruism and civic engagement, whose link with skills has been attributed to civic education. Like trust, altruism can also be beneficial for economic performance, in that it may foster co-operation (Bowles and Polania-Reyes, 2012). Under this framework, higher proficiency allows adults to participate, and to understand the conditions, limits and possibilities of participation (Pallas, 2000).

The association between literacy proficiency and volunteering is weakest in Greece, where adults who scored at Level 4 or 5 were about 10 percentage points more likely to have reported engaging in volunteer activities than adults who scored at or below Level 1. Among the countries and economies that participated in the second round of the survey, Singapore is the country where literacy proficiency is more strongly associated with participation in volunteer activities: an adult who scored at Level 4 or 5 was 36 percentage points more likely to have reported volunteering than an adult who scored at or below Level 1 (Figure 5.13). This is similar to what was observed in the first round in Canada (a difference of 35 percentage points), and only slightly below the value observed in the United States (39 percentage points).

Controlling for other socio-demographic characteristics does not change the picture substantially, although the association weakens. The adjusted difference becomes statistically indistinguishable from zero in Greece. In Singapore it remains large, at 21 percentage points, close to what was observed in Australia (25 percentage points), Canada (27 percentage points) and the United States (23 percentage points).

Political efficacy

When it comes to political participation, a minimum level of literacy is needed to cast a vote. Higher skills are needed to make reasoned decisions, understand and follow political campaigns, and research and evaluate the issues and candidates (Hillygus, 2005). Political efficacy, traditionally defined as "the feeling that individual political action does have, or can have, an impact on the political process, i.e. that it is worthwhile to perform one's civic duties" (Campbell, Gurin and Miller, 1954), is considered as one of the most important factors that sustain and develop successful democratic systems (Pateman, 1970), and can be considered to be a building block of political trust (Almond and Verba, 1989).

Political efficacy is measured in the Survey of Adult Skills as the extent to which respondents (dis)agree with the question "People like me don't have any say about what the government does". This can be considered as a measure of *external* political efficacy (referring to the individual's beliefs in the responsiveness of political bodies to citizens' demands), as opposed to *internal* political efficacy (which refers to feelings of personal competence to understand and participate effectively in societies). Both internal and external political efficacy have been found to be correlated with actual political participation (Clarke and Acock, 1989; Pollock, 1983). External political efficacy, which can be also thought of as a measure of trust in institutions, is clearly crucial for the effective functioning of democratic societies, although the direction of causality between individual political efficacy and the quality of political institutions can clearly run both ways.

Higher skills proficiency is also associated with higher levels of political efficacy. In Turkey, the link between skills proficiency and political efficacy is weakest. The share of adults in Turkey who reported high levels of political efficacy is in line with the international average among adults who scored at or below Level 1, but is well below the average (23% versus 48%, see Table A5.13[L]) among people who scored at Level 4 or 5, resulting in a difference between the two groups not significantly different from zero. Political efficacy is even lower in France, where the likelihood of reporting high levels of political efficacy ranges from 8% among the least proficient adults to 12% among adults with the highest levels of literacy proficiency, resulting in a difference of less than 5 percentage points. Other countries in which the relationship between political efficacy and skills proficiency is weak are the Czech Republic, Lithuania, Singapore, Slovenia and Spain. In these countries, moving from Level 1 or below to Level 4 or 5 increases the likelihood of reporting high levels of political efficacy by less than 20 percentage points.

In Greece, Israel and New Zealand, adults who scored at Level 4 or 5 were about 30 percentage points more likely to have reported high levels of political efficacy compared to adults who scored at or below Level 1. Similar differences are recorded in Australia, Estonia, Finland, Korea, the Netherlands, Sweden and the United States. In Chile and Norway the relationship is strongest, at 42 percentage points (Figure 5.13).

Health

Health is a crucial element of individual well-being, as well as an area that absorbs a significant share of public expenditure. There is also increasing awareness and alarm about rising levels of inequalities in health status, often related to individuals' occupation or geographical location. Promoting practices that favour healthy lives is a top policy priority.

Increasingly complex healthcare systems, requiring adults to process a large amount of health-related information, as well as increased polarisation, by which highly skilled individuals are more and more likely to end up in "good" jobs and to be able to afford living in "good" places, all strengthen the link between health and proficiency in information-processing skills (Borgonovi and Pokropek, 2016).

The relationship between health and literacy proficiency is strong in most countries/economies that participated in the Survey of Adult Skills. On average, the chances of reporting good to excellent health are 22 percentage points higher among people who scored at Level 4 or 5 than among those who scored at or below Level 1. Greece is somewhat of an exception, with the difference between the two groups at only 8 percentage points (further reduced to a statistically insignificant 3 percentage points after differences in other socio-demographic characteristics are accounted for). This is because even among individuals who scored at or below Level 1, 84% reported good to excellent health.

Figure 5.14 ■ **Private health expenditure and association between literacy and self-reported health**

Relationship between the share of the private sector in total health expenditure in 2012, and adjusted and unadjusted literacy skills gradient in self-reported health

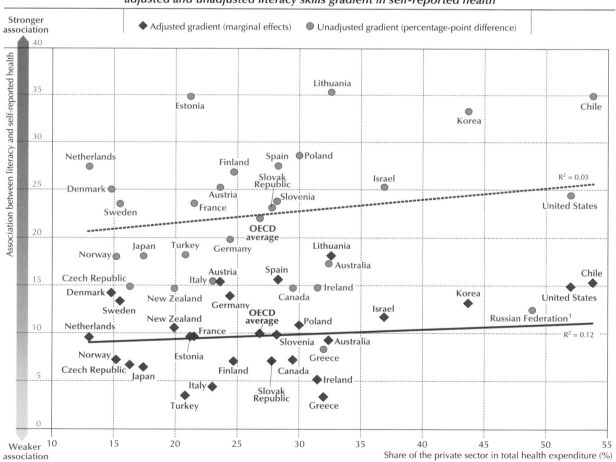

Notes: The unadjusted gradient is the percentage-point difference among adults who reported being in good or excellent health between those performing at Level 4 or 5 and those at Level 1 or below. The adjusted gradient refers to the average marginal probability of scoring at Level 4 or 5 in literacy among adults who reported good or excellent health (reference is Level 1 or below). The gradient is adjusted for age, gender, education, immigrant and language background and parents' educational attainment. Adjusted gradient for the Russian Federation is missing due to the lack of language variables.

Sources: OECD Health Statistics 2015 and Survey of Adult Skills (PIAAC) (2012, 2015), Tables A5.13 (L), A5.14(L) and A5.15.

StatLink ⟐ http://dx.doi.org/10.1787/888933366436

By contrast, the difference is much larger – more than 30 percentage points – in Chile and Lithuania. In both countries, the relationship between literacy proficiency and self-reported health remains strong (at 15 and 18 percentage points, respectively) after accounting for other socio-demographic characteristics. However, because of the low number of adults scoring at Level 4 or 5, differences are estimated imprecisely in Chile, and end up being not statistically significant.

In an attempt to explain why the strength of the relationship between skills proficiency and self-reported health varies across countries, one could look at between-country differences in the organisation of healthcare systems. The role of the private sector in the financing of healthcare expenditure, for instance, can be interpreted as a proxy for the inclusiveness of healthcare, which could have an impact on the relationship between skills proficiency and health. Figure 5.14 shows that the relationship between skills and health tends to be stronger in countries where a larger share of health expenditure is financed by the private sector. This makes intuitive sense. When the financing of healthcare is devolved to the private sector, one could expect to see less-than-universal access to healthcare. The association between skills proficiency and health could thus become stronger, either because income becomes a barrier to accessing healthcare (and more skilled individuals, by earning more, could be in a better position to afford quality healthcare), or because individuals are expected to assume more responsibility for managing their health, and more proficient individuals are in a better position to do so, by making better-informed choices.

SUMMARY

This chapter began with a question: To what extent does proficiency in literacy, numeracy and problem solving in technology-rich environments make a difference to the well-being of individuals and nations? The answer that emerges is clear: proficiency is positively linked to a number of important economic and social outcomes.

Proficiency in literacy is positively and independently associated with the probability of being employed, and with higher wages in many countries and economies. On average, as an individual's proficiency increases, his or her chances of being employed increase too, as do his/her wages. Proficiency in literacy, numeracy and problem solving in technology-rich environments reflects aspects of individuals' human capital that are identified and valued in the labour market separately from other aspects related to education or personal attributes and characteristics.

Proficiency in these information-processing skills is also positively associated with other important aspects of well-being, notably health, beliefs about one's impact on the political process, trust in others, and participation in volunteer or associative activities. There is a clear interaction between proficiency and educational attainment in relation to these outcomes. In nearly all countries/economies, adults with low proficiency and low levels of education show the lowest probability of reporting positively on all the social outcomes considered. Conversely, adults with higher proficiency and high levels of education have the greatest probability of reporting positive social outcomes.

Overall, the results suggest that investments in improving adults' proficiency in literacy, numeracy and problem solving in technology-rich environments may have significant benefits. Independent of policies designed to increase participation in education and training, improvements in teaching literacy and numeracy in schools and programmes for adults with poor literacy, numeracy, skills and ICT may result in potentially significant economic and social returns for individuals and for society a whole.

Findings also point to the existence of significant mismatch between skills and how they are used at work, particularly for some socio-demographic groups. Data show that overqualification is particularly common among young and foreign-born workers and those employed in small establishments, in part-time jobs or on fixed-term contracts. Overqualification has a significant impact on wages, even after accounting for proficiency, and on workers' productivity. It also implies a "waste" of human capital, since overqualified workers tend not to use their skills fully.

However, part of this type of mismatch is due to the fact that some workers have poorer skills proficiency than would be expected given their qualifications, either because they performed poorly in initial education or because their skills have depreciated over time. By contrast, underqualified workers are likely to have the skills required at work, but not the qualifications to show for them. Mismatches in skills proficiency have a weaker impact on wages than do qualifications mismatch. This suggests either that labour market mismatch may be more often related to job-specific or generic skills than to those measured in the survey, and/or that employers succeed in identifying their employees' real skills, irrespective of their formal qualifications, and adapt job content accordingly.

Proficiency in information-processing skills is also positively correlated with important non-economic outcomes, such as trust, political efficacy, participation in volunteering activities, and self-reported health status. These are all important dimensions of individual well-being, both because many people value these outcomes in themselves, and because they are often found to be important ingredients for a smooth and more efficient functioning of economies and societies.

Notes

1. This is in line with findings that precede the Survey of Adult Skills (PIAAC), like those from the British Birth Cohort Studies, the American Longitudinal Study of Adult Learning or the Canadian Youth in Transition Survey (OECD, 2010; Reder and Bynner, 2009).

2. To limit the influence of outliers and extreme values, analyses in this report follow the standard practice of trimming the sample at the top and bottom 1% of the wage distribution in each country.

3. Although literacy, numeracy and problem-solving competencies – the skill domains that are explicitly tested in the PIAAC assessment exercise – are important elements of people's productive capacity, it should be kept in mind that they only imperfectly proxy workers' overall set of skills.

4. Among the countries and economies that conducted the Survey of Adult Skills in 2011-12, the standard deviation in literacy skills was 46 points. Among the OECD countries and economies that have participated in the survey (in either 2011-12 or 2014-15), the standard deviation for the sub-population of workers is 48 points.

5. In some countries, particularly Chile and Singapore but also Greece, Israel and Slovenia, the proficiency in literacy is similar to that of employed adults, a result that might reflect that in some of these countries relatively few unemployed adults participated in the survey or that higher-skilled workers may have more support during unemployment to find a well-matched job.

6. The measure of hourly wages includes bonuses.

7. A compressed wage distribution is one in which the differences in wages among individuals are limited.

8. The set of control variables includes years of education, gender, age, marital status and immigrant background. In the wage analysis, the control set is augmented with tenure. The set of control variables used to produce the estimates presented in this section is more limited than those commonly used in the literature. The reason for this is twofold. First, the results are meant to be as comparable as possible with those on employment (Figure 5.2). Second, the estimated effects are meant to capture a broad notion of the association between wages and proficiency or education. For example, since the control set does not include occupation or industry, some of the effects might be due to the fact that more educated or more proficient individuals are employed in higher-paying sectors or occupations. However, such individuals might obtain these jobs precisely because they are more educated or more proficient, so it is unclear whether it would be more interesting to broaden the control set.

9. This consists in adding the skills-use indicators (see Chapter 4) to the control set of the linear regressions. For brevity's sake, results are not reported.

10. Other human capital attributes not measured in the Survey of Adult Skills may also contribute to the explanation of the variance in workers' hourly wages.

11. Most often, this term is used with reference to apparent overqualification. See for example, Chevalier (2003).

12. While this is complicated by the fact that some jobs may not have an obvious requirement in terms of qualifications or workers may not be fully aware of it, survey experts have found that both workers and employers tend to find it easier to define jobs in terms of required qualifications than in terms of individual skills.

13. Because qualifications mismatch shown in Figure 5.7 is based on workers' views of what qualification is required to get their job, the results may be affected by respondents' bias – i.e. the tendency to overvalue- or undervalue the content of one's work – or by qualification inflation – i.e. whereby employers raise minimum job requirements as a result of an increase in the number of tertiary-qualified candidates without upgrading job content. The latter would tend to reduce the prevalence of overqualification when the self-reported measure is used, while the former may bias the results in either direction.

14. To limit the potential impact of outliers on these measurements, the 5th and the 95th percentiles instead of the actual minimum and maximum are used for computing skills mismatch.

15. The comparison of skills proficiency and skills use rests on the assumption that the two can be measured on the same scale, an assumption that is difficult to defend for concepts that are so clearly distinct theoretically and that cannot be represented along the same metrics. In addition, the measures of skills proficiency and skills use are based on structurally different pieces of information. Indicators of skills use normally exploit survey questions about the frequency (and/or the importance) with which specific tasks are carried out in the respondents' work activities, whereas skills proficiency is measured through information-processing tests. Work is underway to improve this comparison in future waves of the Survey of Adult Skills.

16. Survey respondents are asked "What was the area of study, emphasis or major for your highest level of qualification? If there was more than one, please choose the one you consider most important" with respondents asked to select one of nine field categories: i) general programmes; ii) teacher training and education science; iii) humanities, languages and arts; iv) social sciences, business and law; v) science, mathematics and computing; vi) engineering, manufacturing and construction; vii) agriculture and veterinary medicine; viii) health and welfare; and ix) services. Respondents are also asked an open question about their job title and their responsibilities in the job (for their current job or the one they held last, if they had paid work in the previous five years). These descriptions are used

to derive each respondent's ISCO-08 3-digit occupation. Using Montt's (2015) coding strategy, each occupation is assigned to one or more of the nine fields of study. Whenever a worker reported having studied in a field that is different than the field(s) that correspond to his/her occupation, the worker is considered to be mismatched by field of study. The coding that assigns each occupational code to the corresponding field or fields of study is available in Annex 2 in Montt (2015). Under this coding scheme, certain occupations may be matched to more than one field, as a particular occupation may provide a relevant destination for graduates from different fields (e.g. an author, journalist or linguist [ISCO-08 code 264] is considered to be matched to his/her field of study if he/she graduated from the "Humanities, languages and arts" or "Social sciences, business and law" fields).

17. These differences in skills proficiency within a qualification level are not necessarily related to performance in initial education. Some graduates may lack the generic skills, such as communication, team-work and negotiating skills, that the education system can foster, but that are better learned in the workplace. In addition, some workers may have the skills expected of their qualification level at graduation, but these skills may atrophy or become obsolete over time, particularly if they are not used or upgraded.

18. In principle, this is true for higher-skilled workers too, as could be the case for philosophers from prestigious universities sought after for work in the financial sector. Montt (2015) explores this possibility and finds that, for the most part, highly skilled workers within a field are more likely to remain in the field than be mismatched to receive higher wages.

19. This could be explained by the fact that young people entering the labour market for the first time lack experience and are more likely to be hired for jobs that are below their qualification levels. However, it could also be due to an increase in the prevalence of overqualification over time, such that younger adults are more affected. Unfortunately, the data do not allow for separating these two effects.

20. This is consistent with the mixed results, found in other studies, concerning the role played by gender and family status in explaining qualifications mismatch (Quintini, 2011). Husbands tend to optimise their job search, while their wives' job search is considered – by both the husband and the wife – to be of secondary importance. Also, some researchers have argued that women with children may be more likely to be overqualified because of the constraints on job choice imposed by childrearing. However, there is no empirical evidence to support these claims.

21. Classical references are Knack and Keefer (1997) and Routledge and von Amsberg (2002). Recent reviews of the existing literature include Temple (2003), Durlauf and Fafchamps (2005), Guiso, Sapienza and Zingales (2006), and Algan and Cahuc (2014). We also refer the interested reader to OECD (2001).

22. Recent studies have been able to establish a causal link between trust and economic growth (Algan and Cahuc, 2010). This continues to be an active field of current research (Algan and Cahuc, 2014).

A note regarding the Russian Federation

The sample for the Russian Federation does not include the population of the Moscow municipal area. The data published, therefore, do not represent the entire resident population aged 16-65 in the Russian Federation but rather the population of the Russian Federation *excluding* the population residing in the Moscow municipal area.

More detailed information regarding the data from the Russian Federation as well as that of other countries can be found in the *Technical Report of the Survey of Adult Skills, Second Edition* (OECD, forthcoming).

References and further reading

Adalet McGowan, M. and **D. Andrews** (2015), "Labour market mismatch and labour productivity: Evidence from PIAAC data", *OECD Economics Department Working Papers*, No. 1209, OECD Publishing, Paris, http://dx.doi.org/10.1787/5js1pzx1r2kb-en.

Algan, Y. and **P. Cahuc** (2010), "Inherited trust and growth", *American Economic Review*, Vol. 100/5, pp. 2060-2092.

Algan, Y. and **P. Cahuc** (2014), "Trust, growth, and well-being: New evidence and policy implications", in Aghion, P. and S. Durlauf (eds.), *Handbook of Economic Growth*, Vol. 2A, Elsevier, Amsterdam, pp. 49-120.

Almond, G.A. and **S. Verba** (1989), *The Civic Culture: Political Attitudes and Participation in Five Countries*, SAGE Publications.

Borgonovi, F. and **T. Burns** (2015), "The educational roots of trust", *OECD Education Working Papers*, No. 119, OECD Publishing, Paris, http://dx.doi.org/10.1787/5js1kv85dfvd-en.

Borgonovi, F. and **A. Pokropek** (2016), "Education and self-reported health: Evidence from 23 countries on the role of years of schooling, cognitive skills and social capital", *PLOS One*.

Bowles, S. and **S. Polania-Reyes** (2012), "Economic incentives and social preferences: Substitutes or complements?", *Journal of Economic Literature*, Vol. 50, pp. 368-425.

Butler, J., L. Guiso and **P. Giuliano** (2009), "The right amount of trust", *NBER Working Papers,* No. 15344.

Campbell, A., G. Gurin and **W.E. Miller** (1954), *The Voter Decides*, Row, Peterson and Company, Evanston, Illinois.

Chevalier, A. (2003), "Measuring over-education", *Economica*, Vol. 70/279, pp. 509-531.

Clarke, H.D. and **A.C. Acock** (1989), "National elections and political attitudes: The case of political efficacy", *British Journal of Political Science*, Vol. 19, pp. 551-562.

Durlauf, S. and **M. Fafchamps** (2005), "Social capital", in Aghion, P. and S.N. Durlauf (eds.), *Handbook of Economic Growth*, Vol. 1B, Elsevier, Amsterdam, pp. 1639-1699.

Fukuyama, F. (1995), "Trust: The social virtues and the creation of prosperity", Free Press, New York.

Fields, G.S. (2004), *Regression-based Decompositions: A New Tool for Managerial Decision-making,* Department of Labor Economics, Cornell University, pp. 1-41.

Guiso, L., P. Sapienza and **L. Zingales** (2006), "Does culture affect economic outcomes?", *Journal of Economic Perspectives*, Vol. 20/2, pp. 23-48.

Hanushek, E., G. Schwerdt, S. Wiederhold and **L. Woessman** (2013), "Returns to skills around the world: Evidence from PIAAC", *European Economic Review*, Vol. 73, pp. 103-130, http://dx.doi.org/10.1016/j.euroecorev.2014.10.006.

Hillygus, S. (2005). "The missing link: Exploring the relationship between higher education and political engagement", *Political Behavior,* Vol. 27/1, pp. 25-47.

Kampelmann, S. and **F. Ryck** (2012), "The impact of educational mismatch on firm productivity: Evidence from linked panel data", *Economics of Education Review*, Vol. 31/6, pp. 918-931.

Knack, S. and **P. Keefer** (1997), "Does social capital have an economic payoff? A cross-country investigation", *Quarterly Journal of Economics*, Vol. 112/4, pp. 1251-1288.

Leaker, D. (2009), "Economic inactivity", *Economic & Labour Market Review*, Vol. 3/2, pp. 42-46.

Leuven, E., H. Oosterbeek, and **H. van Ophem** (2004), "Explaining international differences in male skill wage differentials by differences in demand and supply of skill", *The Economic Journal*, Vol. 114/495, pp. 466-486.

Montt, G. (2015), "The causes and consequences of field-of-study mismatch: An analysis using PIAAC", *OECD Social, Employment and Migration Working Papers*, No. 167, OECD Publishing, Paris, http://dx.doi.org/10.1787/5jrxm4dhv9r2-en.

OECD (forthcoming), *Technical Report of the Survey of Adult Skills, Second Edition.*

OECD (2016a), *Getting Skills Right: Assessing and Anticipating Changing Skill Needs*, OECD Publishing, Paris, http://dx.doi.org/10.1787/9789264252073-en.

OECD (2016b), *Survey of Adult Skills (PIAAC)* (Database 2012, 2015), www.oecd.org/site/piaac/publicdataandanalysis.htm.

OECD (2015a), *OECD Employment Outlook 2015*, OECD Publishing, Paris, http://dx.doi.org/10.1787/empl_outlook-2015-en.

OECD (2015b), *In It Together: Why Less Inequality Benefits All*, OECD Publishing, Paris, http://dx.doi.org/10.1787/9789264235120-en.

OECD (2015c), *Health Expenditure and Financing 2015* (database), http://stats.oecd.org (accessed on 13 February 2016).

OECD (2014a), *OECD Employment Outlook 2014: How Does Mexico Compare?*, September 2014, OECD Publishing, Paris, www.oecd.org/mexico/EMO-MEX-EN.pdf.

OECD (2014b), *OECD Employment Outlook 2014*, OECD Publishing, Paris, http://dx.doi.org/10.1787/empl_outlook-2014-en.

OECD (2013), *Skills Outlook 2013: First Results from the Survey of Adult Skills*, OECD Publishing, Paris, http://dx.doi.org/10.1787/9789264204256-en.

OECD (2010a), *Pathways to Success: How Knowledge and Skills at Age 15 Shape Future Lives in Canada*, OECD Publishing, Paris, http://dx.doi.org/10.1787/9789264081925-en.

OECD (2001), *The Well-being of Nations: The Role of Human and Social Capital*, OECD Publishing, Paris, http://dx.doi.org/10.1787/9789264189515-en.

Pallas, A. (2000), "The effects of schooling on individual lives", in Hallinan, M. (ed.), *Handbook of the Sociology of Education*, New York: Springer.

Pateman, C. (1970), *Participation and Democratic Theory*, Cambridge University Press.

Pellizzari, M. and **A. Fichen** (2013), "A new measure of skills mismatch: Theory and evidence from the survey of adult skills (PIAAC)", *OECD Social, Employment and Migration Working Papers*, No. 153, OECD Publishing, Paris, http://dx.doi.org/10.1787/5k3tpt04lcnt-en.

Pinkston, J. (2009), "A model of asymmetric employer learning with testable implications", *Review of Economic Studies,* Vol. 76, pp. 367-394.

Pollock, P.H. (1983), "The participatory consequences of internal and external political efficacy: A research note", *The Western Political Quarterly*, Vol. 36/3, pp. 400-409.

Putnam, R.D. (1993), "The prosperous community: Social capital and public life", *The American Prospect*, Vol. 13, pp. 35-42.

Quintini, G. (2011), "Right for the job: Over-qualified or under-skilled?", *OECD Social, Employment and Migration Working Papers*, No. 120, OECD Publishing, Paris, http://dx.doi.org/10.1787/5kg59fcz3tkd-en.

Reder, S. and **J. Bynner** (eds) (2009), *Tracking Adult Literacy and Numeracy Skills: Findings from longitudinal research*, London: Routledge.

Routledge, B.R. and **J. von Amsberg** (2002), "Social capital and growth", *Journal of Monetary Economics*, Vol. 50, pp. 167-193.

Stiglitz, J., A. Sen and **J. Fitoussi** (2009), *Report by the Commission on the Measurement of Economic Performance and Social Progress.*

Temple, J. (2003), "Growth effects of education and social capital in OECD countries", *OECD Economic Studies*, Vol. 2001/2, OECD Publishing, Paris, http://dx.doi.org/10.1787/eco_studies-v2001-art11-en.

Tyler, J. (2004), "Basic skills and the earnings of dropouts", *Economics of Education Review*, Vol. 23/3, pp. 221-235.

Vignoles, A. (2016), "What is the economic value of literacy and numeracy? Basic skills in literacy and numeracy are essential for success in the labor market", *IZA World of Labour*, No. 229, http://dx.doi.org/10.15185/izawol.229.

Wolbers, M. (2003), "Job mismatches and their labour market effects among school-leavers in Europe", *European Sociological Review*, Vol. 19, pp. 249-266.

Annex A

Skills Matter: Further Results from the Survey of Adult Skills
Tables of results

ANNEX A
LIST OF TABLES AVAILABLE ON LINE

The following tables are available in electronic form only.

Chapter 2 Adults' proficiency in key information-processing skills

http://dx.doi.org/10.1787/888933366458	
WEB Table A2.1	Percentage of adults scoring at each proficiency level in literacy
WEB Table A2.2	Performance in the reading component assessment, by literacy proficiency level
WEB Table A2.3	Mean literacy proficiency and distribution of literacy scores, by percentile
WEB Table A2.4	Percentage of adults scoring at each proficiency level in numeracy
WEB Table A2.5	Mean numeracy proficiency and distribution of numeracy scores, by percentile
WEB Table A2.6	Percentage of adults scoring at each proficiency level in problem solving in technology-rich environments
WEB Table A2.7	Correlation between literacy and numeracy proficiency
WEB Table A2.8	Mean literacy proficiency, by level of proficiency in problem solving in technology-rich environments
WEB Table A2.9	Mean numeracy proficiency, by level of proficiency in problem solving in technology-rich environments
WEB Table A2.10	Mean literacy proficiency in the International Adult Literacy Survey (IALS), the Adult Literacy and Lifeskills Survey (ALL) and the Survey of Adults Skills (PIAAC)
WEB Table A2.11	Mean numeracy proficiency in the Adult Literacy and Lifeskills Survey (ALL) and the Survey of Adults Skills (PIAAC)

Chapter 3 The socio-demographic distribution of key information-processing skills

http://dx.doi.org/10.1787/888933366463	
WEB Table A3.1 (L)	Difference in literacy scores between contrast categories, by socio-demographic characteristics
WEB Table A3.1 (N)	Difference in numeracy scores between contrast categories, by socio-demographic characteristics
WEB Table A3.2 (L)	Mean literacy proficiency, by educational attainment, and score difference between high- and low-educated adults
WEB Table A3.2 (N)	Mean numeracy proficiency, by educational attainment, and score difference between high- and low-educated adults
WEB Table A3.3 (L)	Percentage of adults at each proficiency level in literacy, by educational attainment
WEB Table A3.3 (N)	Percentage of adults at each proficiency level in numeracy, by educational attainment
WEB Table A3.3 (P)	Percentage of adults at each proficiency level in problem solving in technology-rich environments, by educational attainment
WEB Table A3.4 (L)	Mean literacy proficiency among 16-24 and 20-24 year-olds, by educational attainment
WEB Table A3.4 (N)	Mean numeracy proficiency among 16-24 and 20-24 year-olds, by educational attainment
WEB Table A3.5 (L)	Mean literacy proficiency, by age groups, and score difference between youngest and oldest adults
WEB Table A3.5 (N)	Mean numeracy proficiency, by age groups, and score difference between youngest and oldest adults
WEB Table A3.6 (L)	Relationship between age and literacy proficiency
WEB Table A3.6 (N)	Relationship between age and numeracy proficiency
WEB Table A3.6 (P)	Relationship between age and proficiency in problem solving in technology-rich environments proficiency
WEB Table A3.7 (L)	Percentage of adults at each proficiency level in literacy, by age groups
WEB Table A3.7 (N)	Percentage of adults at each proficiency level in numeracy, by age groups
WEB Table A3.7 (P)	Percentage of adults at each proficiency level in problem solving in technology-rich environments, by age groups
WEB Table A3.8 (L)	Relationship between literacy proficiency and problem solving in technology rich-environments, by age groups
WEB Table A3.8 (N)	Relationship between numeracy proficiency and problem solving in technology rich-environments, by age groups
WEB Table A3.9 (L)	Mean literacy proficiency, by gender, and score difference between men and women
WEB Table A3.9 (N)	Mean numeracy proficiency, by gender, and score difference between men and women
WEB Table A3.10 (L)	Mean literacy proficiency, by age and gender
WEB Table A3.10 (N)	Mean numeracy proficiency, by age and gender
WEB Table A3.11 (L)	Percentage of adults at each proficiency level in literacy, by gender
WEB Table A3.11 (N)	Percentage of adults at each proficiency level in numeracy, by gender
WEB Table A3.11 (P)	Percentage of adults at each proficiency level in problem solving in technology-rich environments, by gender
WEB Table A3.12 (L)	Mean literacy proficiency, by immigrant and language background, and score difference between native- and foreign-born adults
WEB Table A3.12 (N)	Mean numeracy proficiency, by immigrant and language background, and score difference between native- and foreign-born adults
WEB Table A3.13 (L)	Percentage of adults at each proficiency level in literacy, by immigrant and language background
WEB Table A3.13 (N)	Percentage of adults at each proficiency level in numeracy, by immigrant and language background
WEB Table A3.13 (P)	Percentage of adults at each proficiency level in problem solving in technology-rich environments, by immigrant and language background
WEB Table A3.14 (L)	Mean literacy proficiency and score difference, by parents' educational attainment
WEB Table A3.14 (N)	Mean numeracy proficiency and score difference, by parents' educational attainment
WEB Table A3.15 (L)	Percentage of adults at each proficiency level in literacy, by parents' educational attainment
WEB Table A3.15 (N)	Percentage of adults at each proficiency level in numeracy, by parents' educational attainment
WEB Table A3.15 (P)	Percentage of adults at each proficiency level in problem solving in technology-rich environments, by parents' educational attainment
WEB Table A3.16	Percentage of adults who score at or below Level 1 in literacy and/or numeracy
WEB Table A3.17	Percentage of adults who score at or below Level 1 in literacy and/or numeracy, by socio-demographic characteristics
WEB Table A3.18	Likelihood of adults scoring at or below Level 1 in literacy and/or numeracy, by socio-demographic characteristics (average marginal probabilities)

Chapter 4 How skills are used in the workplace

		http://dx.doi.org/10.1787/888933366479
WEB	Table A4.1	Average use of information-processing skills at work
WEB	Table A4.2	Average use of information-processing skills in everyday life
WEB	Table A4.3	Adjusted and unadjusted labour productivity and average reading skills use at work
WEB	Table A4.4	Skills use at work and skills proficiency of the working population
WEB	Table A4.5 (L)	Distribution of skills use, by literacy proficiency
WEB	Table A4.5 (N)	Distribution of skills use, by numeracy proficiency
WEB	Table A4.5 (P)	Distribution of skills use, by proficiency in problem solving in tehcnology-rich enviroments
WEB	Table A4.6	Variation in information-processing skills use at work
WEB	Table A4.7a	Information-processing skills used at work, by gender
WEB	Table A4.7b	Gender differences in the use of information-processing skills at work (adjusted)
WEB	Table A4.8a	Information-processing skills used at work, by age group
WEB	Table A4.8b	Age-related differences in the use of information-processing skills at work (adjusted)
WEB	Table A4.9a	Information-processing skills used at work, by educational attainment
WEB	Table A4.9b	Education-related differences in the use of information-processing skills at work (adjusted)
WEB	Table A4.10a	Information-processing skills used at work, by sector
WEB	Table A4.10b	Sector-related differences in the use of information-processing skills at work (adjusted)
WEB	Table A4.11	Information-processing skills used at work, by firm size
WEB	Table A4.12a	Information-processing skills used at work, by contract type
WEB	Table A4.12b	Contract-related differences in the use of information-processing skills at work (adjusted)
WEB	Table A4.13	Mean skills use, by High-Performance Work Practices
WEB	Table A4.14	High-Performance Work Practices, by type of practice

Chapter 5 The outcomes of investment in skills

		http://dx.doi.org/10.1787/888933366489
WEB	Table A5.1 (L)	Workers' mean proficiency in literacy, by labour force status
WEB	Table A5.1 (N)	Workers' mean proficiency in numeracy, by labour force status
WEB	Table A5.1 (P)	Workers' mean proficiency in problem solving in technology-rich enviroments, by labour force status
WEB	Table A5.2 (L)	Effect of education and literacy proficiency on the likelihood of being employed
WEB	Table A5.2 (N)	Effect of education and numeracy proficiency on the likelihood of being employed
WEB	Table A5.3 (L)	Distribution of wages among employees, by level of literacy proficiency
WEB	Table A5.3 (N)	Distribution of wages among employees, by level of numeracy proficiency
WEB	Table A5.4	Effect on wages of education, literacy proficiency and reading use at work
WEB	Table A5.5	Contribution of education, literacy and numeracy to the variation in hourly wages
WEB	Table A5.6a	Contribution of education, literacy and numeracy to the variation in hourly wages, by age group
WEB	Table A5.6b	Contribution of education, literacy and numeracy to the variation in hourly wages, by gender
WEB	Table A5.7	Qualification, literacy and field-of-study mismatch
WEB	Table A5.8a	Overqualified workers who are mismatched by literacy or field of study
WEB	Table A5.8b	Field-of-study mismatched workers who are mismatched by qualification or literacy
WEB	Table A5.9	Overqualification, by individual and job characteristics
WEB	Table A5.10	Overskilling in literacy, by individual and job characteristics
WEB	Table A5.11	Field-of-study mismatch, by individual and job characteristics
WEB	Table A5.12	Effect on wages of qualification, literacy and field-of-study mismatch
WEB	Table A5.13 (L)	Percentage of adults reporting positive social outcomes, by literacy proficiency
WEB	Table A5.13 (N)	Percentage of adults reporting positive social outcomes, by numeracy proficiency
WEB	Table A5.14 (L)	Marginal effects of literacy proficiency on adults reporting positive social outcomes
WEB	Table A5.14 (N)	Marginal effects of numeracy proficiency on adults reporting positive social outcomes
WEB	Table A5.15	Share of total current expenditure on health funded by the private sector (2012)

Annex B

Skills Matter: Further Results from the Survey of Adult Skills
Additional tables

ANNEX B

LIST OF TABLES AVAILABLE ON LINE

The following tables are available in electronic form only.

http://dx.doi.org/10.1787/888933366492

WEB	Table B2.1	Per capita GDP
WEB	Table B2.2	Percentage of adults, by age and level of educational attainment
WEB	Table B2.3	Foreign-born population as a percentage of total population
WEB	Table B2.4	Percentage of adults with no/limited computer experience and participation in the computer-based assessment, by age
WEB	Table B2.5	Percentage of adults with no/limited computer experience and participation in the computer-based assessment, by educational attainment
WEB	Table B2.6	Percentage of adults with no/limited computer experience and participation in the computer-based assessment, by type of occupation
WEB	Table B2.7	Literacy and numeracy mean scores, by experience with computers and the computer-based assessment
WEB	Table B2.8	Percentage of adults with no/limited computer experience and participation in the computer-based assessment, by level of engagement in ICT-related practices in everyday life
WEB	Table B3.1	Percentage of adults, by educational attainment
WEB	Table B3.2	Percentage of young adults, by educational attainment
WEB	Table B3.3	Percentage of adults, by age groups
WEB	Table B3.4	Percentage of adults at each level of educational attainment, by age groups
WEB	Table B3.5	Percentage of adults, by immigrant and language background
WEB	Table B3.6	Percentage of adults, by immigrant and language background and age groups
WEB	Table B3.7	Percentage of adults, by parents' educational attainment
WEB	Table B3.8	Percentage of men and women at each level of educational attainment, by age groups

ORGANISATION FOR ECONOMIC CO-OPERATION AND DEVELOPMENT

The OECD is a unique forum where governments work together to address the economic, social and environmental challenges of globalisation. The OECD is also at the forefront of efforts to understand and to help governments respond to new developments and concerns, such as corporate governance, the information economy and the challenges of an ageing population. The Organisation provides a setting where governments can compare policy experiences, seek answers to common problems, identify good practice and work to co-ordinate domestic and international policies.

The OECD member countries are: Australia, Austria, Belgium, Canada, Chile, the Czech Republic, Denmark, Estonia, Finland, France, Germany, Greece, Hungary, Iceland, Ireland, Israel, Italy, Japan, Korea, Luxembourg, Mexico, the Netherlands, New Zealand, Norway, Poland, Portugal, the Slovak Republic, Slovenia, Spain, Sweden, Switzerland, Turkey, the United Kingdom and the United States. The European Union takes part in the work of the OECD.

OECD Publishing disseminates widely the results of the Organisation's statistics gathering and research on economic, social and environmental issues, as well as the conventions, guidelines and standards agreed by its members.

OECD PUBLISHING, 2, rue André-Pascal, 75775 PARIS CEDEX 16
(87 2016 01 1P) ISBN 978-92-64-25804-4 – 2016